OUR TREACHEROUS HEARTS

by the same author

THE WHOLE TRUTH
(Faber)

FEMALE DESIRE
(Paladin)

PATRIARCHAL PRECEDENTS
(Routledge)

LANGUAGE AND MATERIALISM *with John Ellis*
(Routledge)

OUR TREACHEROUS HEARTS

Why Women Let Men Get Their Way

ROSALIND COWARD

faber and faber
LONDON · BOSTON

First published in 1992
by Faber and Faber Limited
3 Queen Square London WC1N 3AU
and in 1993 by Faber and Faber Inc.,
50 Cross Street Winchester, MA 01890

Photoset by Parker Typesetting Service, Leicester
Printed in England by Clays Ltd, St Ives plc

All rights reserved

© Rosalind Coward, 1992

Rosalind Coward is hereby identified as author of this work in accordance with Section 77 of the Copyright, Designs and Patents Act 1988

A CIP record for this book
is available from the British Library
and Library of Congress
ISBN 0-571-14156-0

Contents

Acknowledgments, vii
Introduction   Heroines or Collaborators:
   women's place in contemporary society, 1
1 'Having It All', Giving It Up, 15
2 Envy, Competition and the 'Unreality' of Work, 31
3 The Pleasures and Perils of Maternalism, 49
4 Buried Emotions, 61
5 The Ideal of the Good Mother, 75
6 The Sorrows of the Mothers:
   how women's feelings about their mothers affect their
   decisions, 90
7 Guilty Women, 105
8 Women Idealizing Men, 119
9 Women and Manipulative Behaviour, 135
10 Slim and Sexy: modern woman's Holy Grail, 147
11 Women as Victims, 164
12 Are Women Passive by Nature? 176
Conclusion   The Complicity of Women, 190
Index, 201

Acknowledgments

This book is based on interviews which I carried out between 1990 and 1991. I have changed the names of all the interviewees in order to preserve confidentiality. However I do want to thank all the women involved. Many women welcomed me into their homes, gave me further contacts and, most importantly, gave long and extremely frank answers to my questions. This book could not have been written without their help and, while I cannot name them individually, I would like them to know how grateful I am.

I would also like to thank certain people for the encouragement they gave me while I was working out the ideas for this book and then, finally, writing it. Fiona McCrae, Antony Goff, and Natasha Fairweather all had great faith in the idea and encouraged me to get the project off the ground, as did Susanne McDadd, who also presided over the painful process of extracting the book from me. I would like to thank Agniescka Piotrowska for the fruitful discussions we had while she turned the ideas in this book into a moving documentary for Channel Four. And I would also like to acknowledge Catherine Kenyon's contributions to that project and her help with the book. I am grateful to Louise Chunn at the *Guardian* and Emma Dally at *She* magazine, who both gave me space to 'try out' some of these ideas in this book.

Finally I am grateful to my friends and my family, especially John, Carl and Harriet who had to live it, for all their help and encouragement.

Introduction
Heroines or Collaborators:
women's place in contemporary society

The 1990s look set to become a decade of massive political upheaval. The old certainties have gone. The Berlin Wall has come down. Communist regimes are in confusion. Unexpected 'enemies' and hot spots have appeared. A new world order is emerging and the process is fluid, unstable and unsettling. But not quite everything is metamorphosing into new forms. Some things – especially social and domestic ideals – appear to be doing the opposite, returning inexorably to how they once were.

If the media is to be believed, the chaos and confusion caused by feminism has abated. That chaos – the chaos of changing sexual roles, the antagonism of angry women – belongs to a different era. The battles have been fought and won. Women, without the pressure of their more raucous sisters, are deciding for themselves how they want to live. Overwhelmingly, it seems, what they really want are the traditional things: children, the family and the confidence of being found sexually attractive by men. They may want to work; they may hope for 'equal' relationships with men; but they appear to want those things only if they don't have to unsettle the traditional relationship between the sexes.

Most people now accept that the battle of the sexes is over. The feminism of the 1970s is seen as a bloody and unappealing confrontation to which men quickly capitulated. The rapid changes in women's opportunities are used to prove that men simply needed to have the error of their ways explained to them. After all, not so long ago women were excluded from voting, or had to resign from certain professions when they married – yet throughout the 1980s Britain was led by a woman prime minister. Margaret Thatcher –

invincible in elections, a formidable foe in political life and the embodiment of authority – seemed to prove that things had changed irrevocably for women. From then on, no one would dare to say that men and women were different and, by implication, unequal.

Thatcher's personal triumphs ushered in the decade in which feminism began to look redundant. Professional, economic and social equality appeared to be finally within women's grasp. In the 1970s feminists had complained that many professions still excluded most women and kept others from reaching the top. But barely had these complaints been backed up by statistics than images of successful career women began to dominate not only our screens but also our consciousness. TV programmes and films portrayed women in the stockmarket, or running companies, or as heads of television companies. And magazine after magazine featured their real-life equivalents, showing us the successful careers, the glossy homes and the lovely children. 'Ordinary' mothers complained about these supermums, whose lives were so unlike their own. Their voices, however, did not reach the press. Instead, newspapers held up these glamorous, ultra-feminine, working mothers as evidence of a 'post-feminist' era.

The media took pleasure in reminding their audiences how coolly feminism was now regarded. Women were turning their backs on the so-called man-haters, and were able to enjoy the home and the family as equals. Younger women, we were told, had decided that feminism was irrelevant to their lives. The more radical of them dissociated themselves from what they saw as the last public vestige of feminism: its fight for professional women. On the political front, other social issues like homelessness, the environment and race took on a greater prominence than women's advancement. Those who continued to dwell on women's issues were labelled laughable, the remnants of an embittered generation. The conflict was well and truly over, we were told – it was now time to move on.

But was it? Had women's lot really improved so much that the majority of women no longer saw any need for fundamental changes? Did women really feel free to enjoy the traditional family structures as equals rather than victims? Or had they fallen prey to a new version of an old myth, in which women yet again were told

Introduction

what they could and should feel about the family, rather than being free to describe the reality to each other?

It is true that the situation has improved so much for women that the demise of feminism seems, at first sight, explicable. After all, many of the constraints which gave rise to the feminist movement are no longer in place. Opportunities are available to women that would have been unimaginable twenty years ago. All professions are open to women. Legislation has been passed to prevent the more blatant attempts at discrimination. And many women have made it to the top. The dismissive 'sexism' which pervaded humour and culture in pre-feminist days, which belittled and marginalized women, as workers, mothers and housewives, has also to a large extent disappeared.

Statisticians confirm that women's lives have undergone total transformation in terms of employment patterns and demography. During the 1980s the labour market needed more women workers, with the result that most women of all classes – even mothers – are now expected to work. There is no longer a stigma attached to the working mother, even if individual women continue to feel guilty if they are away from their children. Family patterns have also been changing. Divorce, mostly initiated by women, is on the increase. The number of single parents has risen massively, and virtually all of these are women. There has been a substantial increase in the number of unmarried partners and 'illegitimate' births.

These changes are invariably interpreted as further evidence of the gradual, inexorable improvement in the lot of women. Women are now more ready to contemplate life alone. They have higher expectations of a relationship and are more likely to take decisive action when these expectations are not met. There is a general assumption that women reject the conventions of marriage because they are unhappy with the connotations of possession, obedience and subordination associated with that state. All these factors – the public achievements of women and the greater fluidity of family structures – tend to reinforce the idea of great improvements in the lot of women accompanied by the gradual overthrow of that bastion of male oppression – the Family.

If this is true, why are women not euphoric about improvements in their condition? Why is it that any conversation with any woman will reveal a 1990s equivalent of the female condition that Betty Friedan identified in the 1950s as the 'problem that has no name'? Why is it that in my interviews for this book I repeatedly heard tell of the difficulties of women's situations, the impossible choices, and, especially, the pressures and stresses of women's lives.

These worries and complaints bear witness to the fact that many aspects of women's lives are just as difficult – if not more so – as they were when feminism first gained a voice in the 1970s. Even women's increased participation in the workforce and their achievements in professional life are potentially double-edged. The pressure for women to work and achieve like men comes as much from the economy as from women themselves and, as with most changes dictated by a market economy, some women benefit more than others. Malcolm Wicks, who has studied family changes for over a decade, has argued that:

What has been needed recently has been an increasing number of women workers. This change looks irreversible, regardless of any downturn in the economy. So the companies are ready to talk about flexible markets and childcare. It's easy for them to give away childcare vouchers, along with other company perks. But it's the Samuel Smiles ethic. No one is really discussing the quality of life envisaged for working parents or their children. And no one is discussing the class dimension. These changes aren't going to help the low paid, the women in grotty jobs with no proper conditions of employment. These changes benefit a few, not the majority of, women. (Kent University, lecture on the family, May 1991)

Wicks is saying that further down the social scale women are much more likely to be having a hard time than men. Single parenthood – which, as we have seen, is massively on the increase – is taken to be the most reliable indicator of hardship, and 90 per cent of all single parents are women, a clear indication that significant numbers of women are living in poverty. At the same time there has been a rise in low-paid domestic service jobs – nannies, mothers' helps, cleaning ladies. All this points to the fact that more 'successful' women have solved some of their dilemmas by passing them on to other women. For non-professional women, low expectations and low pay are still very much the norm.

For those women who are neither high-fliers nor their servicers, some of the old problems remain unchanged. The jobs that women still tend to take, such as clerical work, teaching or health work, remain relatively low paid. There is also a chronic lack of provision for these working mothers. In the UK, 75 per cent of mothers work, the highest percentage in Europe, yet Britain has the worst pre-school care provision in Europe. In response to inadequate social provision, most women still take breaks in their career, or work in less well paid, lower status or part-time jobs that they can shape around their children.

Few would dispute that the last ten years have also seen a deterioration in the quality of life for women and the family. Public spending on health care and special needs declined, and, because women continue to take prime responsibility for the family, even if they are working, increased responsibility for the elderly and sick fell on women. Many women regarded pollution and environmental hazards as direct threats to their families; food scares increased, while worsening traffic congestion meant that the number of child deaths on the road escalated. Parenting also had added stresses. Changing attitudes towards children emphasized the crucial role of the mother in encouraging a child's intellectual development, making many mothers more anxious about the effects of their actions. It is difficulties of this kind that led virtually all the women I interviewed for this book to describe their lot as 'stressful', 'difficult' or 'impossible'.

Given such individual awareness of the new and additional pressures on women, it would have been reasonable to expect a resurgence of feminist protest. But there was nothing of the kind: the political visibility of women, *as women*, was nil. Organized feminism, which in any case had never won over the majority of women, disintegrated. Public debate about women was confined to questions of women and work, such as demands for improved childcare. Discussions about the problems of lower-paid women and the stresses and strains particular to women found no public forum. Apart from a few who risked mockery by the media for their dogged concern with 'wimmin's issues', most people agreed that these issues were a relic from the past.

In addition to this paucity of political and social discussion, there has also been a more surprising development. The family has swung back into fashion. Statistics like those showing the dramatic increase in single parents may have made the family seem precarious. But socially, and especially among those women whose voices dominated the public sphere, the conventional family was idealized by people ranging from Conservatives to erstwhile critics like Germaine Greer, who was heard to sing the praises of the Tuscan extended family.

On a practical level, this meant that many professional women found themselves racing home from work, driven by ideals of mothering as rigid as those of the 1950s and 1960s. Despite the problems the traditional family gave rise to, there was little sign that women wanted to fight to change it. Women were not unaware of the pressures, the dissatisfactions or the dilemmas, but it seemed they would rather live with those feelings than raise the old battle cries. None of the women I interviewed who described their situation as difficult and stressful wanted it any other way.

Examined a little more closely, even those statistics which show significant changes in family life can also be interpreted as evidence showing that the traditional ideal of the family still holds good. Those who divorce quickly remarry. Half of single parents move into other families within five years. And, in spite of the fact that the majority of women live with a partner before marriage, there has only been a small drop in the number of women who marry at some point in their lives – in the 1970s, eight out of ten married, and in the 1990s, seven out of ten will do so.

Neither have roles *within* the family changed very much. Increases in divorce, single-parenthood and working mothers have not led to a challenge to the traditional divisions and expectations of family roles. The larger numbers of working women did not lead to men sharing responsibility for the home. In fact, research suggests that women are still doing 80–90 per cent of domestic tasks. Nor did an increase in co-habiting bring a new equality to work in the home.

All the evidence is that men's outlook, priorities and contribution to the home have remained largely unchanged. The main difference is that men are now thought to be doing more than in previous generations. But the reality in most families is that the man's work still takes precedence. Faced with that fact, a woman's choices are limited. She can either work a double shift herself, or she can fit her own job around the hours and needs of her husband's work. Even in families where women themselves are pursuing successful careers, they still tend to arrange the childcare, do the bulk of the domestic work and all the domestic planning.

The public success of individual women has disguised this fundamental lack of change in the relations between the sexes. Many women who profited from feminism's onslaught on the media and the establishment then went on to discredit feminist ideals. Many argued that feminists had failed to recognize women's true power – the power of childbirth, and nurturing children. They argued that true fulfilment lay in living out their feminine destiny, albeit in a modern form as a 'working mother'. Some working mothers claimed their success had come from their own individual talents and the support of a 'good woman' at home – a 'treasure', as Margaret Thatcher dubbed what for her was the only viable childcare. Amongst these publicly successful women there was almost no recognition of what feminism had done for them, and even less recognition of what they could now do for other women.

Women who succeeded in previously male-dominated domains felt compelled to reassure men that *they* were not man-haters. An anxious, over-feminine style was adopted by many of the women who were challenging men most directly in the world of work. A symptom of this was the way in which the severe power-dressing of the early 1980s gave way to a more consciously feminine look – femininity was flaunted, apparently in order to deny any real challenge to men.

But being sexually appealing to men was no longer enough. Many public women also flaunted their families, and especially their babies. These were the ultimate proof that, whatever their own successes, their traditional feminine needs and priorities were deeply in place. Again, the unspoken agenda was to reassure men that all was well between the sexes and that men were not being asked to change.

This absence of confrontation is surprising because whatever the disagreements among feminists, there had been one point of consensus: nothing would improve the lot of women unless men themselves changed. While state-run crèches and better wages might ease women's lot, feminists knew that any real improvement in the quality of life for women *and* children would involve radical changes in men themselves. But this challenge to men was never consolidated. Organized feminism fell apart in a series of acrimonious divisions over such issues as how much women were 'collaborating with the enemy'. And other women, including those sympathetic to feminism, breathed a sigh of relief when this uncomfortable issue in their personal lives was closed.

In crucial and important ways, women – including once-active feminists like myself – backed off from a confrontation with a system of values which gave certain men real privileges. They fitted in, and found ways of justifying their decisions to themselves. They have shown themselves keener to pass on the unpleasant parts of their life to other women than to confront men with the need for fundamental changes. Many of the women who became high achievers in public life did so by accommodating men, or even, as in the case of Margaret Thatcher, by repudiating other women. They did not challenge the traditional rules of sexual exchanges, nor the ways in which men work, nor the different expectations of men and women in the public and private spheres.

The interviews I have conducted for this book have confirmed an impression that women are scared of a fundamental confrontation with men. They seem to be afraid that asking men to change will involve losing men's love and support. Many women have given up challenging their partners over career choices and domestic arrangements. I have come across startling exceptions – men who have fought for custody and now care for their children, or men and women who reverse roles so that the women can work full-time. And it is clear that most women will no longer stand for extreme displays of 'patriarchal' arrogance or bossiness. But overwhelmingly, the traditional expectations of the family and the woman's role within that remain unchanged.

There has also been a failure of political will to challenge the Conservative government's hostility to allocating any public funds to educational, health and childcare resources – an allocation which might have improved life for all women and children. Indeed, combined with the discrediting of communism abroad, most people seemed to accept this hostility as a necessary antidote to the much feared state socialism. Women might have been the main victims as more and more responsibility was pushed back on to the individual family, but few women objected to this process, certainly not by presenting a coherent political alternative.

Instead, women were central in accommodating the new individualistic philosophies. Women themselves have pasted over the cracks and retreated more and more into the idea of the primacy of their own individual family, paying for private solutions to the woeful inadequacies of a society which does not truly care about the well-being of its children.

These individualistic solutions are difficult to achieve, especially for less affluent women and especially as the extended family is no longer there to fill the gap between these higher expectations of the family on the one hand and the reality of social change on the other. But the difficulties have not diminished women's determination to make things work for their families.

Most women know in their hearts that they delude themselves by imagining that their relationships and compromises will succeed where so many have failed. Polly Toynbee has painted a gloomy picture of the likely consequences for the woman who still invests everything in traditional expectations:

> Women work at the family as if it were a constant rehearsal for something else, as if at the end there was a prize. Easy in the days when people believed in the after-life – but what now? Empty nest at 45, unemployable or some skivvying job for the next decade until retirement? Or husbands leave and marriage disintegrates. If part of the bargain was protection against loneliness in old age, there is no guarantee. The abandoned woman can support herself no better than in Victorian times. The only difference is the welfare state instead of the workhouse and most divorced or single mothers live on social security. (*Times Review*, 14 September 1991)

In spite of this, there is little evidence that the family and the feminine role within it has lost any of its appeal as the central, prime and overwhelming attraction and responsibility for women. Whether women have successful careers or not, they remain just as committed to finding and keeping a man and to upholding the traditional divisions between the sexes. If relationships go wrong, it is often a case of regrouping for the next try. It is women who have been holding the social structure together, doing it willingly or at least without too much complaint. In short, women have been complicit in keeping alive the old forms of femininity in the family, albeit in a new guise.

This area of complicity – women's deep-rooted, fundamental

complicity with traditional family structures and expectations, their complicity in personal relationships with men, in the continued idealization of men and the desire for their approval – is the subject of this book. It is the complicity of continued deep dependence on men, the unwillingness to contemplate change which might improve the lot of all women. Female complicity consents to many things. Sometimes it consents to extreme forms of abuse, like violence, sexual abuse and sexual exploitation. But more commonly it is a hidden complicitly, a way of living our personal lives that protects men and reinforces their habitual ways of doing things.

Why at the crucial moment did women lose their nerve and prefer to unlearn many of the lessons which feminism had taught them? Did feminism get it wrong? Or were women terrified of feminism's image as a painful struggle with an unclear outcome? Why were women so anxious to reassure men that everything was all right after all? Why do women let men get away with it – with keeping long office hours, paying too little attention to the kids, dominating the political and social environment, concentrating on social and political priorities remote from improving the quality of women and children's lives? Why in the end do so many women prefer to accommodate men rather than hold out for social and personal change which might ultimately guarantee a better way of life for most women?

These questions came from a realization that my own life had involved a sort of retreat – from the confident, Utopian feminism of my 20s to a conventional family structure and a lack of any organized feminist politics in my 30s. When pregnant with my first child, I never dreamt that I would contemplate giving up work, let alone be happy to. Yet when it came to a choice between a daily motorway drive to a job which did not fire my enthusiasm, and a small child to look after at home, the decision was easy. I gave up my university job and went freelance, cutting my hours of work, thereby pushing my partner and myself into a conventional division of labour that neither of us had ever anticipated. Once that decision had been taken, virtually every woman I met seemed to tell a similar story. I could no longer avoid the question of how much women themselves collude in keeping the conventional structures in place.

Introduction

There will of course be many people who object profoundly to my asking these questions. To ask about women's complicity, they argue, is to ignore the pervasiveness of male power. They insist that the whole situation should be seen from the point of view of unequal power relations. Men have the power – economically, socially and politically – and women have little choice but to make do as best they can. They would describe women's vulnerability and their loyalty to the old forms as a 'cycle of dependency'. And this economic dependency on men is used to explain most things, from divorcees who remarry to extreme cases of physical and sexual abuse. Such analyses are even enshrined in current United Nations policy, which declares that 'the root cause of abuse of women stems from the position of women in society and the unequal power structure therein'.

This, of course, is the classic leftist and feminist analysis of women's position, which has been repeated on and off for the last twenty years. It asserts that there is a structural economic inequality between men and women that can only be solved by women achieving full economic equality and independence. Most feminists did believe that the traditional patterns of the family were caused and then reintroduced by women's economic inequality. Ultimately, this assumes that women are coerced by men, rather than colluding with them. In the absence of any massive upheaval, women opt for the most satisfying compromise: the love they can find within their own family. This is certainly how most women themselves view the situation, and it would of course be foolish to disagree with aspects of this analysis. Women's dependency is in part due to economic inequalities, but then all women working full-time irrespective of their preferences is no answer either.

The idea that women collude with men because really they are coerced can still be expressed in highly radical ways. Susan Faludi, for example, in her bestselling book *Backlash*, has given it a new and important rendition. She argues that both the belief in a new state of post-feminist equality and the stampede of high-flying women back to their homes are part of a massive backlash against feminism, which can be found in all areas of American life – from politics to films and even contemporary psychology. She argues that a fear of women underlies the media's contradictory assertion that feminist battles for equality have been won but that equality has not made women happy. If feminism's simplest assertions have unleashed such an hysterical backlash, she asks, how much more remains to be done?

Faludi's argument assumes that women make the choices and adopt the postures they do simply because the odds are stacked against them. Women themselves cannot change when the whole structure of society operates to their disadvantage, especially given the hysterical reaction to any attempt to change it. She claims that it is the media who peddle the idyll of the family, the feminine woman and the sexual masochist. Women themselves, she says, consistently recognize feminism's debt and acknowledge there is still a long way to go.

Her argument is relevant to the British situation. The counter-assault on feminism began in the newspapers and on television, where young men, following the typical path to success through the usual schools, universities and networks, had an all too obvious interest in supporting the utterances of their editors – editors like Simon Jenkins of *The Times*, who dismissed women's-issue journalism as 'demeaning to modern women who want to be considered as people not women'. Women journalists and cultural figures were popular provided they distanced themselves from any organized system of thought like feminism and simply fired off witty and opinionated pieces.

But this cannot simply be a question of feminism being muzzled by the media. It is not men alone who have peddled this ideology, but women themselves. In the last ten years women have appeared not just willing but positively eager to assume double responsibilities in the home: they have felt uneasy if their own achievements began to outstrip those of their male partners, and they have been almost frantic to retain male sexual approval. They have done all this in the full knowledge that feminism outlined the pitfalls of such strategies twenty years ago, even if it failed to offer any popular solutions.

Feminist arguments never carried the majority of women. And feminism itself was subverted as much from within as from without. Feminism fell apart not because of bad press but because of internal divisions, lack of agreement, guilt-tripping and political despair within the movement. Nor does the idea of being duped by

Introduction

the media explain why the hopes and aspirations of millions of individual women have run, not quite in concert, but certainly in parallel with the new media images. The media may have been peddling extreme forms of the glamorous, successful but heavily male-directed woman, but there was plenty of evidence that the basic message reflected a popular retreat into traditional values.

I decided to write this book because I wanted to find out about that psychological retreat. What had fuelled it? What are women really feeling about work, men, children and the family? The majority of women I interviewed were neither innocent victims of men's lust for power, nor dupes of the media. In society in general women have enough opportunity, experience and, dare I say it, power to demand great changes. But they have not done so. Nor can this passivity be explained by ignorance. Women themselves are instrumental in educating each new generation of girls into feminine and traditional expectations. The reasons for this passivity lie much deeper, in aspects of the male and female psyche and in how men and women relate.

It is this *internal* account of the family dynamic, and the deep structures of the male and female psyche, that interest me. A good deal has been written on the problems and obstacles confronting women, and on the *external* forces at work. But virtually nothing has been written on the subjective side, especially not by someone sympathetic to many aspects of the feminist project. Very little has been written about the satisfactions, fears and anxieties which determine women's choices. Too little attention is given to the ancient histories which men and women bring to the family. Why does their need for each other take the form of women carrying the weight of social problems and anxieties? Why should half of society find itself anxiously trying to shield the next generation from society's unresolved problems?

This book is based on the personal accounts of women. In what I hoped would be a fairly representative survey, I talked to almost 150 women; slightly over half were from the professional classes. I fear I will be accused of generalizing from a small sample of women, and criticized for including so many interviews with middle-class women. But I am also confident that what I am saying will strike a chord. Some of the fears, pleasures, anxieties and pathologies which women currently experience in the family seem to transcend the differences of race, class and region. Giving voice to these feelings is the first step towards a more honest appraisal of what contemporary life is like for women. And only when women are able to be more honest will they be free from the myths of 'femininity' and 'womanhood' which are at the heart of their collusion with men.

I
'Having It All', Giving It Up

How can I refer to women's collusion when faced with the amazing advances women have made in employment over the last decade? Why would anyone want to assert that there has been a return to traditional values, considering the remarkable changes of recent years? In England women now make up a higher proportion of the workforce than in any other European country. And this is not simply a response to the economy's increased need for women workers. Women themselves now expect to continue working – not only working-class women (who have always worked) but women of all classes. A recent survey (*Guardian*, 25 September 1991) showed that over 70 per cent of all women with very young children expected to continue working. Surely all this is conclusive evidence that a quiet social revolution has taken place – that the 'bad old days – when mothers who went out to work were looked at askance, when employers were unrelenting and nannies hard to find – now seem far away'? The same article went on to record that it isn't just women who have changed their attitudes. Now 'only one in five Britons believe that a woman's place is in the home'.

It is hard to avoid the consensus that the social position of women has changed dramatically, that it has changed for the better, and that it will never regress to those 'bad old days'. Even the Tory Party, some of whose members called throughout the 1980s for a return to 'Victorian values', contained a group of women who insisted that the party should come to terms with the realities of family life. They told us that children will no longer limit women's potential, that women will no longer feel guilty about working, and that the future promises more and more childcare provision, tax concessions and state nurseries.

Yet in spite of all this, the vast majority of women still see the family as their priority and still see themselves as bearing the main responsibility for their children and family. According to the same survey which revealed that 70 per cent of all women with young children expected to continue working, 95 per cent also believed that their family was their main commitment. This continuing priority has until now been the hidden underside of the quiet revolution in attitudes towards women and work. It has been the silent extra burden, the additional pressure, the double shift, invariably discussed as a problem of how individual families arrange things, rather than as a problem affecting women as a whole.

Until very recently, the only public discussion of working women's extra burden has been in terms of finding practical solutions to childcare in order to make work easier for women. But now the media has begun to document – and celebrate – a rather surprising phenomenon associated with new patterns in employment. Just at the point when statisticians began to talk of 'returnism' – women with very young children returning to work – the media discovered the opposite tendency, a form of inverse 'returnism', where career women who have 'had it all' – top jobs and husbands – have given it all up to stay at home with their children.

The first rumblings of media interest in these women came in the late 1980s. In a typical magazine article (*Junior*, April 1989) Victoria McKee interviewed several career women who had 'given it all up'. These women – a solicitor, a radio producer and buyer for Cartier jewellers – were archetypes of the new woman of the 1980s; they had succeeded in careers which were not only previously male preserves but were extremely well paid. The article announced, in terms which have since become familiar, that these women were rethinking the ambitions once made famous by *Cosmo* editor Helen Gurley Brown, that contemporary women could 'have it all' – men, family and a career – if they really wanted. Instead, these women had given up their prestigious careers to stay at home full-time with their children, prepared to sacrifice their personal prestige for what they all called 'an improved quality of life'.

The article noted that the decisions of these women represented something of a trend:

> Could it be something in the hormones or the social climate that is making ambitious career women startle their colleagues – and themselves – with the decision to chuck in the Porsche and the perks and stay at home with the baby they swore was not going to change their lives? Women who a few years ago might have put their maternal instinct on the back burner for the sake of burning ambition are now coolly deciding to take a breather and enjoy their children's brief babyhood instead. Has the era of the executive earth mother ended? Can it be that 'having it all' has had it – at least amongst those who have tried and failed?

This article was written two years before the publication of *Having It All* by Maeve Haran, a novel where the central character swaps her job as a television executive for full-time motherhood and a kitchen with an Aga. By this time the idea of professional women giving it all up was of sufficient general interest for publishers to fall over themselves in competition for the book. As all the publicity for it insisted, the novel 'touched a nerve', whether it provoked scorn and hostility or peculiar utterances of 'gratitude'.

As always, the British were slightly behind the Americans in their awareness of this phenomenon. In 1988 the American magazine *Ita* carried one article by a woman who had opted out of the corporate rat-race 'to gather her children and her mate around her'. 'Having just finished arranging flowers from the garden,' she eulogised, 'and finding that my house smells of these and of ripe peaches, and feeling great satisfaction from my task, I was pleased to discover that this mood is part of a new social movement.'

Giving up good careers is only a 1990s version of what middle-class women have been doing since the 1950s. Then, women had often been in higher education only to marry after college and submerge themselves in motherhood. The main difference now is that women are starting careers, and getting into higher positions, before abandoning them. This is partly because women are on average having children later and partly because some of the professional obstacles have been removed. Women are able to get higher in their careers so that when they do give up work for their children their 'renunciations' seem much more spectacular.

No one needs reminding of the practical reasons why women

with the financial option to do so, decide to renounce or reduce work commitments. More and more women may be working, but little has changed in terms of practical provision for children. Women still have to work out individual solutions to 'juggling their lives', and still run up against the gulf between office and school hours. But many middle-class women appear to be giving up jobs and changing careers not just because of these practical obstacles but because of other, more subjective reasons. Or so they represent it, to themselves and to the public.

These subjective reasons are almost invariably represented as the power of the mother–child bond, a feeling of maternal love. Kathy Gyngell in the *Daily Mail* (1991) gave a typical account of what she saw as a conspiracy of silence about a powerful natural instinct:

Because being 'just a mother' was scorned by my peers and never considered an option for an intelligent and educated woman, I had battled on for twelve months until my natural instincts got the better of me. I quit work, came home and have not once regretted my decision. The flood of letters that followed my article bore witness to the extremely large number of extremely undermined full-time mothers relieved that someone at last was voicing their feelings. Motherhood is an important job of which women should be proud.

Gyngell's is a position which has become increasingly common in the 1990s. Professional high-fliers have very publicly abandoned their careers for their children, explaining this decision in terms of a natural, irresistible force. The pull of maternal love is obviously something which is only supposed to afflict women. And when the pull is obeyed there is little to be said about it. It must be obeyed, for better or worse.

Maternal love, we are told, was neglected by feminism, preoccupied as it was with the need for women to 'climb to the top' of their careers. Maeve Haran's version of this new myth that feminism neglected the powerful feelings of motherhood claims that 'one howling gap in feminism was that it hardly addressed motherhood ... it was wrong about how women's attitudes towards climbing the career ladder would be affected by motherhood. Most women care about their families at least as much as the next promotion.' (*Observer*, 30 June 1991)

The myth that feminism had nothing to say about motherhood has become commonplace. Yet as any woman who was involved in feminism will tell, this could hardly be further from the truth. As one woman I spoke to, who also worked with Maeve Haran, said, 'Neglected motherhood! I don't know what it was about if it wasn't about motherhood! What about all our campaigns for community crèches, what about our emphasis on shared parenting, what about all the support we gave mothers as a routine part of our feminism? The problem with people like Maeve Haran is that they were never really involved in feminist activities. They identified with the bits of feminism which were about women's advancement and ignored all the other bits. Then they suddenly find it's difficult to combine motherhood and career, and they blame feminism, which has actually been saying that for twenty years.'

There is, however, a difference between how motherhood was discussed in the early days of feminism and how it is now being represented by the women who are ready to give up all for it. In the late 1960s and early 1970s many women turned to feminism precisely because they had embraced motherhood so intensely that they felt 'drenched in it', as Margaret Forster so eloquently put it. The early influential novels of feminism, like Fay Weldon's *Down Among the Women*, or Doris Lessing's *The Summer before the Fall* and Marilyn French's *The Women's Room*, all described experiences typical of women who were drawn to feminism in that period. They had been educated but had never pursued their careers; instead, they had married and become mothers, and they felt swamped, constrained and depressed by what motherhood then held for women. They acknowledged its centrality in their lives but they were trying to break out of its confines.

Unlike the women of the 1950s and 1960s, women of the 1990s no longer believe that they are coerced and confined by motherhood. They represent themselves as choosing to follow their instinctual female feelings and regard themselves as having proved, through their work, their equality with men. One childless woman I interviewed, currently working as production manager in a company producing adverts, summed up what appears to be a fairly widespread perception among professional women. 'You must have seen this with all your friends. They have wonderful careers, get pregnant, plan to go back after three months – it all seems terribly easy. And then what happens? They have the baby and their maternal feelings hit them between the eyes. They're just not prepared for the feelings they have and most of them never get back to work. At last they find themselves fulfilled.' She went on to say that it was what she wanted, far more than her career. 'It's what comes naturally to women and I don't think you should feel guilty for saying that's what you want.'

While no one would doubt the intense and often unexpected love which exists between mothers and their children, it is also clear that women's decisions involving their families are much more complex than a simple response to a call of nature. Packed into that 'overwhelming sense of maternal love' are various other feelings. There are emotional structures at play in women's decisions to leave work or downgrade their career expectations, and these are far more complex, much less well-known and analysed, than any simple, natural, maternal instinct. Some of the conditions which lead to women 'putting their families first' are at play long before the family arrives and predate any falling in love with their babies. The portrayal of spectacular career renunciations in the media has obscured the real issues around mothering and work, and distorted the dilemmas and decisions of more ordinary women.

Ann is one such mother. In the course of two years she moved from a well-paid and highly regarded career in magazine production to looking after her 2-year-old daughter all but three afternoons a week. For ten years she had been on a clear career path which had reached a peak when she was offered the job as a production editor for a national newspaper. When I interviewed her, she was expecting another child, whose arrival will lead her to suspend all work plans 'until sensible times return again'. She had neither expected nor been prepared for the change to full-time mothering. 'I've switched from being highly ambitious and getting an enormous buzz out of my work to being practically a full-time mother. I've surprised myself. I've astounded myself, in fact.'

When her first child was born, Ann had continued to work in demanding freelance jobs. 'But I began to think, what am I trying to do? I'd get home at night on a high from work, but also very tired. What really got to me wasn't worry about how my daughter was being looked after – that was fine – but the fact that there was no let up for me. I couldn't come in, pour a glass of wine, sit in front of the telly and say, let's have a take-away. I had to come home, pick her up from the childminder's, give her tea and a bath, and then play before bed. There was no stopping. Then it was off again on the tube next morning, usually after a broken night.'

The process of reducing her hours at work has been gradual but inexorable. Like many women, Ann attributes this change of priorities to an unexpected awakening of maternal feelings. 'There have been many moments when I would willingly have gone back to work full-time but I guess my mothering instinct has emerged.' In her case, it was not a question of an immediate bond with a newborn baby but a gradual increase in feeling. 'I did go back to work quite quickly after her birth. But gradually I began to feel more and more protective. When I look at little babies I think, goodness, I left Laura when she was that little! How could I have done it! I'm not going to with number two, and now I look at my daughter and think, she will only be little for so long. I don't want to miss it.'

As for many professional women, so for Ann the birth of a second child proved crucial. Another woman, a solicitor, described how she worked full-time after the birth of her first child but simply could not bear to 'miss out' a second time round. 'I went back to work as a full-time solicitor after the birth of my first daughter. There were no problems on the nanny front – in fact she was so competent that I realized I knew nothing about bringing up my daughter Emma and was missing so much. I was so knocked out by my maternal feelings when Kate [the second daughter] was born that I didn't know what to do.'

For these women, the feeling which they describe as maternal love grew gradually, although once it was recognized they were determined to have their fill a second time round. For others the experience may be sudden and dramatic. One woman I interviewed, Andrea, told a particularly dramatic story, having changed from being a successful businesswoman to becoming a full-time mother of three children. Andrea had previously run a successful flower-selling business in New York. When her husband was moved to England she came too, but kept on the business, commuting to the States several times a year.

After her son was born Andrea had fully intended to carry on with business as normal. 'But when the baby was two months old I had to go to New York. He was still breastfeeding and I organized the whole trip around his feeds. I expressed enough milk for fourteen feeds — it took me weeks! — and I thought it would be fine. I got to America and I was in top production after expressing all that milk — my breasts were enormous. I was walking around Manhattan with aching breasts doing all these business things and I suddenly thought, what on earth am I doing here? All this concrete around me and my baby is on the other side of the world. I closed the business, there and then. I said, that's it. No way. It was then that the shock of being a mother really hit me.'

My own particular road to Damascus was on a British motorway. I too had no intention of giving up work after the birth of my first child. In fact I had taken a new job at a university while I was pregnant, a job which ultimately would mean a daily drive of forty miles. On one occasion, when the baby was about six months old, I was driving along the motorway — fast, because I was late — when I suddenly thought, this is total madness. I don't want to be this far away from home. I don't want to be doing this job. If I'm going to be spending time away from my child, the job has got to matter more to me. Leaving my job took rather longer than in Andrea's case, but the moment of revelation was accompanied by a similar sense of shock.

No one is surprised if mothers in badly paid, tedious jobs give up work. As one single mother put it to me, 'Who wouldn't choose to stay at home, even on the social, if the only choice is some shitty job being bossed around by some awful man?' These, of course, are often precisely the women who don't have any options — who have to work if they want to survive above the breadline. But are the decisions to renounce it all of successful professional women, who have gained so much recognition and financial reward, really based on something as straightforward as overwhelming maternal passion? Were traditionalists right after all — traditionalists like Mary Kenny, the journalist who celebrated the replacement of Margaret Thatcher in No. 10 Downing Street by Norma Major as the restoration of a proper model of womanhood: 'intelligent, accomplished but firm in her conviction that she likes her place in the home and does not wish to be told she must change'?

On the surface, women exchanging good careers for motherhood appear to be exchanging glamour for drudgery. To men, at least, it may seem like having tasted the heights and chosen the depths. Yet on a closer look, such decisions may turn out to be more complex than they appear, revealing an unexpected ambivalence in women regarding their careers. Ann, for example, turned down the job as production editor of a newspaper *before* becoming pregnant. 'I'd been doing the job already for four months before they offered it to me permanently. It was a great job, but at the end of those four months I was a gibbering wreck. I turned down what could have been a real marker in my career because I realized what I would and wouldn't accept in terms of a way to live and the kind of hours expected of me. That was a turning point, and I realized I might as well go ahead and get pregnant.'

Pregnancy confirmed her deep, although not often apparent, ambivalence about work and career. 'When I announced I was pregnant, the immediate question everyone asked was, when are you coming back to work? And I thought, Jesus, what is this? Why is everyone so obsessed with work? What is so damned important about work over a human being? And I started saying "I'm never coming back to work", because I was so damned angry. I did go back when Laura was 16 weeks old, but I was still trying to prove I could do it. I could have a baby and work and run a home. Gradually I began to ask myself, what am I trying to prove, to whom?'

Even the highly successful Andrea would be the first to acknowledge that other factors predated her sudden conversion. In many ways her career path had typically 'female' elements. She had followed her husband's career moves ever since leaving college. He had wanted to travel, so she had followed him, but unlike many women she was not demoralized but 'enriched' by this pattern. 'Without him I probably would never have left my home town. I just looked for openings in any new situation.' Luck and circumstances, rather than a single-minded careerism, allowed her to discover her business potential. She started to sell flowers on the university campus where her husband was studying, and her success there encouraged her to expand until before long she had a chain of stalls selling in most supermarkets and business foyers. 'A lot of women don't know what they are worth. I was lucky. I discovered I could bring something positive into the world and it was rewarded, and that was a very good feeling.'

Such positive work experience has its problems when that work is exchanged for motherhood. 'I know now that I have two sides and that I'm no longer using the creative business side. It makes me impatient sometimes because I'm not using my whole self. When you have a "normal" job you work towards something, finish it and go on to the next thing. But mothering is a relentless job. You don't see a product or a successful outcome and it can feel very uncreative. But then again, this feels more real. I like the feeling of being surrounded by life.'

Ann and Andrea are affluent women. Neither expected or experienced a drastic drop in the family's income following their decisions to stay at home. But even for relatively affluent women the decision to stay at home is not always easy. They have embraced something which many women have disparaged. They may be frustrated at not being able to achieve or create in the same way as previously, and fear losing their identity by becoming financially dependent on their husbands. Ann, for instance, described how she cried when her husband gave her the first housekeeping cheque. 'That hurt, not because I had no money but because I had no independence left. I thought, I'm just a little kept woman. I said, "You mustn't give me that much," and he said, "It's not that much," and I felt so resentful and upset. I felt as if I didn't have anything left. It wasn't me any more.'

Yet even women who have experienced the advantages of financial independence did not find the drawbacks sufficiently great to challenge their new priorities of home and children. That this should be so points to some of the things which they have in common with less affluent women – namely, the way in which women's working identity rests precariously on a more profound female conditioning. Ann and Andrea have two rather different experiences of work: one was frustrating, requiring a commitment which ultimately, in spite of the pleasures and excitements, Ann was not prepared to give; Andrea's was more straightforwardly satisfying. But there are also important similarities. Even when women achieve at high levels, work is still often less vital to a sense of self than it is for men. It can, it seems, easily be cast off in favour of something 'more real'.

The notion that family and children represent a more important, more 'real' priority was repeated by women from all walks of life. They found it difficult to explain what was meant by 'real', apart from saying they found the issues of daily survival around the home and children more important and more satisfying than some of the less tangible aspects of the working world. Women often perceive their careers as unfolding 'accidentally'. They believe they are career women only when they are already successful. Most women I spoke to with established careers described themselves as 'accidental' career women. This sense that the career is not fundamental to the identity, and rarely integrated within it, accounts for the ease with which work can be cast aside by women. And frustration with work, whether imposed by external factors or subjective preference, means that a new family can offer a timely break. The lack of enticement from work is often just as strong a factor for women as the enticement of the baby.

The factors which make the shift to home and traditional roles relatively easy tend, naturally enough, to be even more pronounced among women with less high-powered jobs. Sarah is in many ways typical. She had a good job as a polytechnic teacher, and although she was not a senior lecturer when she became pregnant, she had some prospects for promotion; she also viewed her job as extremely interesting. It was a special appointment, funded partly for research, partly for teaching. But after Sophie was born she gave up her full-time job, and when the baby was eighteen months old she returned to employment as a part-time teacher. She describes what has happened as fairly 'classic'. 'I had a career with an obvious career path, but now I'm just doing a job. In effect I've downgraded my work in order to be with my child more.

'Before I had Sophie I didn't know much about children and I was totally unprepared for the emotional investment. I thought my life would be much the same but with a sweet little baby sitting in the corner. I found I wanted to stay at home with her. I felt she needed me, even though I hadn't thought I would think that. It was a real pull between the baby's needs and mine. I wasn't really committed to the job. It would have involved a lot of travelling and the people in the department were all really depressed. It wasn't exciting enough to pull me there. I just couldn't face another battle. Life was really hard with Sophie though it was also lovely and overwhelming. I was very tired. I just wanted something easy and I thought part-time lecturing would be simpler. In some ways it is. I don't have to fight battles or deal with people's personalities, but I have no rights, get paid less and have none of the perks a regular job gives you.'

Again, what was at stake in Sarah's decision was a resistance to being asked for a commitment. 'I can see the advantages now of having a full-time job, a commitment to one place of work. You make friends and have a social network and you can enjoy being there because you like to see people and you make a commitment to your working world. As a part-timer you don't have that.' But in spite of this Sarah still doesn't want to go back to full-time work. 'A full-time job is so difficult because people want you to commit yourself to more than full-time work. You have to demonstrate that you love the institution so much that you are prepared to be there all the time, and I can't do that realistically. Some people think if you don't commit yourself 100 per cent you don't want to work.'

Sarah's feelings are highly significant in women's choices about work and children. Women who are following a career with clear stages of promotion invariably experience a conflict of priorities once children are born. They see that their own new priorities of nurturing and protecting a young baby, which feel so immediate and real, will be deeply antagonistic to the career ethos of many professional departments. As one woman said to me, 'All the people at work can make you feel pretty guilty because you're not superwoman and your priorities might be in some little creature who crawls around and makes a lot of noise, and not in their sales targets!'

The woman who made this statement is Judy, who has one daughter and works full-time as a senior editor for one of the large publishing houses. She lives with a man who does the childcare full-time. But in spite of what would be considered by most people a 'good job' in terms of earnings and career potential, and an enviable domestic set-up, her attitude towards her work was remarkably similar to that of most other women I spoke to. Her work was clearly not that integral to her sense of self, and while she had been prepared to give total commitment to work before having children she certainly was no longer prepared to do so. Her partner and she had changed roles simply because she could earn more money than he could. 'I'm not really a career woman,' she told me. 'I'm open to change. The best things in my life have always come as a surprise. I'm not working to any specific goals in terms of career or money, just the usual corny things like wanting to be happy in myself, and honest, and not too greedy. If one thing doesn't work, I'll just figure out something else.'

At some deep level women seem to regard work and a career as dispensable. It is not as vital to their sense of selves as it is for men, and careers are easily exchanged for 'just earning money'. A friend of mine, for example, who has always been extremely ambitious, and who has successfully set up her own production company, took me by surprise when she revealed this attitude after the birth of her third child. On mentioning her career she signalled that she was using the word in inverted commas and on one occasion she added significantly, 'Although, increasingly, I now see what I do just as something I do to get money'.

Ruth gave a clear account of how this attitude towards work often pre-dates the birth of children. She works for an environmental consultancy and now has one boy. She described how she felt her ambition was somewhat on the wane even before she had her child. 'It feels awfully inevitable that it's me who is going to reduce my work and lower my sights, even though my husband and I have talked about this a lot and don't see why it should be like this. He thinks we should find a full-time childminder but I want to take more responsibility for Robert. I want to be his mother. I want to influence his values. I don't want to hand him over to someone else and that's surprised me. And it's easier for me to give up work than for my husband. I'm not absolutely sure why. It may be that I've got to the limit of how far you can get with technical ability and, increasingly, to get further up the firm you've got to be more of a leading type, a manager, and I find that less enjoyable.'

Typically, Ruth's conflicts and doubts at work began to surface at the point where she reached a more managerial level. 'At one stage I had a very high workload and so they encouraged me to recruit somebody. They gave me a totally free hand about where I put the ad and who I interviewed. I didn't get much of a response and I recruited somebody I didn't particularly like. And that was sort of torture really. I had to teach him everything and he seemed very, very slow to learn, and I just thought, if this is what managing is like, I hate it. And I think it was so clever of the firm to leave it completely to me. Because there was nobody I could blame. It would have been so easy to say they left me with a lame duck. But I couldn't. I'd recruited him, and I suddenly realized that my working life was going to be made up more and more of that. I find that kind of responsibility hard.'

For Ruth, the combination of finding the responsibilities of work more difficult and feeling the pull of her small child led to the typical decision of putting her career on a back-burner. She has asked for a job-share, which in effect will slow down her career advancement. These decisions have led her to reconsider herself and her husband as 'automatically equal'. 'I used to think that my husband and I were two equal careerist people. Now I see that my husband's attitude to work is almost the complete opposite of mine. He's the manager type who's always had trouble with the technical side. Part of me now thinks that it's increasingly his sort who get on, having struggled through the technical side and managed to get to the managerial stage. He'll now take off, whereas perhaps I never would have. I used to feel strongly that women were equal to men and what's been slightly disillusioning about having a baby is the feeling that we're not – because of this intervention of a non-ambitious force.'

Like most of the other career women interviewed in this chapter, Ruth found it relatively easy to give up her career in exchange for more time with her child. She felt that the values of work no longer expressed her 'real' concerns whereas they did express her husband's. Ruth puts it down partly to biology; she talked of women's biological functions and her awareness of a biological clock. 'Perhaps,' she speculated, 'I began to get less interested in work when my body was telling me it was time to have a child.'

Such views are typical: women leaving careers or downgrading them have no other language to explain their decisions than the pull of biology, the triumph of maternal bonding over the shallowness of careerism. But while biology is an important factor, it is only one part of a complex set of feelings. These interviews make it clear that at least one other factor is as strong as biology, and that it is often hidden or disguised by accounts of maternal bonding or natural instincts. This attitude to career as dispensable, 'unreal', at some point unimportant, is a deeply held female attitude. It is often there long before a child is born, and the conflict of priorities which a child brings makes it easy for women to jettison things which had previously seemed so important. Almost all these women talked about maternal bonding as the ultimate *explanation* for their decisions. It was the only term they had for the unexpected pleasure and commitment which so effectively displaced their other priorities. Yet these interviews also show that many women feel that the priorities of work have never quite been their own. They have always held a part of themselves in reserve.

Women's ambivalence to work is in part related, if not to maternal feelings, at least to expectations of 'maternity'. Male prejudice, and its attendant frustrations, are certainly connected with such views. And at a very deep level women are programmed to expect breaks in their career. Yet the accounts of these women – who have given up the things most valued by our society – show that maternal instinct involves a number of different converging factors. To understand women's decisions we have to look a good deal further back, into the way in which women are programmed in relation to career, their ambivalence to work and the frustrations and conflicts which work often arouses. If we are to gauge the strength of maternal feelings, we must try to understand what women are hiding from – as well as what they are seeking – in the bond they have with their children.

2

Envy, Competition and the 'Unreality' of Work

In the previous chapter I looked at some of the reasons given by professional career women for their readiness either to give up work entirely or to downgrade their careers once they were mothers. Common to almost all the women I spoke to was an ambivalence about committing themselves to the priorities of the workplace. In this chapter I explore some of the reasons – often hidden and unexpected – why women find it difficult to make this commitment. I talked to women about their ambivalence towards professional values and ethics, the lack of material incentive and, especially, about their fear of competitiveness – with its accompanying feelings of jealousy and envy – particularly when these feelings were experienced towards other women.

The complex and positive emotions which women have towards motherhood will be explored later. For the moment, I am looking at certain negative feelings about work and careers that women repeatedly mentioned to me. These negative themes throw up questions about why women find competition and envy so difficult, and why the family appears more meaningful and somehow exempt from these problems. Their answers tell us much about certain 'feminine' attitudes and shed light on the whole topic of women's complicity in traditional female roles.

Linda has two children and is planning to have more: 'definitely three, hopefully four'. Her terraced house is orderly and quiet. The mantelpiece is covered with photos of the children and the shelves have a few books about interior decoration and art. There is no evidence of Linda's previous working life. In fact, when she got pregnant she was a researcher in an academic department, on course for a prestigious career. It was a job she 'landed' – much to her surprise – after she left university. Attached to one of the country's leading psychologists, she would inevitably have risen with him but left the department when she became pregnant. Officially she is still meant to be finishing her Ph.D but thinks its completion is becoming increasingly unlikely. 'I do work now, two days a week, but I am working for my husband who is setting up a business. I don't think I'll ever go back to academic research.'

Like many of the women I interviewed, Linda describes herself as an 'accidental' career women. When I asked her if she had been ambitious in her career she answered, 'I always did very well at school and university. I don't think I'm especially ambitious. It was rather I felt I ought to be doing something as I had the qualification and the ability and I was offered a really good opportunity.' She describes her particular career as owing as much to luck as to single-minded careerism. 'It just fell into my lap, working with such a prestigious department and such an eminent professor.' She added, 'If I'm honest I never really liked how competitive it was.'

Linda described in very exact terms how her home had always felt more important than her work, even before children. Home was where she went to escape the competitiveness. 'The department was a very competitive place and I never felt I wanted to get fully involved in all that. I couldn't stand the way it *mattered* so much to the individuals if they had more papers published than anyone else. And I couldn't stand their need to put other people down. I couldn't and wouldn't compete, so I withdrew. But I think I felt that before children. Had the opportunity to work with my husband from home come up I would have taken it, even if I hadn't had the children. My home is a higher priority than anything else.'

Linda's story is in some way typical of the interwoven anxieties and emotions of contemporary women. Having a family seemed to make 'perfect sense', given her feelings about competitive work. It also illuminates the way in which the pull of maternal feelings is only as strong as the ambivalence and frustration in a woman's situation. Even so, her decision to leave the field in which she trained has left her with a certain amount of guilt and regret. 'Looking back I can see that it wasn't an ideal moment to get pregnant, but given my career I don't know when an ideal moment would have been. I do feel irritated with myself for having spent five years doing a Ph.D and not having got it. But I wouldn't swap any of it for what I have.'

It is interesting that Linda also feels guilty that the outside world might perceive her as having abandoned her career *because* of her family, when in fact she feels that having children simply made her see her own earlier ambivalence about work more clearly. 'I feel guilty because I dropped out of the research world to have children. What I really ought to say is that I'm not interested in doing it any more; I don't want it to seem that my family is stopping me from doing it. I'm half using my family as an excuse to stop that career. But I'm feeling guilty about doing that. And at the same time, they *aren't* simply an excuse. It's having a family which has made me feel very differently about the work.'

Linda feels no such ambivalence about competitive work in her new role as general factotum for her husband's emerging business. This suits her in terms of working hours and in relation to the house and children. 'Running the business is ideal as far as I'm concerned because it relates to my family. I'm running it with my husband, our office is based in the house and I feel as if I am doing it for *us*. Having a family means that I'm not so interested any more in doing things that I perceive as being of no benefit to my family.' In fact, when I interviewed Linda the family business was not going well. She and her husband had already had to close down one venture and were starting on another. But Linda was still confident, not only that working from home suited her, but also that they could make a lot of money. 'My husband's a great entrepreneur and I'm prepared to work to make things happen for us.' But, I asked, isn't the world of small businesses just as competitive as her previous job? 'No, it doesn't feel like it. This is for *us*. I'm doing this for my family. The academic world felt like pointless competition, just competition between individuals as individuals.'

Linda's account illustrates how alienated and uncomfortable some women feel in overtly competitive situations, especially where recognition and achievement involve pitting oneself against other individuals. Time and time again I heard, with varying degrees of vehemence, how much women *hated* the competitive environments of their professions and how, to some extent, burying oneself in the family felt at first like an enormous relief. One woman, Elaine, gave me a graphic account of the problems which her working environment caused her. Her conflicts and distress about her work led her to make the 'typically' female compromise. Having struggled to continue full-time work while her children were tiny, she has recently reduced her working hours.

Elaine is in her late 30s, and has a girl of 8 and a boy of 6. She works for the BBC as a film editor in the news section. Such a job requires long and often unsocial hours. Sometimes she would be asked to do several twelve-hour days, which were compensated for by time off in lieu. It meant that her childcare needs were irregular and so she and her husband, a teacher, opted for employing au pairs. After a series of disastrous appointments Elaine decided she couldn't cope with the worry any more. She cut her hours to thirty a week and has had to steel herself for the likely consequences in terms of falling even further behind on the career ladder.

You might expect to find Elaine angry and bitter at having to take such decisions. Yet, as with many women, Elaine's decision was not such a difficult choice as it might have appeared. For a long time she had been extremely discontented with her work, and in many ways the decision was an enormous relief. Although the job of film editor is one of the first technical jobs in television where women began to succeed, it is still a male-dominated area of work. Elaine is graphic about how the ethos at work, and especially the competitiveness, 'makes her sick'. She went on to explain, 'When the news has been edited, no one outside can tell who did what bit. It's not as if you can look at it and say, "Ah, Francis Bacon!" One piece of work looks much like another and it's meant to – house style, you know. So how do people get recognized as being good? Well, guess what, they parade their personalities! You get men staggering around with large stacks of tapes saying, "Phew! That was a hard edit," and wiping their brows. I'm just not like that. In fact I hate it. I don't want to be judged on my personality. I want to do a good piece of work and have it recognized for its merit. Only it doesn't happen like that.'

I asked Elaine if this meant that she lacked ambition or was uncompetitive. 'God no! I think I'm very competitive. That's part of the trouble, because it makes me so envious of the others who get on better than me. I envy them their confidence; I envy the way they perform in public; I envy the way they effortlessly "know" the right people. I just couldn't be like that. But at the same time I also despise it. All this devotion to the company and smarming up to people, and all the extra hours you have to put in to appear keen! Well, with kids you just don't have time for it anyway. I take the attitude that people will recognize if I'm any good. But I get passed over all the time. My boss is now a 29-year-old man who started as an assistant only four years ago.'

What Elaine describes here is central to women's experiences of work. She doesn't have the necessary devotion to her self-advancement to make her identify with the institution and its aims, nor can she invest part of herself (as she sees it) in the company. She also has a strong sense of the shallowness of the ethos. She finds it hard to believe that people can take the ethos seriously, while at the same time she is deeply affected by it and resents not having got on as well as male contemporaries. This 'duality' was a repeated refrain. Even the most careerist women I spoke to seemed to be able to pull back from the workplace ethos, to feel detached from it. Yet at the same time they felt downcast at not 'succeeding' in that environment.

There is another aspect of Elaine's feelings about the competitive ethos of her workplace. Her competitiveness and jealousy were worse in relation to other women, something which causes her particular discomfort. 'I don't want to feel like this but I feel even more jealous if a woman does really well. The women who succeed here can be so unpleasant.' She went on to describe these heightened feelings of jealousy towards other more successful women as almost the worst thing at work. 'I feel betrayed. I feel they ought to be like the rest of us, because there is quite a community of us women who support each other saying, "What a lot of shits the men are." You can stand back and feel superior if you are all in it together but not if individual women are buying into those values you hate.'

Apart from the obvious frustration which might result from the fact that Elaine has been passed over at work, there is also an apparently more overwhelming reason for Elaine's discontent with her working situation. It is not, she says, the competitive environment she hates, so much as the uncomfortable feelings this creates in her. 'Sometimes I feel eaten up by the jealousy and competitiveness around me. How can I explain? Competitiveness is a state of being. It's not to do with reality so much as your own feelings. But that makes it worse. It feels as though what is causing the problems is not the situation but the fact that I've let these feelings get to me.'

This is an unusually frank and honest account of what is true for many women who, like Elaine, may despair of and despise professional ethics, not just for demanding so much of them, but also for making them feel bad about themselves. Self-advancement is often based on pitting yourself against another person as a person, and this is something women find extremely difficult. This is what Elaine described as 'trial by personality'. In her profession, the nature of the work dictates why this factor should have entered so forcibly into the work context. But it is no less true in other organizations, businesses and institutions where there is the possibility for career advancement.

Moira, for example, described how she felt hugely disadvantaged as an actor not just because she was black but also because she had no real appetite to compete. 'You think with acting you just get recognized for your talent, don't you? Well, it's not like that. In this business it's who you know. Some of my friends are so easy at chatting and are such good publicists for themselves, and I'm terrible at all that. I feel as if I'm interrupting them and they don't want to know about me. I don't want to sell myself. I'm not as good at publicizing myself.' Again, what Moira found unbearable was not her ambition but her dislike of pitting herself against others and feeling jealous. She, too, found it easier to withdraw. 'I went for a part in a musical and they put about two hundred of us on the stage for an audition. God! What a cattle market! There were all these women practically exposing themselves to get noticed. They can have it. I didn't even wait for my turn.'

It is, of course, a fact that in our society any profession or job where there is a clear hierarchy or an obvious unilinear career structure is dominated by this kind of ethos. And it is interesting to see how much more uncomfortable and full of conflict women seem to find working relations where this ethos prevails, as opposed to those in more menial, less well-paid but less competitive environments. These jobs may have all the problems of low pay, bad conditions and long hours, but at least your worth is less likely to depend on how well your personality compares with the next person's. One nurse I interviewed gave a graphic and upsetting account of her working conditions in a London hospital. But she added, 'I do enjoy it though. The other women are great. When I was pregnant, they couldn't have been nicer.'

The disadvantages that some women experience in unilinear careers are relatively well-known. Lily Segerman Peck has written a book called *Networking and Mentoring* (1991) in which she studies women's attitudes within the professions. She points out how, in spite of many changes, there remain very real obstacles for women:

> In some ways things are going well for women. But in the professional area, especially as women begin to advance up the career ladder, they still encounter a 'glass ceiling'. This is a point at which most women stop in their career and watch younger, often less capable men hop over them. It's not so much that these young men queue-jump, it's that they are in a different queue, and this counts both against women and against some sorts of men who just don't understand the rules.

Segerman Peck attributes this blocking of women's careers only partly to the practical difficulties of combining children with work, and partly to male prejudices: 'Now it's more a case of younger men being promoted because of social attributes and because they will fit the corporate identity and expectations.' Many women come unstuck because they concentrate on doing the job as defined by the job description. Like Elaine they want recognition without having to go begging for it. They often don't understand that senior management has a different agenda:

> Women are doing extremely well in jobs requiring technical ability but subject to higher authority. As soon as you reach general management, companies start looking for someone who can oil the wheels, who can bring in other business and contacts, someone who will socialize with the right people, who is pleasant to go drinking with. And of course this is where certain types of men score.

Segerman Peck believes that men's main advantage lies in the fact that they put more emphasis on this 'networking' aspect of their careers, by which she means making contacts and developing strategies in friendships and work which will advance themselves:

> Everything men do relates to their career. They are brought up thinking in terms of income generation and even their social contacts are often 'strategic', aimed at bringing them good contacts for their careers. Even public works are put to good effect. If they become chairman of the local health authority it's a good way of making contacts and being seen to be the right kind of chap.

And of course behind those men who are able to spend time drinking, socializing, attending extra meetings, taking on unpaid 'public' work on committees are often women – unpaid wives or paid domestics. But while these women are prepared to service career men, sometimes giving up their own career to do so, they are more reluctant to pursue such strategies themselves. 'They consider it beneath them,' according to Segerman Peck. 'They think of such things as cheap and nasty. They call it "buttering up" and don't approve of such considerations coming into employment. So they concentrate on doing their own jobs extremely well and neglect the other aspects which cause management to promote you.'

This is the point at which, in many studies of women and work, and in particular mothers and work, two usual explanations are offered. On the one hand, we are likely to be told about the forms of male networking and bonding, and the narcissistic identification which tends to operate between men, especially in the upper echelons of society. On the other hand, we are likely to meet explanations of women's apparent lack of ambition in terms of the practical obstacles surrounding them. But neither explanation is really adequate. It may be the case that men still do use old networks and employ younger men 'in their own image', but there is a much more nebulous ethos now prevailing. Now companies are likely to look for a person who identifies with the company and its objectives and who has the right profile.

In theory, there is no reason why women shouldn't increasingly take advantage of this breakdown in old establishment values. Some commentators think this is already happening. Nigel Halsey, a head-hunter, argues that 'the beginning and end of why women have been limited in their careers is simply the fact of family responsibilities. Of course if women have five-year breaks they lose out in relation to men. It means that a lot of mediocre men get on better than they should!' Halsey is confident that men are now trying to correct the mistakes of the past because they are missing out on potentially talented employees, and he is equally confident that the problem will eventually go away.

But neither Halsey's optimistic words nor Segerman Peck's cheerful suggestions that women should build their own networks take into account further, more powerful reasons why women often find it easier to bow out of unilinear careers than to follow them through. And it is not just that these theories don't fully take into account the impossibility of ever accommodating family responsibilities, particularly when they are conceived as women's responsibilities. It is also because they don't even consider the ethical conflict which arises from women's own sense that the values demanded by such professions are deeply at odds with family values and caring for children.

Practical difficulties and male prejudice are important and real reasons why so many women should experience such profound discontent at work, but they don't go to the heart of the situation. At the heart are the different feelings which men and women bring to their work experience, and, more important, the different responses which men and women have to the working environment. What is significant here is the discomfort and conflict that women experience when they have to deal with their own competitiveness and envy. These feelings often underlie women's attempts to detach themselves, either emotionally and/or practically, from the work ethos, and their desire to obliterate those feelings in the home.

I repeatedly came across women who described their own competitiveness as a problem. Susan, a radio producer who has three children and a now very irregular career, was vehement when I asked her if she was ambitious. 'Yes, very. That's the problem really. I hate it. I went to Cambridge, which is probably a bad thing in terms of exposing yourself to these things because all my friends are great achievers. I see a lot of them doing very well, and some have even got children, and I find it frustrating that I haven't got as far as them. I compare myself with them and, yes, I do feel jealous. But I wish I didn't. I would feel a lot better if I didn't compare myself with them.'

Catherine, who first changed careers and then gave up paid work to look after her children full-time, described herself as having 'a problem' with always wanting to be the best. She comes from a working-class family where no one else had been to university. 'I did well at school and got to university and I always felt quite special, quite clever.' But she found her work as an administrator in an arts complex extremely frustrating. 'The men had all the best jobs, and unless you were prepared to behave just like a man you didn't get them. I'm not saying the men weren't good at their jobs. They were, but I guess they'd had the support and encouragement and interest from birth. I did feel I'd got to the limit of my own potential so I thought I'd do something else. I got married with the definite intention of having children. And once I was pregnant I thought, well, stuff everybody, I don't have to compete any more.'

Catherine, in common with many women I spoke to, found the possibility of starting a family an enormous relief, not just because she could escape from a competitive environment but because she could escape from her own competitive feelings for a while. 'The minute I was pregnant I changed course completely. That was a good excuse for me. You need a big life event to reassess what you are doing and want, and pregnancy offered that. I think a lot of men are quite envious of that possibility for women. My brother, whose career isn't going anywhere, said, "It's all right for you, you can just go and have children." I think that's part of the decision for a lot of women! It's either too hard or too complicated to go on, trying to make more money, or be more successful, or more famous or whatever they are trying to do. Having a family is a legitimate alternative and everyone seems to accept that, though you might get the odd snide remark.'

Catherine's reference to snide remarks led on to the other area of conflict that she was glad to escape: her envious competition with other women. 'When I told them I was pregnant they were quite negative, not that they said anything, but they weren't enthusiastic. A lot of them were very competitive, wanted to do well themselves. The women with children were nice but the women I was in competition with were not at all supportive. Some women I knew who were and still are childless and are very competitive, said, "What a cop out." But I also chose it for that reason. Because I wasn't having such a wonderful successful career that made it worth pursuing.'

Several of the working mothers placed such competitiveness at the heart of their dilemmas. On several occasions, jealous feelings towards others at work, and especially jealousy and competition among the women, made work seem impossible and distasteful. This situation can be further complicated by the fact that women have to hand over care of their children to other women when they work. For some women, especially those who are frustrated and rivalrous at work, this can be the last straw. They don't want to have to fight for and win their children's love as well, certainly not if there is any risk that such a struggle might be as unsuccessful as the one at work.

I do not mean to suggest by this that women are in some way more competitive at work than men, or unsupportive to other women. On the contrary, most working mothers I spoke to acknowledged great support from other women. This was particularly telling when they had to negotiate job-shares, part-time work or flexitime. On these occasions a female head of department seemed to make all the difference between women negotiating sympathetic arrangements and being forced to leave their jobs. Women are not more competitive with each other. In our society, most people in hierarchical situations appear competitive to all others.

Yet when women feel jealous themselves, and particularly when they feel jealous of other women, they often suffer much greater personal discomfort than men. Paradoxically, women find it peculiarly disillusioning when another woman apparently adopts male values and then succeeds. And that is the point at which they begin to feel they would be happy to escape. Segerman Peck suggested that part of the 'trouble' which women have in advancing their careers comes from the fact that they lack something which men are encouraged to think of as part of their make-up; that is, a drive towards generating more and more income. Undoubtedly such a drive would tend to help men or women overcome any ambivalence they might be feeling about career and self-advancement. The interviews I carried out would tend to suggest that Segerman Peck's comments about this difference between men and women is extremely relevant in terms of the varying ways in which men and women negotiate feelings of competition, jealousy and ambition.

One startling factor emerged in several of my interviews: many women feel extremely uncomfortable about personal wealth – money above and beyond their immediate needs – unless they can justify it as bringing their own family particular advantages. It was strange, in interviews with career-oriented women, to hear how much they enjoyed 'balancing' the family's income. They even sometimes enjoyed the feeling of making economies, of not spending too much, of not consuming too much. One woman whose family income had been hit badly by the recession described this in detail. Her partner had not worked for a year and, as a freelance decorator, she too had been working far less. 'Money is really short. We've had to let rooms out to cover our mortgage costs and we haven't had a holiday this year. But it's funny, I'm quite enjoying some aspects of being careful with money. I'm enjoying looking out for cheaper cuts of meat instead of just buying for convenience in Sainsbury's. I know this sounds mad.'

It didn't sound mad to me. I have met several wives of wealthy men who share these feelings. In a strange way, women often do not fully identify with the available wealth. One such woman, married to a man who earns in excess of £100,000 a year, preferred to live off her own earnings as an archivist. 'He spends his money on family things, like cars and holidays. But day to day, I support myself. I usually travel by bus and find it difficult to be extravagant.' Such ideas crop up in the most unlikely places. Even Maeve Haran implausibly includes a passage where her heroine, erstwhile TV executive and wearer of Armani suits, suddenly enjoys the experience of economizing and being 'mean'.

Such romanticism will strike the single mother on income support as not just bizarre but offensive. But the feeling is not uncommon. In America it has even led to a political manifestation, with women talking of a new goal of inner economy whereby the individual should aim at not using up more energy or resources than the 'planet' can sustain. Such views would have a clear appeal for women with anxieties about having too much, wanting too much, being too competitive. They also touch on the more inexplicable position that many women appear to be drawn to: that they must neither consume nor spend too much; that personal greed is wrong (although family wealth is not); and that being forced to attend to a family's budget is preferable.

Having said that women are no more competitive or unpleasant at work than men, it is also important to insist that they are not any less competitive either. Given a prevalent cultural fantasy of women as 'nicer' people, more caring, more nurturing – something bolstered first by feminism's ideas of uncompetitive sisterhood and solidarity and then by the New Age celebration of the nurturing feminine – there is a readiness to explain women's distaste for competitive situations as arising from their greater natural decency and kindness.

In an article in *Options* magazine in 1991, one woman pondered the absence of any women in a handbook listing the UK's leading entrepreneurs, suggesting that:

> women are basically too honest, decent and too compassionate to make it into the big-time ... As I continued my reading, the reasons why women fail to succeed ... became clearer. How many women would be prepared to sail close to the winds of legality, risking the funds of orphans, widows and pensioners, all for the buzz of a better looking balance sheet? Virtually none, I would imagine. If these are the qualities necessary to make it as a major risk-taker, then I'm proud that not one single woman has yet descended into the premier league.

These views are not uncommon. There's a belief that, however much like men childless women might make themselves, as soon as they have children the 'feminine', caring, nurturing principles will naturally return. A film director described how distasteful her work seemed after she became a mother. This was not because of the practical tensions between work and home (although that was difficult) but because the 'unpleasantness' normally required in her workplace felt too uncomfortable. 'I have to make a lot of "snap" judgments about the people I work with, like the camera crew and the editors. If it's not going well, I just have to change them. Two years ago, I wouldn't have thought twice about sacking people but I can't do it now. Motherhood has made me a nicer person.'

Motherhood probably hasn't made this woman a nicer person, but it has exposed the gulf between two ways of being in the world: the individualism of the professional and the altruism of the maternal bond. Motherhood and leaving work, or making the children one's priority, provides an opportunity for denial, a way of putting those uncomfortable feelings behind oneself. But the ability to make children the priority, the feelings of discomfort at competition and of being sickened by other's ambitions, isn't proof that women aren't ambitious and competitive themselves, only that they find these feelings more difficult to handle than many men do.

It obviously makes things simpler to believe that women don't have 'bad' feelings, or that they have fewer than men. This would be a much less demanding way of understanding the world, but there's no evidence that it is true. Not all women who get to the top behave better than men; we have only to think of the ruthless social policies of Margaret Thatcher to see this. I interviewed a secretary to a female university professor whose account of her working conditions made it quite clear that men do not have the prerogative on domineering, aggressive behaviour. 'She treats me as if I'm not a human being. She never asks me about myself and isn't even polite. She slams documents down on the desk and says, "I want these by four." She shouts at me if I get anything wrong. It's like a parody of the wicked boss.'

But in general competition and achievement are rarely straightforward for women. Even when women do manage to achieve their objectives, they sometimes subvert themselves, denigrating any praise and attention they may receive. They seem to fear that their ambitious urges are destructive. Women do not have a straightforward desire to be best, but instead they mind 'beating' someone else or getting more than someone else. It is as if, in putting themselves up against another woman, they are entering a struggle from which either they or the other will lose out. In other words, what they feel most strongly is not the thrill of the chase, but the destructive spoiling impulses that characterize envy.

For reasons which will be explored more thoroughly later, envy seems to be much stronger in women than in men. Or perhaps I should say sensitivity to envy is more acute, since many women are not so much envious as fearful of other women's envy. Although envy itself and fear of envy are different, they are both distressing emotions. Envy is distressing because it makes you feel bad about yourself and anxious that other people might feel as destructive about you as you do about them. Fear of envy is distressing because you are constantly afraid of another person's destructive rage. Both are archaic emotions of childhood which are stirred up by adult rivalry, especially where the competition is based on personality. They come from the little girl's greediness and neediness which has not been properly satisfied or which fears retaliation.

Why should the emotions surrounding envy be so powerful for women, when envy is obviously common to both boys and girls? The answer probably lies in women's relationships with their mothers. Boys are offered ways to escape their hostile envious love for their mothers; by identifying as boys, and therefore 'other', they cease to feel that their successful separateness might in some way destroy their mothers. Girls, on the other hand, are left with their own rivalry and hostility towards (and from) their mothers and sisters. This means that competitiveness is rarely able to develop in a pure form for women, but is always seen as a destructive attack. Young childless women often seem more able to cope with their competitiveness and rivalry at work, but with the arrival of children a latent agenda erupts – a pressure towards maternal altruism and a fear of competition and envy.

Thus women sometimes run away from work and career because of the uncomfortable emotions generated there. And they run to the family partly because it appears to be the antithesis of everything in the professional world – a place of unconditional love, a place where altruism is not only desirable but necessary, a place where 'the horrible pretentiousness and envy' is absent. This is akin to rolling in a bed of nettles to cure a scratch on your nose. But it is not surprising that women should think they can escape from these emotions within their families. Not only is there a widely held cultural belief that in a good family these feelings won't exist; there is also a deeper, less obvious pressure for women to find their identity in the altruistic, uncompetitive, loving family, rather than in the competitive and materialistic world of work.

The split between the values of work and family is a deep one, going beyond any improvements offered by women's economic and social positions. Historically, our economic system has dealt with its amorality by dividing men and women. Men are allowed (indeed, encouraged) to have a degree of amorality: consider such 'prestigious' careers as solicitor, barrister, politician, stockbroker. Even self-advancement in the more caring professions presupposes a degree of ruthless self-interest. But we claim to be a 'moral' society, in which family decency (human values above competitive and financial values) plays an essential part. Indeed, through the years of Tory government the 'family' has been the only moral category offered against the philosophy of greed is good – and then only as the justification for that greed. But this split goes back further.

Since the Second World War two opposing tendencies have been at work which have put women in a very difficult position. In a society which no longer finds church and state acceptable as moral guardians, the family has become increasingly important as the only remaining 'moral' space. It is within the family that moral values should be preserved. And yet there have been enormous changes in the position of women, not just at work, but because women's expectations have changed, creating greater family fluidity. So women are being educated for work and independence while at the same time internalizing a much clearer sense of the 'moral' agenda than men do – hence the widely shared delusion that women are nicer and more moral than men.

Women still believe that their relationships with their children (what they create in the family) will embody all that is good. Motherhood itself tends to exacerbate what is always a potential conflict for women, between self-assertion and fear of annihilation. But what is particularly difficult is that the moral altruistic notion of motherhood is completely at odds with the requirements for the professional world: it makes for what one woman called the ethical dilemma of the 'impossible 1990s'.

This chapter has focused on the conflict between work and mothering and has tried to explore some of the deeper reasons why traditional solutions often seem appealing. As later chapters will show, some of these solutions involve splitting off and denying the real emotions at play. And emotions dealt with in this way can eventually erupt. But first I will turn to the positive pull of the family and the love between mothers and their children. What are the feelings, values and ethics which women find in mothering, and why are they in such conflict with the self-interest required of us in the working world?

3

The Pleasures and Perils of Maternalism

It is often said – if not so much in public, at least in private, between women friends – that motherhood is its own compensation for any of the social disadvantages that might follow from looking after children. This is not the same argument as the old defence of patriarchy – that men and women have separate spheres of power and influence, men in the public, economic and political, and women in the domestic. But in acknowledging this sense of satisfaction women have to be discreet. After all, if women sing the praises of mothering too loudly, then perhaps it will be all too easy for men to forget the lesson which feminism forced the world to learn; that it is also hard work.

It is undeniably the case that the feelings and experiences associated with the state of 'becoming a mother' are both a powerful lure and a powerful surprise to many women. These feelings and experiences form the basis of many women's agonized dilemmas about work, mothering and childcare. Perhaps the clearest indication of the strength and persistence of maternal feelings is the extent to which women still rate motherhood, in spite of the fact that being 'only a mother' has not been valued socially since the reaction against 'housewives' established itself in the late 1960s. As one writer put it, 'being "just a mother" was scorned by my peers and never considered an option for an intelligent and educated woman'.

In spite of social pressure, the pull of motherhood remains. Sometimes it results in spectacular renunciations of prestigious careers. More often women end up working part-time to accommodate their children's needs. For the most part, any understanding of these decisions is couched in terms of the power of an overwhelming, irresistible feeling of love and maternal responsibility. In the previous chapters I have explored the fact that these maternal feelings are, at least at first, often only about as strong as the complicated – essentially negative – feelings that women sometimes have about work. In this chapter I will look at the other, apparently more positive, side – at the love and sense of responsibility which is central to the decision of women to stay in, or aspire to, traditional female roles. I will look at what maternal love really means to women, to try to find out what women are searching for and finding in that maternal bond.

Why do I want to scrutinize something which is essentially natural and therefore appears to require no explanation? Explaining it in terms of maternal bonding, or natural instinct, closes discussion, closes understanding of what women are really experiencing through motherhood. It stops us understanding the real lures, satisfactions and traps of motherhood and from assessing whether or not the imagined satisfactions correspond to reality. It stops us from being honest about problems we may be encountering. After all, if everything can be explained in terms of a maternal instinct, then surely any problems we encounter must be due to our own failures as mothers. So what are the feelings that women experience in motherhood? What do women say privately about the satisfactions and compensations of motherhood? Are these really sufficient compensation for other, more negative aspects of mothering? Do women have strong fantasies about what mothering will be like, and what it might bring to them? And do the fantasies turn out to bear any relation to the reality?

It is clear that pregnancy itself, again in spite of public representations to the contrary, is often experienced by women as a very powerful state. Of course, there are the detractors, like Paula Yates, wife of Bob Geldof, who has simultaneously extolled the joys of motherhood while complaining about what a revolting condition pregnancy is and how grossly it interfered with her obsession with a fatless female body. And there are plenty of women who will describe the discomforts and incovenience and mess of pregnancy as nothing other than an interference with 'normal' life. Many women long for the pregnancy to be over, or to return to their 'normal' shape, or even, as the pregnancy progresses, want to hide away.

Those feelings are common, and almost all women will recognize them from some part of their pregnancy. But there are other emotions, predominantly feeling powerful, feeling 'interesting', as many women described it to me, and, above all, feeling they are the centre of attention. Helen, now a single mother with two children, gave a clear account of how her first pregnancy gave her a sudden status, not altogether desired but in many ways pleasurable. Helen had her first child at 20, while she was still a student. She describes the pregnancy as a 'sort of accident' and then went on to explain, 'I hadn't been getting on so well with Stephen. We'd been fighting so much that we had practically broken off the relationship. I started going out with another man – a tutor on the course – and this made Stephen very jealous. Somehow that led to us getting back together again. That's when I got pregnant. I remember thinking, this is risky but it doesn't matter. A baby will make everything all right. And I did feel extraordinarily good when I was pregnant. I liked being that big. It made me feel strong and I also felt rather special. I was something of a curiosity on the course, and I have to confess it, I felt clever.'

Two things are fairly typical in this account. One is the sense of being centre-stage, the other is the feeling of cleverness. Women don't often admit to the first. But it is indisputably there, as the many strange jealousies which sometimes erupt around pregnancies bear witness. Helen herself gave a rather startling account of this feeling. 'Recently when I heard my friend was pregnant again I felt terribly resentful but I didn't really know why. But when her little girl was born, I just went berserk. I shut myself in my kitchen and kicked the door. I just felt, this isn't fair. She's got everything. Everyone is looking after her. And look at me! I suppose I felt the only clever thing I've done is have children, and look at how inadequately I did it. The kids' father didn't even stay with me after the birth. He never even cooked me a meal. I felt so deprived.'

Helen felt that her own circumstances had cheated her of something which ought to have been totally special. She should have had a context in which people acknowledged her own sense of cleverness and achievement. When it came to it, being a curiosity on a course was scarce compensation for a relationship where that specialness was acknowledged and celebrated. Helen quickly realized that her student friends and her young husband were unable to understand the changes in her life. It is not surprising that she would then feel desperate when she saw another woman receiving the attention and acknowledgment she had missed.

However, even Helen's difficult circumstances could not take away from what is undeniably an element in women's experience of pregnancy and birth: the sense of physical power and wonder at their own physical processes. Pregnancy is the most natural state imaginable, and yet, in conditions where social, financial or health worries aren't overwhelming, the process can be awe-inspiring, both for women and for the men around them. Feeling proud of themselves, pleased with themselves for giving birth, looking at their babies and feeling clever – all these are common emotions surrounding childbirth. Such positive self-evaluation comes rarely to women who on the whole do not readily regard themselves as particularly clever or congratulate themselves on a job well done.

Whereas for most women pregnancy is mainly a means to an end, some women experience it so powerfully that it becomes a fascination and state of supreme importance in its own right. Mary, a mother of four, describes herself as 'fascinated with the process. After every child, I've instantly wanted to have another. Sure, it's hurt like hell, and while I've had them I've been shouting at my husband that I hate him and I hate babies and I don't want one anyway! But it's the most significant thing I've ever done with my life. I can't think of anything more important or more interesting.' Mary gave up the makings of a career in the film business and threw herself into being a mother. She also broadened her fascination with the process to explore it in other women, and for a while trained and worked as a voluntary teacher for the National Childbirth Trust.

Pregnancy can also bring status. The less social status women have in public in terms of work, the more likely they are to feel that pregnancy confers status. This is often taken to be one of the reasons why teenage girls go ahead with unplanned pregnancies, or even plan them in full knowledge of the likely financial and social problems that might follow. Bea Campbell, in *Wigan Pier Revisited* (1984), describes how some teenage girls reacted to the recession of the early 1980s:

Unemployed girls who've never experienced economic independence are doing the only thing they can – having babies, either getting married or not, but often staying with their mam and dad and, quite soon, getting a council house. They never consider an abortion, often don't use contraception. They want kids. Of course they do. There isn't anything else. Being a mother has a certain status after all, it makes you a grown-up person. Faced with the alternatives of the dole, or the angry aggravation of the streets, motherhood brings a sense of belonging. More important, it offers a transition from immaturity made permanent by poverty, to a state of maturity.

Campbell's book is based on interviews with these young girls. But her impressions have been supported by another research project, the findings of which are published in Ann Phoenix's book *Young Mothers* (1990). She reveals that lack of information about contraception and abortion are barely relevant as explanations for teenage pregnancy. Some girls, for example, enjoyed looking after children and therefore wanted one of their own; others wanted to feel 'more grown-up'. Few regarded their pregnancy as the unmitigated disaster envisaged by the politicians, even though most recognized that their situations were far from ideal.

Kristina, one of my interviewees, also gave a poignant account of how she became a single teenage mother and how it improved her life. 'My first child was an accident. Consciously an accident, subconsciously not. I was the seventh child of nine and my mother became an alcoholic when I was about 6 years old. I left home when I was very young and I needed something to focus my life on. My education had been disrupted because of my parents' situation and particularly my mother's alcoholism so I left home to live with my sister. But I was adolescent and rebellious and she threw me out, and when I went home my parents threw me out too! I tried to keep up my education but it was prettty impossible. But my life dramatically improved when I had Bianca. I established a flat and did it up. I had a nursery place and went to college. I didn't have much money but it was mine, and anyway, the money side of things never really mattered to me. What I loved was having this little girl who needed *me*!'

Kristina's childhood may have been atypical in many ways, such as the large number of siblings and the self-consciously Bohemian existence led by her artist father and Dutch mother, but aspects of it probably resonate with many readers (as, possibly, so some of her subsequent less positive experiences). What is particularly significant and typical here is that looking after a dependent person gave her life new meaning. Again, this is an aspect little explored by accounts of maternal instinct or maternal bonding, but it is a strong element in the power and pull of maternalism.

This 'natural' instinct to look after a tiny dependant is usually regarded as a positive quality, a truly feminine quality, and therefore not subject to any questioning. But caring for tiny dependent people has two sides. Although she has no regrets about her teenage pregnancy, Kristina is now much more suspicious of women's readiness to 'bury themselves', as she now sees it, in looking after other people's needs. Kristina met her current husband when Bianca was 3 and they married shortly afterwards. 'I think when I met Edward I'd had enough of rebellion. I was very angry and mixed up with resentment about my childhood. By the time I was 19 I was very lost and that's when I had Bianca. I did well, I think. I managed. But wanting to manage on my own was all part of my rebellion. I think I must have met Edward and felt I'd had enough. I was tired of rebelling. I didn't really know what I was fighting against any more.'

In what may have seemed like a total volte-face, Kristina married Edward and endeavoured to be the 'perfect housewife'. She gave up college and they moved to a small village in the Home Counties. 'When I married Edward I tried to model myself on "stay at home" women who were completely different from my former self. For about four years we lived in a village and I was hopeless at it all. I couldn't even make cakes properly! I couldn't understand what I was doing wrong and I couldn't understand why I wasn't happy. I kept thinking, surely this is all you ever wanted in life, Kristina. It was a shock when I realized it wasn't.'

Shortly after their marriage, Edward and Kristina had two boys only a year apart from each other in age. 'When I had the second lot of kids it was more of an escape from myself. Often women don't have children for children's sake. It's more of an ego thing – at least I believe there were elements of that in my life. It was certainly true of my mother, who had nine children, and other women who I see staying at home having child after child. That's more to do with burying themselves further and further and it will erupt. What they are trying to hide from will always erupt.'

Kristina now believes that her mother's alcoholism was precisely the eruption of despair. 'The reason my mother started drinking was because of a terrible dissatisfaction in herself. She had been a very artistic and intelligent woman and she just suppressed it and became more and more harried and unable to cope. My father was very domineering and possessive and I believe she married him and had endless children so she wouldn't have to look at herself. That was partly true for me too. I married Edward and had the children in order to try not to look at myself, in order not to acknowledge a part of me that was hurting. I bought into this ideal middle-class state with all the trimmings, but I'm just not like that. I really tried to hide in all that but it didn't work.'

When I spoke to Kristina she was neither regretting the fact that she had had children nor denying her deep commitment to them. She was simply being rather more analytical than many women often allow themselves to be about the factors surrounding maternalism. 'I think having children was fulfilling something very deep for me, that is, finding people who really loved me. This is such a need in me that I even find it difficult to share them. I didn't have to share Bianca but I do have to share the boys and I sometimes find that difficult. I always know that if I'm there to meet their emotional needs they'll love me more than him, because he's very shut down on all that, like a lot of men. And I've used that to my advantage to be secure with them. I wanted them to love me. I don't just mean love me. I mean *me*. Me alone. Maybe I feel no one else did before. I have to be really careful in my marriage not to manipulate or abuse the situation in order to make the kids more dependent on me and less on their father.'

What is particularly fascinating about Kristina's understanding of her situation is how clearly she can capture some of the fleeting emotions that many women experience but which few choose to stop and examine. She recognizes the pleasure in taking care of other people, but also recognizes the dangers. Burying yourself in the neediness of others is not quite the same as an altruistic concern for them. Our culture has difficulty in separating the two, and mothering is an activity which hovers above the narrow dividing line.

Fiona, now in her mid-40s, has also begun to re-examine what she described as her 'obsession' with looking after children. For her, the desire to nurture and protect no longer seems such a straightforward aspect of motherhood. Fiona's background and experiences are very different from Kristina's, but she too has come to recognize that her own neediness was a powerful element in her decisions to throw herself into nannying and then motherhood.

Fiona comes from an upper-middle-class family. Her parents were extremely repressive and believed that 'children should be seen and not heard'. 'My mother and father tried their best for me, but children in those days in that class just weren't considered emotionally in the same way as they are now. They were considered to be rather boring, noisy, dirty people who had to be civilized as fast as possible. I always felt my parents didn't give me enough affection or approval. I always felt I wasn't coming up to scratch.'

But as well as feeling inadequate – not as beautiful as her remote and rather glamorous mother and not academic enough to compensate – Fiona also had to deal with the fact that her mother had 'two if not three nervous breakdowns when I was growing up and was carted off to hospital on each occasion for two or three months. We always had au pairs or a nanny around to look after us and I was at boarding school from the age of 11. But she wasn't there for me as a teenager when I really needed her because that was her worst time. I remember her setting off to take me somewhere in the car, like to another child's party, and then just turning round and going home and back to bed, saying she couldn't cope.'

Fiona describes her reaction to this situation as 'weird'. 'I don't remember ever feeling, this person doesn't love me. But I do remember feeling *I* didn't love *her*. Given that I was only 11, this was an extraordinary reaction. We had a full-time nanny then because my little brother, who was 5, had asthma very badly, and by that point my mother definitely needed that kind of help. Muriel, the nanny, was much nicer to me than she was to my brother because she liked girls more than boys really. I remember going down to her in the kitchen one day – I can't remember what preceded it – and saying, "Did you love your parents?" And she said, "Yes, why?" and I said, "Because I don't love mine." And I burst into tears and rushed upstairs. Very dramatic. And she followed me. But by the time I got to my bedroom the crisis was over and I wasn't prepared to say more. She said, "What do you mean?" and I said, "Oh, nothing." I never talked to anyone else again about it. But I was terribly worried about myself because I had no feelings. I didn't have any feelings of any sort. I didn't have good feelings or bad feelings. I just had no feelings. It went on for several years. I knew I ought to be happy about some things and I wasn't. I knew that I ought to be sad about some things and I wasn't. I seemed to block off completely.'

Fiona's solution, like Kristina's, came, paradoxically, when she found herself looking after children. Her mother sent her off to become a nanny. 'It's what the upper classes did with girls they couldn't think of anything else to do with,' she said. But the course at a smart nannying school was for her a salvation. 'I learnt that what was happening to me wasn't right, that you could do things differently. I recognized that I had to put something right in my life that was missing. And I also learnt how much I enjoyed looking after small creatures who were even more needy than myself.'

Fiona found she was good at looking after children, but she also recognizes that perhaps her passion for it was 'a sort of weakness'. 'People who look after children, who want to look after children obsessively, who can only see themselves as carers, are often, like me, the victims of unhappy childhoods. Some women become mothers or nannies because they *need* to look after children and sometimes that need can be obsessive. It isn't just a normal liking of little things, and wanting to help them.' In her case, she felt she became so absorbed in caring for her own small children that she failed to notice her marriage was falling apart. Eventually her husband left her for another woman. 'I was devastated when he went but I managed well on my own. That was part of the problem really. I didn't actually *need* him in the first place. I was engrossed in the children.'

Fiona is now able to see how her own childhood made her into a 'carer', something which she has not passed on to her own children, now in their early 20s. 'My children are definitely not "carers". They aren't uncaring but they don't want their professional lives to involve caring. When I was their age, if my mother said, "Mrs Smiggs down the road would love to see you," I'd have gone down the road like a little lamb and loved the fact that she needed me. I wouldn't have considered rejecting her because I'd have thought about how sad she would be. If I said that to my daughter she would say, "Bollocks to Mrs Smiggs." I fear that that is probably a rather healthy attitude. She doesn't have the need to be liked by everyone, like I did. I wanted everyone to like me. Even if it was a dependent love. Yes, that's why I liked the children so much, because I liked them to be dependent. I don't like the fact that my 20-year-old isn't dependent any more. He only rings every three weeks. I'd be happy even if he used me to do his laundry.'

Descriptions of this pleasure in taking care of dependants were so common in my interviews that it was hard to make a selection for this chapter. But it is more common for this pleasure to remain unanalysed. It is rarely considered strange, certainly not pathological. After all, dependency is part of the human condition and caring comes most naturally to women, who for nine months have already experienced the close dependency of another's life upon their own. So for many being needed and loved is a state experienced as an 'ordinary' pleasure. But such a set of emotions is highly susceptible to obsessive behaviour. Even in the most adjusted households, meeting the needs of others can take care of, or wipe out, deeper feelings which are more difficult to express.

Caroline, a mother of three in her mid-40s, also thinks that in her case the powerful, almost overwhelming desire for babies came from a deep neediness in herself. 'I always desperately wanted children, it was my main ambition. I longed to have a baby even when I was very small. I had a baby doll I adored more than a toy. I really loved her. In fact I kept her till very recently. I finally wrapped her up and put her in the bin. I thought, she's just a doll and that's finished. But at the time she was very real to me, alive. I used to talk to her and I loved all the business of making clothes for her and putting her in a pram. I was fascinated. I was a "proper little girl" as they used to say.'

Caroline also had a disrupted and difficult childhood. 'It was during the war and my parents were moving around a great deal. My father was stationed at different airbases. I was pretty bewildered by all that. But my parents' marriage was also already in difficulties. I didn't have a lot of direct contact with my mother, especially after they moved to Holland when I was 4, just after the war. My mother had to do a lot of entertaining, and we had Dutch women in to help. I think I must have missed her a lot. And soon after that the marriage broke up. We came back to England and my father stayed in Holland, eventually marrying someone else. We came back to Yorkshire and moved around a lot, to my grandmother's, to hotels, to different houses. So maybe I would have been like that anyway but maybe I desperately wanted to make a close mother–child relationship.'

The pathological aspect of motherhood, revealed in possessiveness over their children, often takes women by surprise, especially more 'modern' women, who have less traditional expectations of men and the family. Kristina touched on it when she spoke so honestly about the danger of exploiting the children's neediness for her. Repeatedly, I heard women describe their children's exclusive neediness for *them* – sometimes with a great deal of self-awareness, sometimes with none at all.

Vanessa, a committed feminist, was shocked at how readily she excluded her partner from caring for their child. 'Bill and I were all ready to share everything half and half. He took six weeks leave off work when Harry was born. We were going to take it in turns feeding the baby at night. Did we heck! I could hardly bring myself to let him push the baby round the block for half an hour, let alone have him deal with the baby's feeds on his own. I felt so critical of everything he did.' What she described was something I recognized very much from my own experience. I too had intended to share parenting equally. But that intention didn't stand a chance when challenged by something far more primitive and complex – the sense, perhaps for the first time in one's life, that it was *you* who was needed, and that you could do it well. One woman described to me how she and her husband had fought physically the day after their child was born. She was beside herself with tiredness. He was trying to help. 'But I couldn't bear to let go,' she said. 'I was convinced *I* could stop the baby crying, not him.'

At its most banal level, this desire – or, perhaps more accurately, ability – to lose ourselves in our children does take care of other, much less resolved questions for women. We have seen that women often don't feel fully able to buy into a system which is simply about self-advancement or money (or not in the way in which men pursue these goals), and that they are encouraged to believe that there ought to be a moral, ethical or emotional purpose to their lives. Clearly, this purpose can be fulfilled in caring for and looking after dependent people, a project which more than takes care of any philosophical doubts. What could provide a deeper sense of purpose than the fact that somebody's life is dependent on your own? Especially if that purpose is affirmed by the prevailing social ideologies surrounding the maternal instinct and bonding.

Women can and often do make themselves the emotional centre of large and complex families. And when these situations are happy there is no reason for a woman to doubt or question her need to take care of others. Even the 'empty nest' syndrome can be postponed indefinitely by women who are able to encompass the expanding needs of their families. Barbara is one such woman. In her early 50s, she is the 'emotional centre' of a complex, four-generation family. Her own three children are now in their mid-20s, with children of their own. All of her children have either been divorced or have married partners who already have children by previous relationships. Barbara works part-time as a cleaner and looks after her grandchildren and 'adopted' grandchildren.

In many ways, Barbara's lifestyle seems highly enviable. It's hard work, there isn't a huge amount of cash for luxuries, and she would like to move 'to a better area', but the house is never empty and all the children and grandchildren actively seek out her company. She is lucky with her husband, a carpet-fitter who, without the relentless commitment to career so typical of middle-class men, has made her priorities his own. More important, she provides a source of stability for a number of children whose first carers have unsettled lives. But although the conflict between her own needs and those of the family are often not so drastic or problematic as they can be in some families, there is still a sense that some deep needs of her own have not yet been met. She still weeps at the memory of her teenage years, spent nursing her dying mother and then being left with an abusive father who provided for his motherless children but showed them no affection. Barbara, as eldest daughter, quickly assumed the role of mother, and has fulfilled it successfully ever since. It is hard to imagine that any job would have fulfilled such needs, but not hard to recognize the familiar pattern of women needing to surround themselves with dependants.

Often women are not so fortunate as Barbara. The interviews in this chapter have more than hinted at the fact that losing oneself in this caring role is often a difficult, even problematic, route to take. Kristina is now 'taking stock' after her changing roles and rebellions, spending time at home trying to think about what she really needs now in her life. 'Everything is up for grabs at the moment because I'm changing. I don't know what the outcome will be. I don't even know if my husband will want to stay with me through the changes. But I know I've got to do this. I've been lost for too long and it's time I found out what I need.'

Fiona and Caroline show greater signs of discontent and anxiety. Fiona fears a time when she may well feel redundant, no longer needed in an obvious way, even though that possibility is further off. Unusually for a woman, she now has a 'second' family, as she remarried eight years ago and has two more children. She says, 'Since I want to be around until the children are 18, I'll be 58 before I can work. I don't really have to face that. And in the meantime I'll do childminding while my children are at full-time school.' But Caroline is discontented and depressed. She is looking around, comparing herself with other women who have stayed with some kind of career and feels like a failure as her children reach school-leaving age. She suddenly fears that, having needed the children's dependency on her so much, she has become dependent on them. 'If the mother is so needy herself, it's a burden for the child. It was for me in relation to my own mother. I think it's terrible for a child to feel responsible for its parents' happiness.' This is the point of inevitable disruption of the relationship between a mother who needs a child to be dependent and a child who wants to be looked after but separate.

These problems afflict women across all classes, but women with less money are particularly vulnerable. It is often not possible to meet the children's needs in quite the planned or anticipated way, and the consequences make women emotionally very vulnerable. Pauline is in her early 50s and works as a childminder. She describes herself as loving babies, so much so that whenever one of her charges reaches the age of 3 she immediately advertises for another newborn. This pattern in her working life repeats her own family experience. She had five boys, each separated from the other by three years. The youngest two were both born with a

The Pleasures and Perils of Maternalism

serious genetic illness and she still feels extremely guilty that she continued with the last pregnancy even though doctors advised her against it. Her husband left her with the children when the eldest was only 12 and the youngest just born, and for numerous years her life was taken up with caring for them and coping with extreme hardship. When her fourth child became seriously ill, she devoted four years to nursing him, scarcely leaving the house. But when he died she was confronted with a crisis. Her youngest had grown up without her noticing, and two of the older ones had left home.

It was then that she discovered childminding, and to some extent 'solved' her sense of being bereft, of no longer being indispensable and needed. 'I thought, what can I do? and then I thought, there's only one thing I know how to do well and that's look after children and be in my home. And I don't want to leave my home because I still feel my boy who died is here in some ways. And I like it most of the time. Only sometimes I get so depressed I can't get dressed. I feel ill and I just sit in the kitchen and think, why has it all been so hard? I can remember when I just had the three boys and I went one day with my husband to the beach. It was lovely. I'd got the family I always wanted and I thought it wouldn't be long before we got a house of our own. We were short of money and we lived in a very small flat – I did all the washing-up and washing on the landing. But I remember it was a happy time. Then my husband started drinking and I couldn't bear that. And ever since then it's all been such a struggle.'

For women like Pauline, working with children or in domestic-related jobs is often the only possibility. This isn't solely due to lack of educational opportunities; it is also because of deep emotional needs. Lives like Pauline's seem a long way away from the privileged choices of the professional women hanging up their briefcases to answer the maternal call, but there are points in common. What is being satisfied is often not the child's deep neediness but the mother's own need to be needed. The difference between Pauline's life and that of the professional woman is that Pauline cannot shield herself against the difficult times, wrap herself in ideologies of maternal bliss. Lacking the resources to pay for freedoms and respites, she has to take the rough with the smooth. And if life deals, as it did in her case, a rough hand, there's no easy way out. Maternalism may satisfy deep needs, but it also brings hardships – low pay, living off benefits, the demands of grown children; for Pauline, the price she has to pay is often hard struggle and depression.

This is the crux of the matter. Like any lure, that of being indispensable can also be a trap. At some point the children will cease to be dependent. And children's needs are various and complex, so that their interaction with a needy mother is unlikely to go smoothly. Most of the women interviewed for this chapter found some 'balance' in espousing maternalism – meeting the children's needs was something which they could more or less accomplish. But that is not always the case. For many women, the difference between their expectations of a baby and its reality may be too great. Some women are overawed at the responsibility, can't cope, and above all cannot handle the child's own neediness in relation to their own.

Few women can accurately anticipate the feeling of maternal responsibility, a difficulty exacerbated by the lack of real information about children and child development made available to young women. Instead, presented with a terrain criss-crossed by media fantasies, distorted images and personal dreams, women may often spend more time trying to force little children to correspond to the fantasy than to finding out what is really needed for their care. Confronted with a tiny dependant, a set of overwhelming inner needs and these unreal fantasies, there is far more potential for getting it terribly wrong than there is for any longed-for maternal bliss. What may start as a desire to meet the child's needs may end in total disarray.

Investing your hopes for an answer to all your needs in motherhood is dangerous. Children are unpredictable creatures; they are not simple, passive recipients of a parent's fantasy. It is the exception rather than the rule for a true symbiotic match to be made between a mother's need to mother and a child's need to be mothered. In the following chapter I will look at some of the most dramatic ways in which the reality of the family undermines some of the fantasies and hopes and needs that women bring to it.

4

Buried Emotions

In the previous chapters I looked at how women sometimes turn to mothering and caring for dependants when faced with problems and conflicting emotions in other areas of their lives. Sometimes these conflicts are brought on by work, sometimes by deeper, less conscious emotions within themselves, sometimes by a combination of the two. This is not to say that if things were easier for women they would all choose not to have children. However, it does mean that in a society like ours, where different sets of morals and emotions are expected from men and women and where individualism is set against caring for others, women often find themselves trying to solve unbearable conflicts by burying themselves in taking care of their children's needs.

But does the family as we experience it now really provide the *solution* to some of these conflicts? Does burying yourself in the family in order to avoid ambition, competition and envy really work? Or do these emotions simply resurface within the family, causing confusion and disappointment? And what happens to the relationships between women and their children when the waywardness of children's development runs up against the needs and denials of their mothers?

In the attempt to make the family a haven from 'unsafe' emotions, conflicts re-emerge between women over their children. Competition and rivalry is often rife in groups of mothers. As a worker at a one o'clock club told me, 'If you want to see a good punch-up, hang around here for a while.' I didn't need to; I'd seen it all often enough before: sometimes one woman cold-shouldering another, sometimes an exchange of words, sometimes

times even physical pushing and shoving. There are any number of things which provoke fights between mothers when they get together, but they frequently have the same cause: one child does something that is perceived as bad behaviour but that goes uncorrected by its mother. 'Didn't you see your boy pull my little girl's hair?' I heard one mother shout. And when she was ignored, the mother flew across the room and pulled the little boy's hair herself.

This may sound extreme, the type of behaviour that only a 'disturbed' woman would engage in – the sort of woman prone to flying off the handle, always likely to get into arguments. But the fact is that actions like this only display what goes on beneath the surface all the time, and across all the social classes – a profound identification between mother and child through which much of women's own hidden emotional agenda, including aggression, competitiveness and envy, re-emerges.

Presently, there is no greater social minefield for women than the relationships which they form for and with their children when these children are very young. I say this in spite of the fact that many women, including myself, recognize that the friendships and networks centred on their children may also be their lifelines. But developing and maintaining real friendship and support around the children is not an easy process. It is well worth it, but to achieve it sometimes involves women in facing and having to break through their old patterns of behaviour.

To say this is to run counter to a prevailing ideology. Feminism is partly responsible for having peddled an ideal of female solidarity and friendship that would transcend hostile competitiveness, which was seen as a largely male characteristic. What was stressed was the common bond between women, rather than the rivalry. And although these views are no longer widespread as specifically feminist ideals, the notion still prevails that the automatic networking and support which women give each other in their shared work as mothers is founded on mutual identification and love. Hostile and competitive feelings are supposed to be absent here.

Yet the same people who praise these networks are often those who also readily admit that maintaining them is not without its difficulties and pitfalls. Even where women have started meeting with the specific aim of supporting each other, there is no guaranteed immunity from difficulties. Competition often erupts over how fast a child is developing, how well it is doing at school, its behaviour – not to mention all sorts of trivial issues like how long each child is left to cry, how many sweets you give it, what time the child goes to bed. Each and all of these can be taken as reflecting on women's mothering abilities and are a potential source of conflict.

One woman, Clare, described to me a tangled and difficult friendship she'd formed with another woman – a friendship which makes it clear that some of the simplistic views about what mothering will entail are wide of the mark. In this friendship, defensiveness about their children and identification with them led to the two friends falling out. Clare met Val in her local childbirth classes and the two of them hit it off immediately. Both were teachers, and they had similar interests. Their children, both boys, were born within two weeks of each other. For their babies' first year they met at least twice a week. Clare described the friendship as 'extremely important. We talked about everything – the babies, our husbands, our feelings about going back to work.'

But as the children became more active and mobile, Clare began to find their socializing more and more difficult. 'My Daniel is much more outgoing and independent that Val's boy Luke. Luke is quite passive. When he was little he clung to Val all the time and she would never leave him. Then we got to the stage when the children were constantly snatching toys from each other and hitting each other. I suppose it was all quite normal but Val and I didn't manage it very well. I felt resentful that whenever my little boy did anything aggressive, there was the most enormous scene. Val made him apologize and then we had to have a post-mortem about why he was behaving like that. But if Luke did something aggressive Val never noticed and never told him off.'

Resentment built up until Clare finally challenged Val about double standards. 'There was a terrible row, basically about whether or not Daniel was "playing" or being "nasty". Val implied Daniel was too aggressive and that I should give him more attention – I was back at work by then. I was furious. We didn't see each other for over a year. Eventually a mutual friend invited us round together. And we still like each other. But we'll never meet up with the children again. Sometimes we have dinner with

Val and her partner. We talk about the children all the time, but I just don't want to get involved with them as a family again.'

It may seem incredible that a friendship and relationship was jeopardized by such trivial incidents, but the history of female friendships is littered with such casualties. One mother described to me how she fell out with another because she felt slighted over her children's choice of breakfast cereal. Another described 'the final crunch' as when the mother of her daughter's friend sneered at her for allowing her daughter to read Enid Blyton! These incidents are merely the epiphenomena of a deeper anxiety which women feel about their children's behaviour and activities as reflections on themselves. This difficulty in acknowledging a separate existence and identity for their children leads women to interpret other people's reactions to them as reactions to themselves.

Perhaps the most dramatic illustration is provided by the friendship of the mothers of Anna and Catherine, two 5-year-old girls. The two mothers had met at work and had the babies within three months of each other. It seemed inevitable, with such similar backgrounds and two daughters so close in age, that they would gravitate towards each other. But the girls had extremely different personalities. Catherine was shy to the point of withdrawn, while Anna was extremely loud and boisterous. As Catherine got older her antipathy to Anna's aggressiveness became marked. By her 5th birthday, Catherine's mother, Sue, decided to have a small party and to exclude Anna.

Sue gives this account of what happened. 'During the party, Anna's mother rang up and started shouting at me. She said, "Can't you hear how upset Anna is?" and she held out the phone so I could hear Anna sobbing in the background.' Instead of dealing with a child's reasonable pique and natural desire to have everything nice, Anna's mother obviously identified with 'the rejection' and used her child's feelings as a cover for her own. The two women have not spoken to each other since then. Again the story sounds extreme, but it is by no means atypical. Many of the women I spoke to had a similar story to tell of how, when dealing with their children's feelings and developments, they fell out with their friends.

This is the stuff of raw identification, of women unable to perceive any difference between their own slights, hurts and feelings and those of their children. There is little difference between the protected world of Anna and the mother who storms into school to scream at the headmaster. Both are founded on a muddle between the parent's and the child's emotions which goes way beyond a straightforward empathy. This is more than sympathizing with your child's frustrations and hurts; it is feeling them as if they were your own. Indeed, in Anna's case it is also imposing on the child's experience of the world your own emotional history.

Women's identification with their children is rarely discussed as anything other than a positive, blind 'bonding', a vital element in survival, like that of the ferocious tigress protecting her young. Yet it is a powerful and often problematic force. Women have described to me how the birth of a child, particularly a first child, awakens buried feelings from their own infancy. These feelings are usually overwhelming and rarely other than confusing and inchoate. Mostly they guarantee that a child will be well cared for, because in taking care of the child's needs the mother is taking care of her own.

But reliving their own infantile feelings and re-experiencing their own infantile needs does mean that the identification between mother and child can subvert a more straightforward caretaking relationship. Sometimes it means that women cannot tolerate any frustration for their child. Sometimes it will be the opposite feeling – a hostility to the child's neediness as a too painful reminder of their own. Whichever it may be, the results are complex and unexpected. So much so that in some cases the normal rules of social interaction can go by the board. This chapter started with the example of the mother who pulled the hair of another woman's child. That waiving of the 'normal' conventions which adults observe is typical. I know one woman who waded into a toddler tussle, snatched a toy from her son's tiny antagonist, and gave the other child a hefty shove.

In these two instances, it was the children's aggression that caused the women's relationship to founder. This was not just coincidence. Children's aggression is an explosive area and affects women's relationships with each other. Because women have an extremely complicated relationship with their own aggression and fear, they are often thrown by and sometimes simply cannot handle the normal aggression which is part of the child's universe.

Women often overdramatize children's aggression, which is probably quite a straightforward emotion until it is channelled and distorted by the adult response. But as has already been seen in discussing women's antipathy to aggression and competitiveness at work, it is an emotion which throws women if they feel it themselves and/or if they provoke it in another.

Aggression, even in these supposedly post-feminist days, still causes an enormous muddle for women, a muddle which exceeds the difficulty of seeing your own child inflicting pain or being hurt. If the aggressor's mother does little to stop her child from hurting yours, it is hardly surprising that bad feelings follow. But I spoke to one unusually frank woman who made it clear that these feelings are more complex. Anne has two children, a boy and a girl, and she 'admits' that she often despairs about her son Michael. 'I feel incredibly embarrassed by him and I always have. Even when he was little, he used to hit other children a lot. Whenever there was trouble at the playgroup or nursery, there in the middle of it was some child wailing, "Michael hit me." Sometimes I hit him, sometimes I try to reason with him. He has got better but he's still in trouble a lot at school – getting into fights. And he's got a filthy temper. I'm a bit scared of him. But at least I don't have to worry about him being a wimp. I'd hate if if he was the one getting beaten up at school. But I sometimes hate him for doing it. At my worst moments, I want to wash my hands of him because I'm scared of what might happen.'

When I talked to Anne about her own childhood, it was clear that other things were fuelling her response to her son's aggression. She was the third daughter in a family of four; her youngest sibling was 'the boy my parents always wanted'. There wasn't much money around – 'All my toys and clothes were hand-me-downs.' She described herself as a child as 'pretty pathetic' and 'a real goody-goody'. 'I was too shy to go anywhere, and I was scared of everything. I suppose I'm glad Michael's not like that. At least he sticks up for himself.' It wasn't very difficult to realize that Anne felt pretty ambivalent about her son's aggression. One moment she seemed almost to admire him for 'sticking up for himself', the next moment she seemed to hate him for it. Perhaps hers is an extreme case of what women often feel about their forceful sons – pleased to feel their sons are not losing out as they once did, but hostile and anxious about any expression of emotions which they have come to regard as bad. Perhaps here too is one way in which women collude in ensuring men possess all the qualities which feel impossible for women.

It would be possible to see children's early aggression and volatility as a necessary evil, something to be overridden for the sake of group solidarity, something requiring collective responses and collective standards. But there are important ways in which this understanding of children is completely absent in contemporary Western approaches to mothering. On the surface, aggression is frowned upon, and for the middle classes has become yet another issue in the general competitive ethos of whether or not the children eat healthily, talk early or read well at 6. Feminism is particularly culpable here for endorsing a notion that the good child – the best child to have, in fact – is the child who is peace-loving and non-aggressive. As with everything else surrounding children's behaviour, however, aggression isn't easily channelled according to the ideologies of the parents. Many feminists have had to learn the salutary lesson that a simple conditioning in 'feminine' values is about as likely to produce non-aggressive children as planting potatoes and hoping for beans.

But while some of us have felt inclined to back off and consider the situation more complex than previously imagined, for others it has been the best possible evidence to reinforce traditional views of the natural division between boys and girls, men and women. I've heard feminists 'boasting' about their non-aggressive little daughters – using them as proof of women's natural superiority. This has been accompanied by protracted public moans about the difficulty of overcoming the natural aggression of little boys. Polly Toynbee in the *Guardian* gave a typical example of this. She bewailed the fact that her daughters were nice and co-operative but her boy only loved fighting and aggressive stories. It wasn't clear whether at a deep level she was pleased or unhappy about this state of affairs. What was clear, however, was that the age-old split whereby boys can become the repositories of feelings unacceptable to the mothers themselves was still well and truly in place.

The consequences of these unresolved ambivalences in women are dire for girls, not least because it means that in subliminal ways mothers transmit to their daughters the same distrust and fear of aggression which has been part of their lives. It is extraordinary how prevalent this denial and policing of girls' aggression still is. The consequences for girls if they show aggression – often in ways which would be considered natural for boys – are severe . Jo, who describes herself as an anarchist and New Age Traveller, told me that part of her decision to live as she now did was because she couldn't see her daughter fitting in anywhere else. 'I've encouraged her to feel strong and fight with the boys if they pick fights with her. I don't think swearing and fighting is any worse for girls than boys. I don't approve of fighting but she's no worse for doing it than some of the young lads round here. One of my mother's friends told me that Rachel is foul-mouthed and delinquent. I don't want to hang around people like her.'

It is ambivalence about aggression which underlies not only the unclear messages that boys are receiving, but also many of the conflicts which erupt between the mothers of young children. That 'aggression' could become a source of so much muddle and competition should warn anyone who believes that women transcend competitiveness on becoming mothers. Any study of the exchanges, especially between middle-class women and their assorted children, would reveal not so much a minefield as a battlefield, upon which the protagonists conduct themselves in numerous tangled, deflected, but nonetheless damaging ways. Mothers are often unable to put any emotional distance between themselves and their children; what children do and act out is often a theatre where their mothers' own inner dramas appear to be played out.

The examples so far are clear about two things – namely, that emotions suppressed in the mother often re-erupt around children, and that having children is just as likely to stir up, rather than finally quell, the mother's inner warfare. But the examples also hint at another aspect of mothering. For not only do women bring to bear on their mothering aspects of their own infancy, but they are unable to predict or control the consequences of their actions. Sarah, who had her first child at 37, gave a typical description of how women bring to the child compulsions, anxieties and repetitions from their own childhood, and also of how, when the child fails to respond as predicted, the mother feels anger and resentment.

Sarah describes how she felt the most important things she had to do as a mother was to give her own daughter 'a feeling of being competent, good, attractive and happy'. She added, 'It's something I didn't get. I always felt I hadn't done well enough. I can see now that my parents wanted the best for me, they had high aspirations. But I always felt it was conditional, that I had to do things well before they accepted me.' Reacting against this, Sarah believes she should pay full attention to everything her daughter does and affirm even her smallest achievements, never 'nagging' her to make her feel a bad person.

This strategy was evidently not without its complications for those around her. Her husband felt she was 'obsessed' with their daughter. This was his second marriage and he had two teenage children already. 'He's just not that fascinated by her and thinks I pay too much attention to her. He thinks she should just go off and play on her own.' Sarah admitted great strains were being created in the family. 'I think I probably put my partner's needs incredibly far back. It is an issue, I know, but I've been so overwhelmed by her that he comes a very poor second. I've been lucky he's been tolerant so far but I can see the balance needs to be tipped in the other direction now.'

What is typical here, and it is something I heard often, is the sense of trying to protect the child from the aspects of one's own experiences which are painful. Linda, whose experiences have been described in a previous chapter, was also clear that the deeper aspects of her mothering were 'reactions' to her own early experiences. Her overriding desire was to keep her children 'secure', to which end she would sacrifice just about anything. Her notion of security meant two things. One was to maintain a 'happy' atmosphere in the house, which she feels never existed between her own continuously arguing parents. The second involved making sure that her two children were never submitted to frightening experiences.

This desire to protect her children from fear was deeply rooted in Linda's childhood experiences. When she was little her parents separated, a separation which lasted for several years. During that time, her mother worked in a hotel, taking Linda with her in the evenings. 'I didn't like that at all, being put to bed in a strange room. I didn't like the fact I had no other choice, it was imposed on me. I was frightened a lot of the time. One night my mother had gone out but I still slept at the hotel, even though she wasn't there. A drunk came into the room. I was on the top bunk and he got into the bottom bed. He didn't take any notice of me but I was terrified. It disturbed me for some time. I would hate to put my children through that kind of experience. I have very strong feelings about how I want my children to be. I want them to feel very, very secure and I wouldn't do anything that knowingly made them feel insecure. I feel my mother did, although I now understand that she didn't have any real choice. But for a long time I felt terribly angry with her.'

While Linda, like many other women, may know quite a lot about her own past and what she does and does not want to repeat, her children do not always oblige. She was determined to keep the house quiet, peaceful and free from argument and aggression. But later she went on to describe how she sometimes felt enraged with her son. 'He's so argumentative and angry sometimes. And I sometimes almost hate him.'

Many responses to children are conditioned by hidden emotional agendas, which the children's own emotional development runs up against and has to form around. But the problems come not just for the children, but for other women. Sarah's intense involvement with her child is by no means atypical of a certain kind of middle-class mother, and it creates all kinds of anxieties in the women around her. Sarah described her own mother's punitive hostility to the fact that Sarah was still breast-feeding her daughter at 18 months. Other women, she said, thought she was 'stark staring mad' because of her child-rearing strategies, like 'not hitting her, not leaving her to cry, letting her disturb my nights, letting her take over my life. I think they find it unbelievable.' Most of the time, though, she says she detaches herself from such criticisms. 'I think these are people who terrorize their children into good behaviour and I don't want to take their advice. But once we went on holiday with another friend who criticized me for breast-feeding too much and too often and for giving in to her too readily. I felt disturbed by that because maybe deep down I think it too.'

In this particular example, Sarah's apparently 'obsessive' attention to her child happens to correspond to prevalent fantasies about how much attention a child should receive. For the traditionalists like her mother, Sarah clearly represents contemporary mothering, with all its drawbacks. Traditionalists have a sense that the more attention the child gets, the more its demands will grow to fill every available space. Her mother complains that the little daughter has 'got to get used to life', the traditionalists' aim being to acclimatize a child to accepting little by way of adult attention. But contemporary attitudes towards mothering have swung almost to the opposite extreme. Writers like Penelope Leach have placed so much emphasis on the importance of a child getting adult attention, response and stimulation that many contemporary middle-class mothers believe they are 'failing' in some way if their children do not receive constant adult stimulation. Of course, reality is more complex and demanding, and few parents have time or energy for such undivided attention. Hence the fact that the majority of women I have spoken to describe their own mothering as falling short of an ideal.

It is hardly surprising that Sarah's response to her daughter should trigger anxiety all around her. Her mothering may be driven by her inner need to reverse how she was treated, but the attention she gives her daughter corresponds to a contemporary ideal. No wonder it provokes some resentment and opposition. But like Linda's child, Sarah's does not always respond with the expected happiness and contentment. 'Sometimes I feel I've done everything that I can to be a good mother. I couldn't have read more books about it, thought about it more, talked about it more – and then Sophie won't let me put her clothes on and has a massive tantrum. I feel really resentful then. She has so much of me yet she can be really difficult. I sometimes get surges of feeling: it seems so unfair that mothers who beat their children round the head and give them three seconds attention a day get them to sit quietly while they dress them. Here I am giving her the best possible environment, and here she is, screaming her head off.'

What is voiced here is both incomprehension at the child's autonomy and resentment that the child fails to fulfil the mother's expectations and ambitions. There can be little doubt that Sarah was also competitive in her mothering. Her aim was not only to reverse the way she was looked after, but also to produce good results. Competitiveness with her mother was extended to other women as well. 'I do compare myself with other mothers,' she said, 'and I think I am pretty good.' In this respect, Sarah is typical of her generation. Much fashionable contemporary mothering involves a reaction against the values of the previous generation. But it is a reaction with a clearly competitive edge, a desire to do it better, since the previous generation of women are often blamed for not having given their daughters sufficient confidence in themselves.

However, Sarah's comments are also salutary. Driven by compulsion and competition, and running up against the child's autonomy, the parent can rarely control the outcome without crushing that autonomy. As another of my interviewees said, 'I suppose we all desperately want to succeed as parents, as even people who batter their kids do in their own way, and in the end we have very little control over our own children. If I make a cake, I have a certain amount of control – nine times out of ten, I can achieve the result I set out for. But with parenting I can do X, Y and Z, and still I might not get the results. I might do, but I might not because my child is a separate person whom I don't have that much control over, and I think that does produce anxiety.' In Sarah's case, there is a desire to give her daughter everything she feels she never had – confidence, attention, a sense of intrinsic worth – yet when the child fails to behave as Sarah hopes, she feels resentment towards her daughter for having so much. It is yet another example of how, however hard we may try, we are always at risk of being subverted by our *own* needs.

Nowhere is this clearer than in the issue of competitiveness and envy between daughter and mother. Like Sarah, many mothers are anxious to instil in their daughters a sense of valuing their own looks and, as they get older, their own sexuality. Yet this is rarely as easy or as straightforward as it sounds. In a culture where the value and respect accorded a woman decreases with age and the loss of 'looks', it is often difficult for any woman to affirm the next generation of women in a straightforward way, especially as mirroring and identification often occurs between mother and daughter. One woman who came to mothering late described to me how she had been cuddling her little daughter and looking in the mirror. She was shocked when she realized that she was thinking, not only how gorgeous this tiny, fresh-faced creature was, but also how dreadful and old she looked beside her.

Another woman gave an even more poignant account of how competition and envy can exist between mothers and daughters, however hard you might try consciously to resist these feelings. Jackie, in her 40s, describes how as a teenager she despised her own mother's 'lack of style'. 'I was embarrassed by her. I thought she looked dreadful – unfashionable and unattractive. Now I know she was depressed and confused at the time, but then I just hated her for it. She also made me feel really bad about my own sexuality as it was the sixties and I was quite fashion-conscious and influenced by what was happening at the time. I was experimenting sexually and she called me terrible names. I suppose it didn't help that her relationship with my dad was so bad. But what is especially difficult is that I feel my eldest daughter who is now fourteen sees me as I saw Mum. I've tried to make her feel confident and good about herself and now I feel she despises me.'

It is evident from all these accounts that trying to bury envy and competitiveness in the family is akin to lighting a match to look for a gas leak. It is within the family that these feelings often arise, and the family is a perfect breeding ground for them. Women may think that all they are bringing to their tiny dependants is an altruistic desire to take care of another, but what they often overlook are their own suppressed feelings and ambitions. These feelings may not manifest themselves in exactly the same way as the overt competition and aggression of the workplace, but they feel all the worse for surfacing in unexpected places, in individuals whose survival is tied up with not being swamped by those needs.

There is nothing new about women channelling ambition and competition into the family. In the past, when women were required to give up their own careers and education, it invariably happened that their own frustrated ambitions would emerge focussed on their husbands and their children. But while these feelings and conflicts have always existed in the family, some of the possibilities for identification and competition have been infinitely expanded in recent years. Now competition surrounding children is no longer simply a matter of academic achievement, although this is certainly very much in evidence. The prospects for identification with the child, and therefore projection of the mother's own needs, ambitions and desires on the child, have been infinitely extended with new philosophies of childcare.

This is not simply a question of academic competition starting earlier and earlier, with questions about whether your baby will be the first to crawl, walk, talk. It is also an extension of competition into the terrain of behaviour and emotions. Will she or he be well socialized, aggressive, dominant, too passive? And, paradoxically, at a time when women's freedom from the family has been highlighted, psychologists now stress how absolutely central the role of the mother is in this emotional adjustment, stimulation and development. It must be obvious that this new emphasis expands the potential for muddle and difficulty. There is more scope for identification with the child when what is at issue is no longer just a matter of how well she or he does at school, but of how he or she behaves as a person. How well the child does and behaves is seen as a direct reflection on the mother's abilities *qua* mother.

Child-rearing allows women to experience and show altruistic and loving feelings which transcend the apparent pettiness of the material values around us, but it can also evolve into a spectacular mixture of competition and compulsion. The family is often not the safe place that it is supposed to be. Women turning their backs on the hostile rivalry of professional ethics often find themselves assaulted by feelings of competitiveness towards other mothers and of insecurity at being judged and found lacking as a mother. Indeed it is very often the retreating professionals who bring the greatest degree of anxious competitiveness into their relationships with their children and their children's friends.

As with everything else they do, women are constantly looking over their shoulders, evaluating what they do and comparing it with what other women do, a habit that is grotesquely reinforced by the prescriptiveness with which women are always treated. Mothering, or to use the more contemporary term, 'parenting', is the area where the prescriptions about how women should be and what they should accomplish are most intense. That women should buy in so wholeheartedly to prevailing ideas makes their difficulties in the family much greater. Their willingness to follow these competitive ideals raises crucial questions about women's collusion with the structures which oppress them. It is to these questions that we now turn.

5

The Ideal of the Good Mother

We have seen how much anxiety attaches to women's perceptions of themselves 'as a woman', and also how much envious hostility is directed towards others who are apparently more successful. Both of these issues show women internalizing messages about their roles and responsibilities that create often unnecessary difficulties. This aspect of the female psyche is at its clearest in relation to mothering, where definite and widespread ideals and pressures actively prevent women from coming to terms with their emotions and the realities of contemporary family life.

As women we are constantly comparing ourselves with other women, and re-evaluating ourselves accordingly. These comparisons spur us to make changes and to try and pull ourselves into line with the prevailing ideal. Although men are also envious and given to evaluating themselves against ideals, for women this feeling is often more central – and more damaging. Women are assailed by images (we used to call them stereotypes) of ideal bodies, ideal health, ideal children, ideal homes. These operate simultaneously as a lure and a source of dissatisfaction, spurring desire but at the same time creating discontent. This endless courting of female desire is partly to do with the crucial role which women's subjectivities play in a consumer society, but it also produces women who have difficulty in accepting themselves.

Women's readiness to make changes could be an extremely positive force. But, more often, their pursuit of ideals is negative, externally, rather than internally, imposed, and creating destructive, jealous and self-critical emotions when the ideals are at odds with reality. This is particularly damaging with regard to motherhood. Middle-class women seem especially susceptible to prevailing ideals of motherhood, but most women I interviewed, from all classes, had a clear picture of what a good mother would be like, the kinds of things she would do, and how their own lives would be greatly improved if only they could meet this ideal.

I don't mean to suggest that contemporary ideals are as rigid as the notion of motherhood which childcare manuals, adverts and advice films promulgated throughout the 1950s. Few women I spoke to regarded their ideal as something imposed on them by social workers, health visitors or state functionaries, but rather as coming from within themselves. For most, the prevailing ideal is nebulous, something spotted in other women, something which stirs their regret and often their envy. It means they are constantly berating themselves for falling short, rather than tackling the real source of their problems.

What, then, is the contemporary ideal? Interestingly, the issue of whether or not women work is slightly at a tangent to deeper aspects of the ideal. A Gallup survey conducted in June 1991 found that more than half the women interviewed felt guilty about being 'just a mum', while four out of five full-time mothers felt they were second-class citizens who lost status when they gave up work. These findings were confirmed by numerous similar stories I heard on this subject. During my interviewing for this book, one of the most consistent themes was women's fear that they should be seen as 'just a housewife or mother'. Hilary, for example, who recently gave up her job as a community nurse, said that the most difficult part of the decision was being seen as just a mother. 'There are a lot of "career women" in my husband's area of work and I go as often as I can with him on social outings. I don't think I'm imagining it, but the conversation always seems to stop dead when people ask me what I do. I almost invariably say I used to be a community nurse but I'm taking time off to be with the children. But that isn't completely accurate. I want to be a full-time mother but I don't want to admit it in those sort of circles.'

Among the women I interviewed there were those who felt they had to brazen out their decisions to be at home with the children, making themselves indifferent to the values of the professional world which they used to inhabit and their husbands still do. Others told me they dreaded parties when someone might ask them what they did. Invariably they answered, like Hilary, with accounts of what they did *before* they had children. Most often, though, women were determined to continue with some kind of work, and avoiding being seen as a 'stay at home wife' was a principal reason. A surprisingly large number of women told me that they thought their husbands did not want to be married to a stay at home wife. Pam, for instance, has four children under 5, including a set of twins. She works part-time as a civil servant but finds the double role extraordinarily hard-going. Five mornings a week she leaves the house at seven-thirty, works four hours and races home to take over from her mother's help at lunchtime. At that point she has to do all the things expected of a full-time mother – the shopping, cooking, cleaning and entertaining of the children. A large part of her decision to live like this seemed to come from anxiety about her husband's opinion. 'I don't think he'd like to be married to just a housewife.'

If the ideal is not the stay at home mother, what is it? I was struck by how many women had similar if not identical anxieties about motherhood. Most of them knew at least one other woman whose life seemed easier and more comfortable because she had 'got it right' as a mother. Most believed that if they could become more like this good mother, their lives would change from bad-tempered survival to idyllic peace. The most important element in the contemporary notion of the good mother is the boundless energy which she devotes to her children, in particular the endless enthusiasm she has for creative activities designed to further the child's development. The ideal mother doesn't just survive motherhood, she shapes it, encouraging her children to find their potential in a number of stimulating and educational activities. Most of the middle-class mothers I talked to expressed envy of women who are prepared to devote themselves to 'being creative' with the children. They were often made anxious by other mothers who demonstrated this ability – painting with their children, thinking of stimulating games for them, and generally enjoying them in a way that the interviewees often did not.

There was extraordinary consistency in the qualities these ideal families were supposed to possess. Primarily it is their good-natured readiness to eschew mass culture and find entertainment and stimulation geared to personal development. One woman spoke for many when she described the creativity of her friend's household. 'I admire my friend ... She's got four children and she is always doing things with them. All the children play musical instruments, and they often play together. I just don't have the same energy for doing things as her. I'm relieved when my children sit in front of the television.'

When I asked where women felt they were falling short as mothers, most answered in the same terms; they had neither sufficient time nor energy for doing stimulating and creative things with their children. Worse still, if they were honest, they didn't always have the inclination. Over and over again I heard, 'I don't do enough with my children', 'I don't give my child enough individual attention', 'I don't have the energy to teach her the violin, to read, to speak a foreign language'. One mother of three who at the time of the interview was trying to decide whether or not to return to full-time work said, 'Half of me thinks it would be nice to really nurture the children all the time, to sit down and invent little games for them and make things and be creative, stimulate them and all the rest. But even now, not working full-time, I don't do those things as much as I feel I should, as I thought I would before I had children. The other half of me wants to go back to work and do proper stuff, proper work and really use my brain.'

What seemed to hurt women most was that their responses to the family situation fell so short of the ideal. They were often bad-tempered and shouted at the kids. Ideally, most felt this should never happen; most berated themselves later for what they saw as their mishandling of family life. One mother of two described her perception of the mismatch between the ideal and the reality. 'I often feel I don't give enough time to my little boy. We always seem to be rushing round doing things. I work in the mornings and I say to myself, "Well, the afternoons are for him." But it never works out that way. He sleeps and then we go out somewhere. We always seem to be dashing somewhere and there never seems to be time to just sit down and do things.'

Even though the ideal seems to be clearly understood, or at least internalized, by so many women, it isn't just the stresses and strains of everyday existence which stop women from achieving it. Several women 'confessed' guiltily to me that they often found these pursuits boring, and many admitted that they frequently preferred to turn their backs on the children. Even cooking and cleaning was preferable. 'At least you can think while you are doing it,' said one. At the end of these activities there was at least a vague sense of accomplishment, whereas most felt their own identities and interests disappeared if they gave themselves up wholly to the children's play and activities.

Only a handful of the women I interviewed said they enjoyed devoting themselves to their children's developmental endeavours. One said that children's activities gave her the chance to rediscover and enjoy earlier childhood pleasures. Another said she had found abilities which had never previously developed, such as learning to make toys when she attended a family workshop with her little boy. The outcome was a period where she made and supplied dolls and clowns to large department stores. But these two were the exception. For the most part I heard tales of guilt and resentment about failing to live up to this ideal.

Such exhaustive attention to children's development is not something which ends when they start school. If anything, school-children have to be introduced to more, and more varied, activities. Children are enrolled in swimming lessons, pottery classes, French clubs. And for the middle classes there are the obligatory violin and piano lessons, which seem to be real flashpoints in the edifice of middle-class beliefs. Across the country, hordes of disgruntled children are dragged to music lessons, forced to practice their instruments, berated by anxious mothers who believe they will one day be thanked for giving them this pleasure and talent. The children complain and resist for months on end, but if they make the mistake of ever showing enjoyment, they have had it — two lessons a week instead of one. This is the so-called privileged life of middle-class children today, hounded by their mothers' anxieties and aspirations.

Increased affluence and leisure opportunities for children and the loss of confidence in state provision have resulted in a deterioration of the mother's lot. But she is not just papering over certain cracks in state provision. A contemporary mother takes on a whole new set of roles. She is expected to manage a child's social life in a society where the opportunities for this are much more extensive, and expensive, and where street culture for children has become an increasingly precarious option. Yet few women see this as a social problem. Instead they continue to berate themselves in relation to the ideal mother. The fault, they say, is in their own attitudes, not in what they are being expected to do.

At the heart of these feelings about the ideal mother is a fantasy that the really good mother is someone who *enjoys* mothering so much that her enjoyment would override all the stresses and strains of family life. Surprisingly, given how many mothers now work and how many of my interviewees worked, there is still a deep and persistent idealization of the woman who has opted willingly and wholeheartedly for motherhood and no longer submits to the contradictory demands of work and home. Marie, a mother who works full-time for British Telecom, spoke for many when she described which of her acquaintances seemed to be the best mother. 'One friend I know is quite happy to stay at home and she organizes games and makes playdoh and loves it. Yes, I envy that. It would be nice to feel easier. It would be nice to say, what I really want is to stay at home full-time and look after the kids. But there are lots of things I want to do. I don't think I could be happy making those decisions but I wish I could be.'

There is a strong and persistent belief therefore that what is crucial in creating the ideal mother is *attitude*. Women who express dissatisfaction with their lot, either because of the stresses and strains of their circumstances or because of their decision or need to work, feel convinced that things would be better if only they didn't feel such difficult and contradictory emotions. Lorna, whom I talked to when her first child was just a year old, expressed this feeling in a particularly clear and self-analytic way. 'There's someone who lives nearby who has given up a good job in the City just to be with her baby. But she seems to enjoy it and I do find that quite difficult to comprehend. I suppose in one way I do – what's the word? – well, envy her. When I say envy, I don't envy her lifestyle because I don't want to be not working. But I envy her ability to be a good mother because my perception of being a good mother is that you adore being with your children all the time. I think that's probably a false perception but that's what you are brought up to believe – that a good mother devotes herself to her children and really loves it and is totally fulfilled. And I feel guilty because I can't live up to that ideal. I'm just not like that. I wish I *could* be like that . . . It would make life simpler.'

Behind these thoughts on good mothering is often the view that women could change their circumstances by changing their own feelings and attitudes. Women spoke regretfully about wishing they could change themselves, so becoming able to 'attend to the child more wholeheartedly'. Marie, again, identified mothers' own feelings as the problem. 'I am ambitious, and that's one of the big problems. You don't stop being ambitious because you've got a family. You don't stop wanting to do well in other areas and it's hard to put a brake on it.'

What is startling is that, despite decades of changing attitudes and employment patterns, there persists a traditional notion of good mothering. Truly good mothering still evokes ideas of total altruism, in the form of one who ferries the children about endlessly or one who crawls around on hands and knees being included in the fantasy games of a 4-year-old. Here, for example, in an article on 'fashionable' mothers, Georgina Godley, 'a notably elegant and unhysterical fashion designer', describes her ideal as her own mother, who was a 'brilliant, loving, putting-everybody-before-herself mother' (*Evening Standard*, December 1990). There is no exploration of how unrealistic this ideal is in our contemporary economy. But however difficult and impossible the ideal, women still experience any falling short of total altruism as personal failure. No wonder everyone feels so guilty.

In the past, maternal altruism might have been perceived in relatively basic terms, in the sense of a woman who would give up her own needs in order to feed and clothe her children and keep them secure. In contemporary fantasies, this altruism goes further. It is assumed that children want and need deep, exclusive and full attention; they need an adult at their disposal, who will listen and hear and play.

The ideal of 'early learning' has probably been the largest single concern of mothers in contemporary life. So much of what has been written about childhood over the last forty years has stressed the need to recognize early development of perception and intelligence and the need to stimulate the child through its environment. I am not calling this into question. What is interesting, though, is how much of the responsibility for such stimulation has fallen to the mother. 'You Are Your Child's First Teacher', one book reminds us, and the message is reinforced in virtually all the current writing on children's development. Indeed, in many of the theories it is not simply that the mother is the best because she happens to be the adult most usually on hand; she is the best because the maternal environment is seen as ideal for stimulating the child's brain.

This enmeshing of emotional and intellectual development means that contemporary ideals of motherhood are a good deal more demanding than were those of the 1950s. Then, at least, the main demand on the mother was that she provided security, often quite literally in the form of simply being present. Feminism emerged partly as a challenge to that restrictive ideology. In the late 1960s and the early 1970s, novelists like Fay Weldon and Doris Lessing charted the frequent disasters of maternal self-sacrifice. How, they asked, did these dependent child-women survive the traumas of their children growing up and leaving home in a society that increasingly valued work-based identity? How would they survive divorce if they had no other identity than as a wife? Why should girls and young women who had been educated as boys' equals suddenly be expected to give up everything for husbands and children? And why should mothers who worked be ostracized and blamed for anything ranging from neurosis to 'delinquency' and social unrest? In response to this feminist challenge the restrictive ideals are supposed to have melted away, leaving women much more free to find their own solutions without fear of social stigma and disapproval.

But the story is much more complex. Contemporary ideals are in many ways much more exacting for women, even if the mother is not required to be quite literally present 100 per cent of the time. The underlying requirements can be gleaned from the numerous childcare manuals which are proliferating on our bookshelves. Like most books on childcare since the Second World War, the emphasis is on getting it right emotionally and psychologically, rather than on moral or physical issues. But the current emotional agenda is very different from that of the 1950s and 1960s. Then, Freud and Winnicott were the driving forces behind anxieties that a child might be tipped irreversibly into psychosis by bungled potty training or the washing of its comfort blanket. The ultimate objective was always the child's security. Now, although the

The Ideal of the Good Mother

woman is no longer required to be so totally tied to the home, she has nevertheless to attend to a whole series of educational and psychological needs. The terms that most commonly attach themselves to mothering these days are full of promises of personal growth for the child. Good parenting is 'creating a nurturing environment', 'reducing conflict within the home', 'developing a child's self-esteem' and 'allowing space for personal growth'. But behind this liberal and relaxed jargon lies a much more gruelling agenda. The family environment in fact has to be managed, with 'listening time'. Space has to be created, needs met and objectives assessed. Everything has to be done to facilitate the child's personal growth, and this means a complex orchestration of emotional and educational needs.

Anyone who threw themselves wholeheartedly into this kind of approach to mothering would indeed be committing themselves to a pretty arduous task. Mothers have to become the child's first teacher, its therapist, a home manager, as well as its altruistic mother. It is as if all those attributes and skills which previously were given to a child in the outside world are now to be found, or at least organized, through its home. Most women recognize the impossibility of attaining this ideal – either consciously, or just by failing to do it – but it doesn't stop them feeling guilty.

One American programme sums up the gap that exists between the ideal of parenthood and the reality of contemporary women's lives. It sums it up not by exposing the two as mutually contradictory but by offering a solution, a plaster to put over the wound. Reality Attuned Parenting (REAP) is a 'psychological programme' directed at working women. If you hoped that reality attuned parenting might entail a little realistic coming to terms with one's own shortcomings, you would be sadly disappointed. Instead, it amounts to making yourself into a full-time mother, psychically at least, even if you can't be continuously present. The idea is that you train yourself into a state of supersensitivity to your child's needs so that the child believes that you always understand everything he or she is feeling. This enables the child to carry 'an evoked' companion inside itself, a companion who will always understand its needs.

This imaginary persona is always on hand to dole out comfort, usually of a kind that 'mirrors' the child's mood. So, for example, when a child is screaming on the floor in a tantrum, the mother's response should be, 'I can see you are feeling really angry,' instead of one of confrontation. By being sensitive to the child's moods and needs, the mother can create a secure 'other' who will be retained whatever happens. At base this is not so different an idea from Melanie Klein's notion of internalizing the good mother, which then allows the child to make other relationships and feel secure in the world. But in Reality Attuned Parenting, creating this good mother is more than riding the infantile storms and being perpetually present. Now it is learning the tricks so that you can, in fact, be absent. The child can be in day-care or with a minder. This will not harm him or her so long as the evoked companion can be summoned up at any point in the day. Techniques to keep the mother omnipresent include a regular mid-morning phone call, during which the child's 'care-giver' is trained to let the child sniff at your favourite perfume or hold your clothes.

For the most part, though, mothers are not enrolling on such programmes to solve the mutually contradictory ideals of the working mother and the omnipresent educator. Instead, they are either torturing themselves trying to do both or feeling guilty about their failure to do either. It doesn't take books or behavioural programmes to tell us that contemporary notions of motherhood are complex and burdensome. Everyone I spoke to had a strong, if not overwhelming, notion of an ideal which they were trying to live up to, or a previous ideal which they were trying to overthrow. Few women were able to say, as one did, that she 'felt herself to be a better mother than most'. Most felt themselves to be inadequate in general ways and often inadequate in relation to one or two specific friends.

So, as more and more mothers work, the notions of the consequences of bad parenting and the duties of good parenting have become more and more alarming. And together with these obligations, duties and inadequacies, which hang over virtually all mothers, many also have a sense of being watched, usually by their own mothers, sisters or other women. One slip-up (in terms of the child's behaviour or educational failures) will be taken as proof that the mother's choices were wrong. Thus women's lives, rather than improving, have become worse. Many seem to feel obliged to function as general taxi-driver and office manager. They attend birthday parties; they attend classes and extra-school activities; they feel under obligation to provide outings, and to attend school functions.

With a family of any size this life can really be quite arduous. Cathy, who after a hysterectomy was finding it difficult to pick up her old patterns, said, 'Sometimes I think I'm going mad. I can't keep all the arrangements in my head all the time. It sounds terribly trivial but there's so much filling up, not just of your time but of your head. I have to drive up and down to the school six times in one day delivering children to various classes. Then there are all the complicated exchanges we have arranged about taking the kids to other activities like Brownies and extra maths coaching. Then there are the endless social arrangements and birthday parties. Most of the time you just keep going, but if you take a step back and look at your life, you do wonder, what *am* I doing?'

The story of Mary is also revealing about the gulf between the ideals and the reality of life. As described in Chapter 3, Mary has four children. She described herself as 'fascinated with the whole process of childbirth' and gave up her job in film production to become a full-time mother and National Childbirth Counsellor. Now she is deeply dissatisfied with her life. 'I've been ferrying kids to and fro for ten years now and I don't think I can stand it any more. Because we live in London, I wait in a traffic jam on average six times a day. I think all the things the kids do are important – gym, music lessons, wildlife club and so on. But I just can't stand it. I'm bored and I'm a bit lonely, because most of the other mothers seem to be working now. Some days it seems worth it, but other days I just don't care. I'd rather the kids sat and watched soap operas all day than have to get in that car one more time.'

It is interesting that the issue of whether or not a woman is working is at one stage removed from this deeper question on what makes for good mothering. Clearly there are ideals and competition surrounding whether or not to work, but in an odd way these seem less tortured than the deeper question of whether or not one's mothering is even-tempered, altruistic and committed to the child's development, intelligence and creative potential. Working mothers feel pressurized by the worries of childcare and the difficulty of ever finding time for themselves. But full-time mothers seem to feel the same. The problem for both is how to preserve something for yourself in the face of the ever-expanding demands of children, declining public provision and the philosophy of totally altruistic childcare.

Women may no longer be the slaves of men, but there's a very real danger that they are now becoming the slaves of children. Many women I spoke to seemed to think that one of the best reasons to work – usually part-time – was because there at least your own identity was slightly less at risk. There, too, would be the possiblity for time of your own, time to think, time to have a cup of coffee, time to use your mind rather than be constantly attending to the minds of others. In this bizarre situation, work is seen as an escape from the insistent and draining demands of the home.

How has all this happened? How, at a time when they might have pushed men and the system to change, have women come to put themselves at risk of being swamped by the insistent demands of their families? Perhaps it is, as Susan Faludi suggests, the backlash against feminism, where pyscological precepts about childcare have re-emphasized the mother's centrality in child development. It certainly does seem suspicious that this new view of the mother's role arises at the moment women have a bit more freedom. But a semi-conspiratorial notion of why things have happened like this simply doesn't address the active part women themselves have played in shouldering these ideas. How can we blame men for promoting self-negating ideas of motherhood when so many women themselves are so actively espousing those views?

Veronica gave me a clear illustration of how women themselves collude in trying to force reality to fit this impossible ideal – which may have disastrous consequences for other, less affluent, women. Veronica is in her 30s, a typical career woman of the 1990s. She is an interior designer whose business has been extremely successful. When I interviewed her, she was pregnant with her first child. Like many women in this condition, some of her plans were doubtless unrealistic, but she claimed she had 'thought about this a lot' and had decided on the best way of going into motherhood. 'I'm really looking forward to having a child. I've always wanted a family. I'm planning to be at home as much as possible with the child. I've got a business manager in my office and I'm going to stay in touch from home. But my husband and I have agreed that we're going to pay someone to do all the boring domestic bits – the cleaning and the washing and ironing. If I'm going to be at home, I want to attend to my family fully. I don't want to be spending my time on the drudgery.'

Veronica is not representative of women in general, but in an odd way her plan seems to express some of the crazy logic that currently prevails. Contemporary notions of motherhood don't allow for drudgery and routine. They comprise a mixture of work outside the home, and full, stimulating attention within it. Gone is the notion that a mother might spend her day according to a routine whereby the house would get cleaned, the shopping done and the children be given some fresh air and a bit of play. I, for one, never thought I would find that picture appealing until I met the Veronicas of this world. But what could possibly be worse than a society where one woman buys another woman's time so that she can attend to her own child's intellectual advancement in such a single-minded way?

Veronica's 'solution' is an extreme version of the collusion inherent in contemporary ideals of mothering. Instead of challenging how much psychological and educational responsibility has been passed to them, women have taken it all on board, as their absolute responsibility. And when the responsibilities are too arduous, women either buy out if they can or feel guilty about their failures. All around women can be heard discussing solutions to the pressure they feel in terms of what can be bought – they are paying for home tuition, for extra lessons, for music and language provision. Even erstwhile socialists and feminists send their children to private schools so that they no longer have to live with the worry of failing their children.

At the beginning of this chapter I mentioned Pam, a mother of four who works part-time as a civil servant. She comes from a poor Irish family, and the cultural difference gives her a different perspective on the ideals of mothering into which so many Englishwomen have now bought. She described the situation succinctly, and in passing gave a strong sense of how women are colluding in keeping up the pressure on themselves. 'I feel under pressure all the time to do creative things. A lot of my friends do that kind of thing. Some pick up their children from nursery and fit in something educational before getting their older children from school. Thank goodness work gives me an excuse not to do that. But I do feel pressure all the time, and a sense of failure. If I just let the children play or watch TV I feel guilty. Women feel they should be constantly stimulating. But it wasn't always like that. I was worrying about whether or not my 5-year-old could read and whether I was doing enough to help him and my mother said, "Well, I didn't teach you to read." She didn't expect to have to do it. Her day consisted of taking us to school, doing a bit of housework, cooking a meal. And we were expected to entertain ourselves. My kids can't entertain themselves for more than twenty minutes.

'I think that women do have a very tough time now. In Ireland, if women work, it's not a career job. But their lives are more relaxed, they can have a chat and they don't attend so closely to their children. I don't know if the children's lives are better. Possibly not. But I think we've swung too far the other way. We're so concerned about our children's lives and their needs that we don't allow ourselves any time or position. All this worrying about education and whether our children are getting the best. It's part of the general competitiveness. We are always comparing our children and competing with other mothers all the time, often without realizing it. Obviously it's wrong to leave children unstimulated, but what women are doing now is not good for themselves or for the children.'

Pam's words sum up this chapter. Women collude by trying to follow unrealistic ideals, and when they find them impossible to achieve, instead of challenging them, they have tried to find ways of compromising. Some see part-time work as that perfect 'solution', not just for financial and social reasons but to draw boundaries in their home that they feel incapable of making for themselves. Some have paid for private solutions rather than attempt to resist deteriorating public facilities. There has been little or no resistance to the additional responsibilities women now have in the family. The build-up of this pressure has been partly external – new coercive ideals of childcare and especially a running down of state services and provision – which opens the way for private and personal solutions. But women's willingness to shoulder these responsibilities has come from within. Perhaps some of these high expectations women have for their children reflect what they themselves have given up – intellectual stimulation and the development of skills. But they also seem to derive from an ideal of the good mother which seems to have its roots in an earlier time. How can this be, when the choices available to the current generation of working mothers appear to be so different from those of the previous generation?

6

The Sorrows of the Mothers: how women's feelings about their mothers affect their decisions

One of the crucial factors influencing women's attitudes towards both competitiveness and the ideals of good mothering is their relationship with their own mothers. For although women are responding to changed political, social and economic pressures, they are also working to a different agenda — one drawn up according to their individual emotional history and, in particular, their relationships with their mothers. This relationship can have stormy, difficult and unpredictable results. But why should our mothers' feelings and opinions *matter* so much to us now? Why should it be that, deep down, our mothers still have us by the heart?

Everyone knows that a good relationship with their mother is what most women want, regardless of whether they are 15 or 50. But few claim to have it. There are the odd few who say that everything is all right and that they want to emulate their mothers in every way. But for many women the situation is much more complex. Changes in the social and economic position of women mean that they no longer simply repeat the experiences of their mothers. Into the gap created by change floods a muddle of emotions. There you will find, mixed up together, the desire for love and approval, the desire to do things differently, anger, and, overwhelmingly, an anxiety about their mother's pain and suffering.

Therese seemed to sum up this situation. In her late 20s, and already with a considerable reputation as a theatrical agent, she literally wept every time she mentioned her mother. She described her mother as the happiest, most wonderful woman in the world.

'I'm only crying because I love her so much,' she said. But her inner conflict was pretty mild compared with what I heard elsewhere. For many women, the relationship with their mothers can be openly difficult and often painful. Sometimes there are dramatic conflicts; sometimes there is simply an ever-present sense of pain. Much of the time the feelings are confused and unresolved, a fact which presents a very different picture from the popular mythology of a generation which overthrew its mothers' values without so much as a backward look.

We all know about the broad outline of sociological changes affecting women, but at their heart are real human relationships between generations of women. Each generation that takes a new direction to some degree takes a position against the previous generation. On a practical level, this means women take different decisions from their mothers – about marriage, children and work. On an emotional level, it means the daughter breaking the possibility of her mother's total identification with her. What undoubtedly makes this situation acutely painful is that women are extremely sensitive to prevailing ideals of 'womanhood', so that when the ideal by which one generation has lived is overthrown, so is their sense of self-worth. This anxiety and insecurity creates an atmosphere in which envy, jealousy and resentment can be rife.

Feminism is usually blamed for this rupture between the values of two different generations, but the changes themselves have a wider context. England has moved fast – relatively speaking – from promoting the traditional patriarchal family, where women have few rights, to a modern, more egalitarian family. In particular, social changes during the First and Second World Wars have played an important part in changing views of women's sexuality, their working opportunities and the forms of mothering expected. But it was modern feminism which produced the quantum leap. In the 1970s, when women organized to fight for change, change became urgent and inevitable.

Feminism is almost invariably seen as a struggle – or head-on collision – with men. But the truth is that the deep struggle of feminism was with the previous generation of women. Feminism could be called the daughters' revolt, so central has been the issue of women defining themselves against the previous generation and distancing themselves from their mothers. It is no accident that feminists used the language of 'sisterhood', evoking an image of siblings in revolt against parental authority. Much more important than women's relationships with men were the hidden agendas existing between the different generations of women.

Feminists themselves often perpetuate this image of daughters in revolt, eager to topple the last traces of their mothers' world. Germaine Greer has described her feminism as having arisen in revolt against her mother's 'bobby-soxer' generation; she saw those women's lives as wasted, squandered on trivia and swallowed up by their families. Even twenty years after publication of *The Female Eunuch*, Greer is still writing from the perspective of the daughter. In *Daddy, We Hardly Knew You* she reveals herself still angry with her mother, still resentful that her mother appeared to collude with her father's vague and unloving authoritarianism.

However, other writing of the 1980s and 1990s which has feminism as its starting point has shown itself to be more sensitive. It is unrealistic to suggest that there is a clear and painless break between the values of two different generations. In 1978, Marilyn French wrote the influential novel *The Women's Room*, which at the height of feminism charted the 'typical' story of a housewife, Mira, who emerged from a frigid and oppressive marriage. Mira's parents are barely present in the novel. More recently, in *Her Mother's Daughter*, the relationships between generations of women has moved centre-stage. Her heroine reflects:

> My mother was so careful to give me those things she had painfully lacked in her own childhood that she can't imagine that the thing she really lacked wasn't attention or education, but ... that close embrace. Never having had it how could she give it? For a baby rat taken from its mother ... before its mother has time to lick it clean, will in her turn not lick her infant clean when she gives birth. And so on down the generations ... The truth is, it is not the sins of the fathers that are descended unto the third generation, but the sorrows of the mothers. But when I was a young woman, I believed that I could break this chain by sheer will.

For many women, the subject of their identification with and differences from, their mothers is something that can engross them for hours. But although most acknowledge the importance of their mothers to them, there is little real understanding of the effect of the gulf between two sets of values on their own emotional lives. And there is even less recognition of the significance of the previous generation in determining the deepest decisions around femininity and family. It is no wonder, in the absence of this understanding, that there is scope for misunderstanding.

The conflicts between the changing ideals of women and work are often seen as a crucial point of conflict between two generations of women. The usual image is of the generation of immediate post-war mothers, tight-lipped with disapproval as their daughters have pursued careers, especially when there are children involved. But this area is far more complex. Melanie's account of her relationship with her mother is typical of the mixed messages and ambiguities which can become acute when a daughter has her own children.

Melanie is 33 and has two young children, Luke and Emma. She also has a successful career as a translator, much of her work being for the European Commission. This means she sometimes has to spend up to a fortnight away from home. 'I have a full-time nanny who thankfully has been with us five years. But I still rely a lot on my mother. She comes over when I'm away, takes the children out and gives them treats. But her help is very double-edged. She constantly says, "I worry about you, Melanie. You work too hard." I know what she actually means is she's worried about the children because she always calls Luke, "poor Luke"! I sometimes feel as if she is waiting for something to go wrong.'

Melanie feels undermined by her mother's implied criticism. 'Yes, I feel guilty about the kids most of the time. That's a general guilt that most working mothers seem to feel. But it's also peculiar to me and my mother. Because she helps out with my children when I'm working, it's a constant reminder. Mum stayed at home for me and helped me achieve things. She presents it as a sacrifice she made consciously because she says things like, "You only got on so well at school because there was someone at home and you didn't have to worry about me not being there."'

Melanie went on to outline the dilemma her mother's 'sacrifices' left her with. 'If I gave up my career now, Mum's sacrifices would have been for nothing. Do you see? I'm in an impossible situation. I *have* to do well to make her feel better about her choices. But by being a career woman, I appear to be undermining her choices.' She described some of the things her mother said to her when she was growing up. 'I think Mum was pretty unhappy really and *very* resentful of my father. Dad was a bank clerk when I was little, nothing grand, but he gave himself airs and he was a bit of a tyrant at home. Mum used to say to me things like, "Don't end up like me, girl," and, "Get yourself an education. You can't rely on men to look after you." She even told me that I should never have a joint bank account when I married!'

What Melanie describes here is reminiscent of a litany which the feminist generation seems to have imbibed with their mother's milk. The mothers of the 1950s may have opted for, or been driven into, staying at home full-time and devoting their lives to their children, but they managed to tell their daughters that they were not happy about the situation. Above all, they conveyed that their daughters should not 'make the same mistakes'. Time and time again, I found that women's decisions about work and the family involved more complex factors than those surrounding 'financial independence' or 'equal rights', and that they ultimately revolved around the question of their mother's satisfactions and discontents. 'I don't think my mother's choices ultimately made her very happy,' says Melanie. 'She's got very little except the family to amuse – or more often upset – her, and it makes her so vulnerable. I don't want that to happen to me. So even when my guilt is at its worst I feel sure I'm doing the right thing.'

I heard repeatedly stories that women maintain some kind of career – even when there are difficulties – mainly in order to avoid 'my mother's unhappiness' and especially to avoid needing their children as much as they feel their mothers needed them. In many ways, this fear of loss of identity was crucial to the feminism of the late 1960s and early 1970s. The social impetus came from increased educational opportunities, from the political language of the American civil rights movement, and from new affluence. But the internal impetus, the reason why so many women recognized themselves in this movement, was because of the contradictory messages they had received from their mothers. On the one hand they heard a tirade of bitterness, but on the other a sense of their mother's pain, emptiness and need for their children.

Historical and social changes have left a residue of uneasy and unspoken accusations and guilt between generations. These often become particularly uncomfortable with the arrival of grandchildren. Because the full-time mothers of the 1950s and 1960s invested so much ambition in their daughters, their daughters' careers often tend to be a source of pride. It is when the grandchildren arrive that many of the submerged conflicts may erupt, as both sides relive and react against their own situation.

Sandra, now in her 30s with two sons, describes how, when she had her children, she felt overwhelmed by anger. In her case, there is more than sadness at her mother's lack of any separate identity. There is also a sense of distress at how deprived her own childhood had been. 'I suppose I always knew that somewhere. But it was only when I had children that I realized how deprived I had been.' Sandra works as a childminder in Streatham. Although she trained as a nurse, she has given that up in order to 'be available' for her boys. Childminding seemed a good solution – as it is for so many women. It meant in effect that she remained a full-time mother while making a contribution to the family income.

But Sandra's decision to structure her life like this arises from a complicated inner debate with her mother, and a determination not to be like her. 'Not only did my mother have six children – I was number three – but she also had several miscarriages. She always seemed to be pregnant, or miscarrying and ill, or recovering from childbirth. If she was well she was always busy. She never spent time with the children, she never read to us or played with us. I felt I had no intimate contact with my mother. She was always busy with things to do with the house and food. She was obsessed with "good food" and spent a lot of time making home-made jam and pies. That probably sounds idyllic – stay at home mother and all this home-baked food. Well, it wasn't. Who cares about home-made jam? I'd rather have had a mother.'

Sandra shares this acute sense of how frail a woman's identity is when built exclusively round a family, even a large one like her own. 'My mother has been a widow for twenty years but she's never worked. She's rather remote and she just doesn't seem to have any outside interests. So even though I've opted for basing my life, including my working life, around my children, I think it's vital to keep a sense of my own interests and take time for myself. I do a woodwork class, and several weekends in the year I go away and leave everything to my husband. I don't think my mother had any time for herself, and it's very damaging for children, especially boys, to see their mother as unimportant and having no independent existence.'

For many women this fear of losing their identity is still strong. Sue, who had her first baby in her late 30s, has had a very successful career. She is the director of an international charity and spends her working life mixing with politicians and 'powerful' people. Like many women in this position, she is supported by a partner who takes on the traditionally female role in childcare. He takes time off work for illness, he takes and collects their child from the childminder, and he often puts the child to bed when Sue is late in. Again, it's one of those situations which sounds enviable but is more complex than meets the eye.

Sue in fact finds the lifestyle very stressful. She has had a lot of illness since the baby was born, which doctors are constantly telling her is 'stress-related'. She also feels deprived of the baby. 'I do find it very difficult that he turns to my husband for comfort. Yes, I find that very painful. It's not really surprising. He spends so much more time with him than I do. If I ever have another child, which I don't know if I will, I don't think I could do the same again. I feel as if I've cheated myself, really.' Why, I wondered, had she taken the decision to do it like this? 'Well, it's complicated. I've done well in my career. That means it is very difficult to give up because the job is good, interesting and I earn a lot. I also think I shouldn't waste what I am good at. But I'd probably have taken the same decision even if the job had been less good. I suppose I'm scared of ending up like my mother. She had a lot of ability that she just invested in looking after Dad and us lot and she's dreadfully lonely now.'

In spite of this typical reaction to a mother's self-negation and apparently willing submission to an unreasonable father, most women still often internalize their mother's attitudes and expectations, even in the face of profoundly changing social ideals. Sue is a good example of this. In many important ways she tries to provide the kind of environment her mother provided for her, even though her mother's situation was quite different. For example, she makes her own jams and pies, which she cooks in large batches and stores in the freezer. She tries to give her child the same kinds of pleasures and pastimes, and she also recognizes the kind of things she will and won't allow him to do, the expectations she has of his behaviour. 'I hear myself talking to him just like Mummy talked to me. "Come on, eat up your greens," "Don't leave food, there are millions of starving children in the world." I sing him all the songs and hymns from my childhood.'

This instinctive copying or remembering is very common. Women describe singing songs they'd forgotten to their newly born babies, or telling them off in uncannily similar tones to their mothers'. But what is internalized is often more complicated. Caroline, who was also quoted in Chapter 3, offers a particularly vivid illustration of some of the complexities in the passing of ideals and expectations from one generation to another. She describes herself as one of 'a decreasing circle of stay at home mothers in trendy, supermum Putney'. As her three teenage children have become more independent, she has been finding the situation increasingly unsatisfactory. Recently she has begun to question why she made the choices she did.

At Cambridge Caroline not only started a promising acting career in Footlights but achieved a First in English. But after college she never worked. 'I think I was probably looking for an escape from competition. Most of all I wanted to get married and I was on the look-out for a husband all the time I was at Cambridge. When I met Ian I knew immediately he was the one. He was very confident. He knew exactly where he was going and it was obvious he was going to be successful. Most importantly, I knew I could rely on him.'

For many years Caroline believed that her fear of the professional world and her desire to lean on a successful man was caused by her own insecure childhood. Her parents had divorced when she was 4 and her childhood was unsettled and unhappy. But recently she has come to recognize another element in her decisions – her mother's feelings. 'I always felt torn. Part of me wanted to make her feel she had achieved something in her life. But now I have begun to realize that I always felt that I must not achieve more than she did. If I had gone out and had a successful career or something, she would have felt she hadn't done enough. And that would make her feel bad and I'm still very protective towards her.'

Not surprisingly, given this quicksand of envy and frustrated ambition, the 'closeness' of Caroline and her mother involves much tension. 'When she comes to stay she keeps up this monologue. "Oh, you're so clever, how do you cook like this? I could never do this." She seems to be asking me to say, "Well, you taught me everything, Ma." But I can't bring myself to say that. I'm still struggling to be separate and have my own ways of doing things. And when I do things my own way, especially concerning the children, she is very undermining.'

Caroline's is a classic example of the ways in which involvement with our mothers and their desires and needs structures our own choices, often in favour of repeating those traditional structures. Post-war mothers, like Caroline's, were taught that mothering was the be-all and end-all of their existence, so that having a successful daughter proved their own worth. But at the same time theirs is a generation of low self-esteem, and they sometimes fear their daughters' different decisions, partly because of their own missed opportunities, but partly because different decisions about mothering can be taken as implicit criticisms of their whole lives.

Classically, the conflict manifests itself in innuendo and veiled criticism around issues like the routine of young children, demand feeding, diet and children's behaviour. In Caroline's situation the only 'solution' is not to challenge her mother, not to provoke her envy. Yet even changes in fashions of parenting and households – especially the increased affluence and relaxed attitude to discipline – have the potential to unsettle her mother's precarious sense of self-worth.

Low self-esteem is a particularly lethal, though common, element in mother–daughter relationships. It almost invariably ends in mutual criticism and unhappiness, because ultimately, whatever the daughter does, she can only partially 'complete' the mother's needs. To achieve *and* mother is to challenge her own mothering. Not to achieve is to run the risk of unleashing the mother's own disappointment. Fiona, now 43, has two children in their early 20s by a previous marriage, and a little boy and girl from a second marriage. When her first marriage broke up she had to rely on her mother but describes the time as 'very, very difficult'. 'My mother was really supportive about the hard time I was having with my divorce but she was awful with the kids. She criticized me all the time for what she called my "casual attitude" and the kids' behaviour. She brought me up very formally – no, coldly. But I totally rejected her ways.'

Fiona's conflict with her mother went a lot deeper than changing social values around morality and behaviour might suggest. Fiona also felt she had never been given enough affection or approval as a child. 'My mother always made me feel I wasn't coming up to scratch. She kept saying, "What on earth can we do with the girl?" They kept trying to find things for me to do in a way that made it clear that they were just trying to find a practical solution to a hopeless case. Also, everyone thought my mother was very beautiful and they would say to me, "Aren't you like your father." So I knew I wasn't coming up to scratch there either!'

In Chapter 3 Fiona described how her mother eventually sent her off to train as a nanny. 'It was the sort of thing that that class of woman did when she couldn't think of anything else. The idea was that I'd be nanny to a smart family and perhaps see a bit of the world before I found a man to marry. But the course taught me that there were other ways of being with children. It gave me words for something that had happened to me. I'd always known something was wrong but I hadn't got any explanation for it. Once I began to learn about maternal love, and bringing up children, I knew what I'd been missing.'

Fiona believes that her experiences in childhood, combined with what she learnt on her course, gave her a sense almost of mission. She was determined to have children of her own, and determined to mother them in a way that 'undid' her own feelings of inadequacy. 'When my daughter was born I thought the only thing that was important was to show her love and make her feel beautiful, even if she wasn't. I felt if I told her enough she probably would turn out gorgeous. I think I was right. She's much more confident and less hung up than I was.'

The older generation is sometimes right to feel criticized. Fiona's attitude to her own children *is* a criticism of her mother, and this is typical. The new generation of mothers not only disagrees in an intellectual way with previous methods, but often reacts in an emotional way, determined not to continue the legacy of damaged self-esteem. Julia, who has what she called a 'cosy and friendly' relationship with her mother, also describes how her decision to continue to work as an office manager after the birth of her first child was driven by a reaction against her mother. 'The more I saw my mother sitting around doing nothing, the more it made me feel, I'm bloody well going to do better than that. Everyone needs their own parameters. Everyone needs some independence from their own situation. My mother didn't have anything outside the family so she had no affirmation from outside. She has no confidence really.'

Yet criticism and hostility is by no means confined to the younger generation trying to make the break with the past. Such criticisms, especially when embodied in the feminist cause, have attracted the most attention, but the counter-offensive has been equally forceful. For some of the older generation the new, apparently materialistic values are intolerable. Victoria Gillick, who although still in her 40s became a spokeswoman for traditional values, constantly comments on the selfishness of the feminist generation, who are prepared to give up nothing for their children:

The feminists loudly and insistently declared that since, in their opinion, there was nothing very special about biological motherhood, all women should therefore have a right to State-funded crèches and childminding facilities, so that they could go back to work as soon after the birth as possible. You could sum up their argument in more or less one word, repeated endlessly – ME. (*A Mother's Tale*)

Gillick, like Margaret Thatcher, refers to the feminist generation as the me-generation, the women who wanted to have it all. Of course, even a cursory glance at both these women emphasizes the point I am making in this chapter: that decisions about the family often have deeper causes and that public views are not always consistent with private behaviour. Gillick's own parents separated when she was 14, and her sadness about that clearly has some relation to her desire to create a stable and large family. Yet she claims that one of the reasons she so profoundly opposes divorce and laments 'broken marriages' is that the children of broken homes can't form stable relationships. Thatcher is equally inconsistent. She gave little support to working women, but admits that it was at the moment she saw her newly born twins that she decided to become a lawyer.

On a more mundane level, other women described to me the paradoxical actions of their elders which could only be understood in terms of resentment. One woman spoke of how her mother was always ready to babysit if it was a 'family occasion', such as a funeral or a marriage, but refused point-blank if she was going to work. Another described how her mother would never give presents to the grandchildren – '"Children today have got so much," she would say.' Sometimes the older generation looks more like the envy generation than the kindly, altruistic one they would have us believe in.

Andrea, whose decisions about work I recorded at some length in Chapter 1, also gave some interesting insight into the paradoxical nature of generational conflict. 'I think I am both reacting against my mother *and* copying her at the same time. Sometimes it's as if I'm on automatic pilot. When things are busy, I just hear my mother, and I look very like her too, which is odd. I look in the mirror and see my mother. I repeat a lot of her ways of being with us. I react like her a lot of the time, but I'm aware that the reasons for the reactions are with her, not me, and I try to change that. She wasn't able to reach us children and I sometimes feel I don't like anyone near me. My parents were often unreachable but they had had very bad experiences in the war. They lost a lot of their relatives and friends – my grandparents were killed in an air-raid. I think my mother was bereaved. She was switched off from us children. That comes to me naturally but I don't want to be like that, I fight it. I want to be reachable for my children. I have to sort out what is my own experience and what is my mother's.'

Although Andrea's parents had especially bad experiences, the legacy of the Second World War, even for those with less trauma to cope with, cannot be underestimated. Feminists have recorded the contradictions of increased opportunities and freedoms, followed by pressure on women to return to the home. But this experience should also be seen as a psychological event. It is interesting to notice how much the war still features in women's accounts of their lives, not just for women who lived through it but for the post-war daughters who internalized their mothers' fears, hopes and anxieties. Surely it is not far-fetched to imagine that these feelings, surrounding the stay at home mothers of the 1950s, produced the new generation of feminists, the first women to turn on their traditional family structures.

The war was clearly important as a psychological trauma, a period of fear and anxiety which meshed with the practical exigencies of restoring the traditional family. That was true for men as well as women. It meant that the children of that generation were exposed to contradictory expectations, in particular the enormous push to live out fantasy in the face of reality. It meant desires were lived out through children, conflict was denied for the sake of appearances, and ambitions were postponed for future generations. Traditional morality and gender expectations had been unsettled, but there was a massive desire to put everything securely back in its place. No wonder the next generation received such contradictory messages. The conflict that was pushed aside re-emerged through the children.

For the women of that generation, the new changes often seem destructive. First there was the fear that sexual freedom would devalue women. To some extent their fears were justified. Inequalities in power relations meant that sexual freedom had different implications for men and women, as even the most ardent supporters of sexual liberation realized. Now they fear that, in overthrowing traditional rules of discipline and routine, women are making themselves slaves to their children. The older generation may be right in realizing that some of the old ways, although not ideal, might have had some benefits for women. At least old attitudes to marriage ensured support for your children; at least not working allowed them some rest.

Margaret is a widow in her 60s who now lives outside Manchester. She has two grown-up children who were young in the 1950s. Her daughter, Marilyn, who became an active feminist, lives a very different life from her own. She is divorced, works full-time and leaves her children with a childminder. Margaret is very concerned about the changes – the benefits and disadvantages – in what is happening on the home front, and about the conflict she has with her own daughter. 'When I had young children, we just took it for granted we'd stay at home with them. Everybody did. I didn't know any working mothers. We talked about them but we were *very* disapproving. Actually, I wasn't unhappy when the children were little. I feel muddled about

Marilyn. I do admire her. I don't know how she does it. She's got a full-time job with a lot of responsibilities, she runs a home and she hasn't even got her husband to help her. But then again it doesn't seem much of a life to me. She says she likes her job. But she looks exhausted. And it doesn't seem much of an existence for the children. She knows I don't approve, that's why we aren't as close as we ought to be. My fault, I suppose.'

When I spoke to Marilyn I heard the by now familiar litany of grievances against her mother's generation. Marilyn doesn't want to be 'vulnerable' like her mother, relying so much on her children. She wants a life outside the family. And she resents how little help she gets from her mother. 'I just don't understand why Mum won't help out more. She's got the time. She knows how difficult it is for me. I wish she'd just offer to have them for a weekend. It's not that I never have any time off – their father has them every third weekend. It's just that I'd like her to make a gesture. I'd like her to show she liked the kids more. I'm never sure about that. I wish she could approve of me more.' Interestingly, though, Marilyn 'confessed' that she would like to give up work for a while. 'In my heart of hearts, I'd love to meet another man, perhaps have another baby and spend some time at home. Well, at least Mum would be happy.'

Common to the accounts from both generations is a sense of pain. I was struck time and time again by the number of women who found the idea of their mother's or daughter's suffering, bitterness or unhappiness the most unbearable of all emotions. The thing the younger generation most fears is their mother's need of them. They fear that they cannot provide the goods, that in growing up and separating they necessarily disappoint a mother who has invested in them in this way. They are often driven by the desire not to inflict this on their own children.

Yet it may be that this anguish is inherent in the mother – daughter relationship, although exaggerated by the particular family changes over the last four decades. It is interesting that the daughters of careerist mothers had a complaint that was the opposite of the anxious over-identification of the stay at home mothers. Paula, whose mother had continued working through the 1950s and is now a well-known doctor, described her childhood as 'bleak'. 'My mother wasn't really interested in us. She was much more interested in the latest article in the latest journal. When she was with us, which wasn't very often, she was either buried in a journal or on the telephone. I think I'm as normal as I am only because there were five of us kids, and we gave each other a lot of support. I work myself, but when I'm with my children, boy, am I with them! They get 100 per cent of my attention.'

In spite of the problems and grief between mothers and daughters it seems that there are few women who do not still, at some deep level, long for their mother's approval. As Fiona says, 'It's funny, it would mean absolutely everything to me if my mother actually *liked* my children.' Reacting against a previous generation is not, or should not be, in itself a problem. But it becomes so in the context of the perennial anxiety which women of both generations feel about being judged and found wanting. Mothers and daughters measure themselves up against 'ideals' of mothering, asking, did I do it well enough? or, can I do it better? With such self-doubt and anxiety at play, it is hardly surprising that the peaceful relationship for which many women long is often the most stormy. Nor should it be surprising that, in seeking to reassure themselves and each other, women make decisions about their work and family life to appease those inner conflicts, rather than to follow an immediate fashion.

7

Guilty Women

In previous chapters I have looked at the different anxieties and dilemmas confronting contemporary women which often push them in traditional directions. The feeling most frequently found underlying these anxieties is guilt, a guilt which seems to go way beyond specific inadequacies in any individual's life. Guilt about working, guilt about not working, guilt about children, guilt about mothers, guilt about husbands. I didn't find much evidence for the existence of the confident 'have it all' women of the 1990s. Instead I found women trying to find a way of living that held their guilt at bay. If there was a sign that all is not quite well with contemporary women, it is guilt – a sign that women are internalizing the conflicts of their current position rather than finding social solutions.

Guilt, guilt, guilt. At one point I felt as though I would never hear about anything else. One after another, women claimed they had 'the monopoly on guilt' or they had 'invented it'. One woman told me that she felt guilty that her first husband had left her – she must have neglected the relationship. Many told me they felt guilty for not having sex often enough with their partners. Equal numbers told me they felt guilty about their mothers or sisters, especially if they felt their own material circumstances and opportunities were better than those of other members of their family. There was guilt from women who had loved their childminders more than their mothers, guilt from women who felt they loved their mothers too much, to the detriment of their relationships with their husbands. Overwhelmingly there was guilt at not doing things well enough – '*anything* well enough', said one woman, speaking for the ranks of ordinary women who neither receive satisfaction from their work nor feel that they are being particularly effective in the home.

Melanie Klein, the psychoanalyst, has said that 'ambivalence breeds guilt and guilt in its turn fosters masochistic submission'. This comment seems to have direct relevance to the question of why women comply with the traditional sexual division. Guilt seems to accompany any attempt to break with traditional structures, and indeed any *thought* of breaking that structure. And ambivalence does seem to be central here. When there are two strong impulses in play – such as the desire to follow a career and the belief that a child benefits most from its mother's attention – then the feelings of guilt are particularly intense.

What exactly is it that women are feeling so guilty about, and why? Women's guilt about leaving children while they work is well documented – it is widely referred to as 'this guilt thing'. The guilt involves anxiety about depriving the children of maternal attention, which is thought to be superior to that of any other adult. Sometimes the feelings women describe as guilt are actually anxieties about responsibility for the children. There is a feeling that women alone take the psychological and physical responsibility for the kids in the home; having recognized that responsibility, most fear passing it on to someone else.

This feeling should not be belittled. Especially when children are small they clearly need at least one person who is attuned to their physical and emotional well-being in a constant way. Sometimes women take up that role exclusively, sometimes they are supported by the children's father to a greater or lesser degree. But whatever the local variations, it is still seen as a woman's role. For those who have assumed this sense of continuous psychological responsibility, it is difficult to imagine that anyone else could do the task. The situation is exacerbated by the haphazard organization of childcare in our culture. It is usually up to individuals to find other individuals. Often those individuals are 'untrained', and few are supervised by state bodies. Given that most women choosing a childminder rely on instinct rather than professional guidance, their anxieties are hardly surprising.

Strictly speaking, though, this sense of individual responsibility should produce anxiety rather than guilt. So why should women feel guilt as well as a reasonable anxiety about their child's safety? Women seem to suffer acutely from the belief that achieving or doing things for themselves is potentially damaging to other individuals. Could this be the reason why, when some very successful women give up everything for the family, they do it with a vengeance, taking on all the trappings of traditionalism? It is as if they feel they have to compensate – almost masochistically – for having wanted things for themselves. Certainly one persistent factor in contemporary female guilt is a conviction that in leaving their children, women are thereby running the risk of retarding their development. Many women reported to me that one of their main anxieties about working was the possibility that their children might exhibit behavioural difficulties, or not get on well academically. But as well as their own guilt concerning this possibility, they also felt that they would be open to other women's guilt-provoking judgments, especially those of the previous generation.

Lorna summed up a common fear when she described her mother's attitude to her own career. 'I don't think she's actually worried about Brendan, but if he started showing behavioural problems, she might well say, "Aha!" For example, my sister-in-law had a miscarriage while working as a dental receptionist and all the women in the family were very quick to say that it was the work. My mother wouldn't criticize me to my face, but I'm sure she doesn't approve of my working. While things are going okay people will tolerate it, but if anything went wrong with Brendan, the finger would get pointed.' This guilt was a fear of 'failing' according to the standards of the older generation.

Several women told me that their decisions to leave work were influenced by their children not 'achieving' as well as they hoped. Almost all the working mothers I interviewed felt that if their children were slow to read or were not doing particularly brilliantly at school, this was attributable to having been denied that special maternal interest. Anna, who worked as a medical secretary, said it was her nanny leaving after three years that marked the time for her to stop work. 'My little boy was having a lot of trouble with reading and writing at school. We were wondering at that point whether he might be dyslexic. He was needing a lot of extra help and so guilt started to creep its way back into my head. I'd spent a lot of time thinking, he doesn't read because I don't spend enough time reading with him. I knew that was stupid because I knew that I'd read to him every day of his life.'

Working mothers also feel guilt – and, more understandably, regret – about missing the children's significant moments and achievements. One of my interviewees told me that guilt at missing events at her child's school was one of the crucial factors in making her decide to give up work. 'I can remember once pretending that I was at the harvest festival at school. That's awful, isn't it? That was when I knew I'd have to leave work. The childminder had taken our little girl and they sat at the front. And I'd said I would definitely try and get there and I would probably have to slip in at the back and slip out before it finished. But there was just no way I could get there. No one would cover at work. So I rang up the childminder and said, "What hymns did they sing and what happened?" Then when James said, "I didn't see you, Mum," I said, "Sorry, I was there but I did have to leave early." It was a complete lie. And I felt awful about lying but knew that it was really important to him that I was there. It sounds funny now, but at the time I felt absolutely awful about that. And very, very guilty, you know, for lying and for actually not being there.'

There are those who would be baffled by such antics, but this is by no means an uncommon story. Indeed, so prevalent is the working mother's guilt at missing a school event that Maeve Haran in *Having It All* could make her heroine's dash from her high-powered job to her son's private school to be there for his hundred-yard race one of the moments of high sentiment. Needless to say, he responds to the maternal stimulus and wins! Guilt-ridden though this absurd executive mother is, she could at least feel smug that she doesn't experience the more common and routine guilt of most mothers – that they very often don't want to be there in the first place!

Mothers who don't have paid employment have their own version of guilt about children's achievements, but they tend to blame the schools if their children are not 'achieving their full potential'. Even this, however, can become fodder for self-criticism – they must have made 'the wrong decision about schools'. Nowhere is women's complicity clearer than in the way they take personal responsibility for issues which should have social and political solutions. By setting themselves impossible targets, women are doomed to feeling guilty when they fail to achieve them. But guilt is an unproductive emotion, yielding only self-criticism and individual solutions, and is a clear indication that women are preventing themselves from thinking socially and politically. It represents a source of misdirected energy, which could more effectively be employed by placing these worries in their proper place.

More surprising perhaps than guilt about failing to live up to the prevailing ideals of mothering is a widespread, more nebulous guilt that mothers have failed to give adequately to their children. This guilt functions at a deeper level, and is about getting things wrong emotionally. Women are enormously self-critical of their failure to establish and maintain harmony within the family. Several women described how they put their children to bed, only to be overwhelmed by intense guilt that they had mismanaged the day: they berated themselves for being 'emotional failures'.

Faye, whose spotless house, organized manner and apparent enthusiasm for her children seemed to indicate a deep satisfaction with family life, took me by surprise when she said that the main emotion she experienced in the evening was guilt. She was talking about how she missed the sense of accomplishment she had had at work – 'The satisfaction one gets from putting up something and having people's comments back on it.' I asked her if she ever put the children to bed and felt the same sense of accomplishment. 'No, not really, because I always feel guilty about them. I always feel guilty about Amy, my eldest, because she makes you feel nothing is enough. But I also feel I haven't given them enough time and I haven't sat down and made something with them, and then I find a book when I'm tidying up that one of them asked me to read and that I hadn't. It's probably because I've got three very demanding children very close together, but no, I never feel satisfaction. Only guilt.'

I wondered what it was that she felt she was getting wrong. 'Well, it's easy to do stupid things like clean the floor, clear the table, tidy up something that's untidy, because I can't bear to have it like that. When I was growing up our house was always untidy. I didn't like the mess and chaos. I'd like a much neater house. If I'm going to be here all day I want it to look reasonably neat. So I'm probably wasting time doing that while I could take one on my lap and read a story. That's the sort of thing I feel guilty about. That I haven't got my time right. Not managed it properly.'

I listened to similar comments across all classes and types of women. The content was not always the same – instead of spending too much time tidying the house, others might feel they had done the opposite, perhaps by 'not having made the house a welcoming place', as one very busy mother of five said. But the self-critical sentiment is always there. Jane, a mother of two boys living on a Peckham estate in London, said that she never felt a sense of accomplishment when the children were finally in bed. 'No, it never gives me great joy. Sometimes I look at their little bodies and think, look, I did that. I feel quite proud and think, goodness, aren't they beautiful! But I don't feel achievement. I suppose I might if I felt I was a bit more successful at it. But I don't. I think, oh, I should be able to cope. I had people coming this morning and I didn't even get the Hoover out. It's just little things like that. I feel I'm quite inadequate. I feel my mother would cope much better than I do.'

Theresa, a single mother, said she also suffered from a constant sense that she wasn't doing right by her children, a sense exacerbated by the fact that her ex-husband was disputing the custody arrangements which had involved her children in a welfare assessment. 'It makes me feel terrible. I try my best but I'm on my own and I haven't got much money. All the time I'm asking myself, am I doing it right? Is this how other mothers do it? If I lose my temper when Chantel has been playing up, and I shout at her and tell her to go to bed, I feel terrible. Sometimes at my worst moments I even think, maybe he's right. But he doesn't want the kids really. He thinks it's a point of honour to have his own children with him, and he's angry with me because I left him. I feel very guilty that this is what the kids have got to deal with. It isn't how I imagined my life would be.'

This guilt is more than the sense of failing the middle-class ideal of perpetual stimulation, harmony and order, where the mother is totally altruistic, totally giving, and never ruffled. This deeper guilt is evidence of the ambivalence described by Klein – of the existence of two contradictory feelings towards the same object. One woman described to me how she stopped feeling guilty only when she gave up trying to fit together two incompatible elements – her frustration with being a stay at home mother and her ideal notion of motherhood. Linda, who has one teenage boy, now has a well-paid and interesting job in computer training. But her route to this position was hard and involved her having to tackle her guilt head-on, to ask herself whether this guilt wasn't in fact trapping her in a situation in which she was very unhappy.

Linda comes from an Irish Catholic family. 'My husband also has a Catholic background – he's Spanish. When Claudio was born, we both assumed I'd stay at home. We were delighted to have a child and anyway I was only a secretary then and it didn't seem worth going back. But I was really unhappy. It got me down. Claudio was a very unsettled baby and he screamed solidly for three months and then slept badly for ages. I was exhausted and bored at the same time. I got involved in a lot of local things. I helped set up a crèche and a family workshop – which I got a lot from. But I just felt more and more as if I was wasting my brain.'

Linda decided to go back to work, first as a school secretary, then progressing to the job of administrative officer. 'When I was in admin, I got interested in computing and managed to get sent on a course. I loved it. Everyone said I couldn't do it. The more they said it, the more I wanted to show them. I've been working in computers ever since and I'm now working for the Civil Service doing training in computers for various offices. It gives me unbelievable satisfaction when they ring up and ask me to "send the chap". I say, "Perhaps I'll come myself." The last person they expect is a woman with a cockney accent! But the big thing is I don't feel guilty any more. I know it sounds strange, because a lot of mothers feel guilty about working. I felt more guilty about being at home and hating it. Once I started working I started enjoying my home. And I never left Claudio with people I didn't trust. Now he's older I think he admires me. He likes telling his friends his mother is a computer buff!'

Linda's case is interesting because the guilt was at its worse when there were two contradictory impulses – on the one hand a sense of what a good mother ought to feel, and on the other a growing frustration with her life. Her guilt stemmed from her not enjoying it, and in this there is something typical. Those women who appeared to experience the most guilt were the ones whose basic impulses most drastically contradicted the ideal. This, I think, is a not very conscious aspect; it was more that I picked up a sense that the stronger an impulse for self-advancement, the more violent the latent resentment towards the child. The greater the resentment, the more likely this is to appear as guilt about not being a good enough mother. Most often the guilt would focus on the superficials – the state of the house, 'inadequate schooling', not doing enough 'creative' things to make it all worth while.

Catherine, a mother of three, gave an interesting description of how drastically her idyllic picture of family life was shattered by the birth of their first daughter, who cried and was very unsettled from the beginning. At first she had thought, 'This baby isn't going to change my life. I'm going to keep on with activities and meetings. I had redefined my career to fit in with children but I basically kept working. John and I were never in the house at the same time. We didn't think it should take two to look after a baby. But it became obvious when she was quite little that she's a miserable sort of girl. And I began to feel guilty and responsible for that.'

Things got so bad for Catherine that she eventually turned to an organization which helped parents with 'parenting', and especially with understanding their own emotions. 'I went because I had real problems – I felt angry and guilty all the time – and the problems really focused on my eldest child. I felt persecuted by her. She hung on to me all the time and I felt like screaming, "Let go of me. Go away!" And I kept hitting her, though I didn't believe in smacking, and I knew this was making things worse. I was hitting her too hard. I was worried for me and her. The classes really helped me as they allowed me to acknowledge I had needs, rather than trying to be available all the time to the children and then resenting it like hell. I was able to say, "I'm tired, I need a break," not what I had done previously which was say to the kids, "You're tired, go to bed," and then get beside myself when they didn't. Most important for me was learning not to feel guilty because I've got needs as well as the kids.'

Catherine's comments give a clue to some of the elements involved in this pervasive sense of guilt. Very often women expect to be totally available to their children. They will not consciously admit that they expected to negate themselves, but equally they are not good at setting limits for themselves, often using work to establish boundaries when they are desperate for some respite. The danger of losing a clear sense of boundaries is chronic when the children are young. Then the needs and demands are so intense that it is easy for women to lose a clear identity, which in fact few women have to start with. And of course women are predisposed to looking to the family as a place where their own neediness, their own difficult feelings and desires might well be buried under the overwhelming needs of everybody else.

Guilt arises not just because the ideals of mothering are impossible to meet but because, subconsciously at least, there is a powerful agenda of resentment. Hilary, who described herself earlier in this chapter as having a 'problem with guilt', noted how placing women at the centre of all the family's needs was asking for trouble. 'You are pulled in lots of different directions and you don't know which way to go and how to get it right. And sometimes you ask yourself, who are you getting it right for? Are you getting it right for yourself? Or for all the others? I think there is an element of my staying at home in order to get it right for everybody else so I can have a more peaceful structure to home life. But I am frightened that I am going to resent them all because they've made me give up work. They haven't at all, but this is how I rationalize it. I am worried that I will resent them because I have stayed at home. Actually they didn't really care, and it doesn't make any difference anyway. Everything is still as chaotic and I'm still yelling, "Hurry up!" all the time.'

It would be easy to see the guilt which flows from women's central position of responsibility in the home as a simple by-product of the sexual division of labour in our society. I lost count of the number of women who said to me that their male partners didn't feel the same way about the children and were uncomprehending about women's guilty feelings about work and children. This 'difference' was invariably offered as the reason why women ended up doing the lion's share of the work, and taking the psychological responsibility for the home. Lorna summed it up. 'My husband is very happy to see Brendan at the end of the day, but equally happy if it's just for fifteen minutes. He doesn't perceive it as a loss. Sometimes he goes for days on end without seeing him. If I were in that situation, I would perceive it as a loss.

I'd feel dreadful guilt. He doesn't feel any guilt. He thinks I shouldn't feel guilt. He has female colleagues who work full-time and have nannies and he thinks I should be like that. Maybe that's partly me – maybe it's because society expects women to stay at home and look after their kids.'

Lorna's guilt is typical. In part it is an anxiety created by the division of responsibility between the sexes. But it also goes further, merging with a guilt about general inadequacies and failings. These feelings extend beyond the specific problems of individual families and beyond the issue of whether or not women work. They also relate to the anxieties women have about fulfilling their own wants and ambitions, something touched on in Chapter 2. Women are often terrified of the consequences of their actions, and in particular that their own needs and ambitions might deplete other people around them, especially dependent people. Work can become the ultimate pressure since it confronts women with their ability to set priorities and to accomplish things for themselves.

Melanie Klein has put forward an important theory regarding the origins of guilt in the infant's early relationship with the mother. She claims that the early experience of dependency generates hostility and destructive rage towards the mother, which in its turn generates guilt. 'We all know that if we detect in ourselves impulses of hate towards a person we love, we feel concerned or guilty. As Coleridge put it, "to be wroth with one we love, doth work like madness in the brain"' ('Love, Guilt and Reparation', 1937). Klein says that the baby experiences the mother as alternately good and bad – in Kleinian terms, as 'the good and bad breast'. By this she means that the same source of satisfaction (usually the breast) is also potentially a source of dissatisfaction. The breast (and mother) may appear and bring the longed for comfort and food, but it also disappears and frustrates. In short, the breast, and hence the mother, is a source of ambivalence. The baby in its state of dependency is both gratified and enraged – it experiences the breast as attacking and has fantasies about striking back.

These hostile fantasies are followed by fear of retaliation. According to Klein the baby reasons, 'If I feel this destructive hate towards my mother, she might feel it about me.' This is the source of guilt (at the destructive thoughts) and of reparation, the desire to put right the relationship with the mother, to give back to her in order to make up for the destructive fantasies. Such theories may sound fanciful – and certainly the way Klein advanced them is off-puttingly dogmatic – but they do seem plausible as an explanation for the pattern of guilt and anxiety which characterizes contemporary femininity. In all the accounts of guilt I heard, a repeated element was fear – fear that women would be punished for having too much, and for *wanting* too much. Any attempt to stake a claim in the world, to take things from it, to set limits whereby they weren't just 'taken from', all unleashed this strange, self-punishing guilt.

There are other psychoanalytic theories which also have something to say about guilt. Freud, for example, sees the main source of guilt as 'Oedipal desires and hostilities', feelings which he claims have to be repressed into the unconscious as the child grows up. What is critical in Freud's account of the girl's development is his notorious theory of the castration complex. He claims 'feminity' is ushered in by the girl's version of the castration complex; this involves disappointment and anger at the mother for having deprived the girl of a penis. More recent theorists have modified or combined Klein's and Freud's accounts. Nina Herman, for instance, in *One Mother's Daughter* (1990), writes, 'no sooner have the manifold infantile grievances linked to all the frustrations which were inevitably experienced at the breast been partly modified, than the resentments come up that here is a sexual mother whom the daughter has to share with the father, as with other babies.' The underlying emotions, she claims, are anger at her mother for depriving her of the penis, and identification with the father as offering a way out of painful disappointed identification with the mother. But sublimating these emotions leaves a residue of guilt.

In Herman's account there is, theoretically at least, no difference between the guilt of the boy and of the girl child. Human beings of *either* sex suffer rage and grief against the mother for loss of oneness. Yet Herman goes on to record that in her clinical experience she has found women to be far more susceptible to *explicit* guilt than men:

Men seem to have an escape from it while women suffer generalized guilt and anxiety-depression, and emptiness. It may in psychotherapy often only take longer until a man will admit to feelings of emptiness, low self-esteem, to that lack of personhood habitual to the woman, for all the power he may wield, all the success he enjoys in his brittle world 'out there'. The experience of outrage at having been short-changed by 'mother', leading to attacks of guilt, is a universal one, but will have different repercussions in the case of the girl. She will subsequently live in dread of retaliation from her maternal object; but rather than focus on this claustrophobic fantasy – the female castration complex – will deny it to live in a more free-floating guilt and generalized anxiety with degrees of depression, whose dynamics remain unconscious without psychotherapy.

If Melanie Klein is right, then the different responses of the sexes have to do with their different abilities to tolerate ambivalence and the expression of destructive, aggressive feelings. In particular, guilt has a lot to do with the ability to tolerate ambivalence. In Klein's account – indeed, in most psychoanalytic accounts – the 'healthy' individual is the individual who can most easily tolerate ambivalence, who can integrate hostility and aggression with love and reparation.

This brings us back to the very intense hostility, love and guilt that characterize a woman's relationship with her mother. Is it possible that the 'normal' ambivalence of an infant towards its mother becomes in our culture something which is very difficult for the girl child to deal with? As Herman says, 'A daughter's guilt ... reaches back to an early phase ... when it is intimately linked to fears of retaliation ... Malignant fantasies underlie a daughter's sense of guilt, fantasies of having sucked dry the maternal husk, put it to one side, scooped out life to put it to selfish use, damaged her by our self-preservation.'

This is a deep, possibly universal, process, but in our culture it is exacerbated by the fact that women have made and continue to make themselves responsible for their families' well-being, at considerable personal cost and sacrifice. It means that the unconscious fantasies of having depleted or destroyed the mother are overlaid with more immediate and real fears – 'Perhaps', a girl might ask herself, 'my mother has neglected herself and disappeared while looking after me.' And here the unconscious takes over again. 'Perhaps I personally have destroyed her.'

This unconscious logic goes on to produce a cycle of guilt in which the daughter will attempt to compensate her mother through her own child, giving back everything she felt she took away from her mother or wasn't given willingly. The unconscious compulsion behind excessive guilt from a mother to her own child is an obsessive fear that her baby might feel the retaliatory rage towards her that she once felt towards her own mother. No wonder a mother suffers such anxiety and guilt. Any amount of sacrifice is worth it to avoid unleashing such hostile, destructive feelings. What professional achievements could justify such a risk?

Here too is a clue to women's current obsession with their children's 'creative' accomplishments. If a child can be creative, surely this is evidence that the child has not been destroyed. Indeed, a child's creativity is felt as evidence that the mother has 'put something in' to the child. It is the negation of destructive, depleting rage. Of course there is something of a muddle here. Teaching your child the violin or doing clay modelling is not really the same as feeding that child emotionally, especially if such extras are accompanied by a feeling of resentment. Anxious guilt cannot be put right by self-abnegation in favour of the children. As we have seen, that has already played a part in maintaining a guilty, depressive and self-perpetuating cycle of feelings for women.

This chapter has looked at the guilt which holds women willingly in their place, a guilt which means that the traditional sexual division cannot easily be challenged. To some extent these feelings of guilt and anxiety are universal, an inevitable part of any dependent relationship. But they are heightened in our culture because of the division that is enforced between men and women, where women are always at risk of being devalued or rendered invisible or insignificant. In such a context, a daughter's destructive fantasies appear to have a basis in fact, and this makes women doubly eager to make reparation to the next generation.

It might be thought that the drift of this chapter is in favour of women developing a strong and secure working identity so that they no longer feel quite so threatened by underlying destructive fantasies. But the issue of whether or not women work is secondary here. What is crucial is women's internal sense of their boundaries and needs. Work sometimes provides that for women, and sometimes women use work to set boundaries in relation to their children which they cannot find within themselves. The real problem for women is when their guilt is so intense that they cannot maintain their identity in the face of a child's normal demands, which include destructive rages and fantasies. That can happen whether a woman is working or not.

Interestingly, it was a woman who was not working at all who had the most to say on this subject. Kristina, who it may be remembered was a single parent before marrying and throwing herself into full-time motherhood, described how much of her time as a mother had been spent feeling guilty. 'I've swung from feeling guilty about passing responsibility for my children to someone else when I was working to feeling guilty about neglecting myself when I've been at home. But I've begun to realize that guilt is destructive itself. It's been stopping me coming to terms with who I am and what I need. I'm not saying that attending to my needs is more important than looking after my children. It isn't. I don't think that passing your responsibilities to someone else is any solution. What's important is finding a balance. Now I think it's about attending to myself within the limits of my responsibilities.'

8

Women Idealizing Men

In spite of the many changes in women's relationships with men, women are still adapting themselves not just to traditional family structures, but to men themselves. Women are still following the logic of the traditional emotional agenda in which they often have as much at stake as men in keeping things the way they are. In the previous chapter we have looked at the way in which women often deny their real feelings about their family situations, which then return to them in the form of a nebulous and generalized guilt. Nowhere can this female inclination to deny or project feelings be more clearly seen than in the ways in which they engage with men. What this means, in practice, is that women often manipulate men and project certain attributes on to them, so that the needs and desires of men, which women may appear to disapprove of, may in fact come from the women themselves.

The familiar feminist argument runs that men have manipulated women in order to meet their own needs. Women, we are told, have been the victims of sexual conventions which trap them in the subordinate domestic role. Men tell us that they also feel restricted by the roles they have to play. They feel limited by notions of masculinity which tell them they should never cry, be tender, look after children, or be vulnerable. But what has rarely been explored is what women themselves are bringing into that construction of masculinity, both as mothers and as lovers.

My own research has convinced me that women's needs and projections on to men are important, unexplored areas, helping to explain how male–female relationships often stay in familiar, repetitive and traditional patterns. I have found that men are often actively 'idealized' in women's imaginations or fantasies in order to meet women's subconscious needs. This idealization is as potent as any of the fantasies which men have about women. Accompanying that idealization is another equally important aspect of women's feelings about men. In many women there exists a deep fear of challenging men, not so much on the public and social front, but, paradoxically, in their private lives, where one might imagine the tensions would be greater. As a result, when relationships do break down, women's disappointed idealization is often so acute that it is accompanied by extraordinary, uncomprehending bitterness.

It may seem strange to talk about women idealizing men. Indeed, taken as a superficial statement, it might seem the exact opposite of what has happened over the last twenty years. Certainly many men, especially those who had close contact with feminists, initially found my suggestions preposterous. One said to me, 'I thought all women thought all men were the lowest form of human life!' There *is* something of a public discourse along these lines – public in the sense of its being a fit subject for jokes and collective solidarity (as it always was) between women. But when we come to more intimate revelations, a completely different picture emerges. Especially among middle-class women, individual men are still a source of potent fantasies.

While researching for this book, I received the strange impression that a large number of the women were actually married to the same man! One after another, women repeated, often verbatim, the same feelings about their husbands and partners. These men were described as more stable, more balanced, kinder, nicer and more fun than the women themselves. They were 'successful', 'ambitious', 'secure', 'kind', or 'the perfect father'. The women described themselves as 'lucky'. Far from listing men's inadequacies, women seem pathetically grateful for any small amount of domestic input. And many still seem to partake of 'the exempted man' syndrome identified by feminism many years back – all men are dreadful except the one you happen to live with.

Most of the women I spoke to who were in stable and apparently happy relationships described themselves as 'exceptionally lucky' even though some of the conditions they described sounded far from blessed. Ann's husband, for example, does more than many, but even so his contribution to domestic life would appear only reasonable. Ann, however, views herself as 'incredibly lucky'. 'I have a husband who will come home in the evening and put our daughter to bed if I am tired. Sometimes he will get up in the night if she needs it and get her up in the morning. Sometimes he gets in and flops but on the whole I do feel fairly equal. I have to remind him that what I'm doing may not be the most fascinating thing in the world, but it is his child as well. We have breakfast together always, he's always late, but he's always home by seven. If he isn't, I'm desperate.'

Some women described themselves as lucky because their husbands or partners cook the evening meals most nights. Others were lucky because their husbands always share nappy changing when they are at home. Others because their husbands will play and show deep affection and attention to the children. But even those who were most effusive about their good fortune complained that their partners expected to 'clock off' from the children in a way that the women never could, and that these same husbands did not fully share domestic responsibility in the form of day-to-day planning, organization and running of the family. Susan, who also considered herself lucky, said that their situation was pretty unfair. 'I feel he doesn't do enough. The thing is, he gets very tired by the work he does, so making an effort with the children seems like an enormous effort at the one time he wants to relax, which is the weekend. I constantly push him as much as I can to keep him on his toes and to keep him helping, but the funny thing is he has a different perception of how much he does contribute. If we sit down and discuss it he thinks he is contributing an enormous amount, but that's probably because he's never had to look after them the whole day long.'

The statistical evidence about how much men contribute in the home is contradictory. One recent survey showed that men do virtually nothing in the home, while another showed that both women and men now *expect* to share more domestic tasks. But leaving aside whether or not these husbands are exceptional, it is clear that women's expectations of men are minimal, and that many women want to believe that they are indeed married to the perfect 'new man'. That women sometimes enter the realm of fantasy when describing their partners is all too evident. One mother of three describes herself as 'exceptionally lucky' because her husband is 'such a good father'. 'He is so involved with his children and really cares about them. He is always showing around their photos at work.' It emerged later that her husband worked from six forty-five in the morning to eight-thirty at night, and that showing the children's photos around at work was about all he *did* do with them.

This is the kind of idealization you might have expected in the 1950s, not the 1990s. Yes, the language has changed. Women no longer talk so explicitly about men as distant providers who should be obeyed and serviced – but they do describe themselves as 'grateful' if a husband earns well and provides a 'good standard of living'. Susan admitted, 'I would mind if he was less successful because it's great and useful having a good income. Isn't that awful? Actually he's not that successful. He's just a normal boring old banker. He's not one of the high-fliers. The fantastic thing is he doesn't work too long hours: eight-thirty in the morning to seven at night. I'm resigned to getting them up in the morning and putting them to bed but it is a niggle and I find it frustrating that he can't be the modern man enough to really pull his finger out as far as looking after children goes. But the argument is that he really does have to work pretty hard and the income is important so one just has to accept that.'

Like Susan, many women are inclined to describe this situation as *faute de mieux*. They accept their husband's reduced contribution to domestic life as a sad fact of life. Their husbands can earn more because of the inequalities of the job market and inadequacies of childcare provision, so the division of labour in the home seems like a rational response to an unfair world. True enough. But as an explanation, it doesn't go far enough. These women are *thankful* that their partners have some decent human attributes, *thankful* that their partners show an interest in their own children. And at some level, they also seem to *want* their husbands to be more successful than themselves.

There's more at stake here than women having minimal expectations for themselves, although to some extent that does enter into it. Along with this gratitude comes a whole series of projections. These men are not just exceptionally kind and helpful with the children; they are often also seen as 'better' in some way than the women. Repeatedly I heard husbands described as more ambitious, more successful and more single-minded; but they are also described as stronger, saner and more straightforward.

Women's attraction to 'successful' men has been well explored. Attraction to powerful men, rich men and men with social status is at the heart of romance. In the past, feminists have interpreted this as an emotional and sexual pattern that reflects women's economic dependency and vulnerability – women are attracted to men who will prove the most efficient 'mates'. The more money, or power, the greater his capacity to attract women. But it is surprising how prevalent such feelings still are. Time after time, middle-class women admitted to me that their partners' success not only mattered to them in terms of money, but was a crucial component in their respect and desire for these men.

For many women, including career women, the desire for their husbands' success was a vital part of the relationship, and they were prepared to do a lot of work and accommodating to help that success. Hilary, who gave up her career as a community nurse to look after her children full-time, described how an element in her decision was that she could help her husband get on in his career. 'I think my chaos was getting him down. I was always tearing about in a hurry, trying to get ready for work. Often I'd have to ask him to do things for the children. In the end I decided to give up work so that I could get things right for the others. And don't get me wrong, there are lots of advantages. He sells advertising space and his job requires him to do a lot of socializing, going to lots of functions. I go to a lot of things and I enjoy it. We get to do a lot of interesting things and meet interesting people. And I feel proud of my husband.'

Hilary is by no means unusual. Even in these days of the working woman, a husband's career usually takes precedence in terms of where the family will settle and who will give up most for the children and dependants. In Hilary's case, her husband's social status reflects on her in more than simply material terms. This is typical. Another woman, married to a successful and well-known businessman, seemed to have absorbed his identity. She had identified with his business interests and talked obsessively about him and his schemes, mentioning his name whenever and wherever she could. All his triumphs and accomplishments were offered as reflections on herself for being married to him.

None of this is new. What is surprising is that the desire for successful men is supposed to be neither so blatant nor so desperate among contemporary women. Nowadays, women are expected *not* to invest their whole well-being and ambition in men, and most women deny it as a fact of their relationship. But in more searching conversations it is clear that this psychological structure is still alive and well. One woman I spoke to was a successful designer, married to a freelance writer who at the time of this interview was struggling to get work. At first she insisted that the difference in their income was irrelevant. 'We're both just pleased I've done so well. It means we've got a high standard of living, better than either of us expected.' But later she told me, 'I do worry about Ian. I keep trying to suggest where he could get work. He just won't sell himself, and I'm afraid that's what counts in his world. Yes, I do nag him to try and achieve more.' Is that for you or for him, I asked. 'I don't know. I suppose I would like it if he was more successful.'

In most families it is still the exception rather than the rule for women to earn more than men, and for the woman's career to take precedence over the man's. What is even more surprising is how many of the younger women I spoke to seemed to confirm that many women still *wanted* this situation, even if they resented it. Jackie, who is 22, has been working as a secretary since she left school at 16. Her boyfriend of six years has, during that time, been to university, gone abroad, and moved towns in pursuit of employment. Jackie, who in many ways supported him financially through this period, has moved with him every time, even though these moves have interrupted her chances of promotion. Why was she doing it, I wondered. 'I think he will establish himself soon. He's ambitious and he's good at what he does. I'm just earning money until we start a family. Then he can look after me for a bit!'

One of the most common and striking elements in the way women still allow their partner's career to take priority over any reorganization of domestic life is that women are allowing men to carry all the careerism of the family. The man then has to take care of all the competitive and ambitious feelings of the woman as well as his own. It means that women often insist that their partners are somehow 'naturally' more careerist and ambitious.

Some women still project various social attributes on to men, and these attributes are then seen as part of the man's personality make-up. This makes it easier, for example, to let a husband's career take precedence on the grounds that he is 'naturally' better at certain things. Linda, who is quoted at length in Chapter 2 is typical. She described her husband as a 'brilliant entrepreneur' whom she wanted to help. She also described his ambition as much greater than her own. Yet as we have seen earlier, she was extremely ambitious for their joint company while at the same time feeling uncomfortable with her own competitive feelings at work. It was one of the reasons why she was glad to leave work. Projecting these attributes on to him, and idealizing him, means that he can carry all the ambitious, competitive and careerist attributes of the partnership.

Lorna also describes herself as married to a very successful, self-motivated and careerist man whose career has now taken precedence over her own, even though she is still working. But she feels more ambivalent about the consequences of this than Linda. Her description of how she and her husband have dealt with ambitions and career is classic. She too describes herself as 'lucky' and believes her husband Robert is naturally more ambitious than herself, but at the same time she recognizes the pressures which accepting this division can create for women. 'My own career is on a "back-burner" at the moment. I am ambitious but not conventionally so. I don't want to go into management.' Her husband, on the other hand, has had no such qualms and career breaks. 'He works long hours, and often travels abroad for several weeks. I want him to do well because *he* wants to. He is ambitious in the more conventional sense of wanting to get to the top. He wouldn't be happy putting his career on hold for five years. It pleases him, working hard and doing well. And I accept that. If you live with someone you have to accept the way they are or you run into problems. And it has positive aspects. He's well paid, so I enjoy a high standard of living, and I could choose to give up work. Lots of people don't have that choice.'

But Lorna feels that their way of living has great costs for her. 'The down side is I do see a lot less of him, and I've got more stress. I've never liked the long hours he keeps. I don't like coping on my own. I get lonely. Since Brendan was born I've felt I've been coping with the stresses of a single parent, the total childcare, never having a break from him day in, day out, night in, night out, coupled with the loneliness. Going back to work improved the situation because at least I get some adult stimulation. I suppose because of his career I have to accept that I do the major part of the parenting. My husband is wonderful, very interested. It's just he's not here much and I have to accept things as they are. I don't want Brendan to be brought up by someone else. So I've had to compromise my job in terms of doing fewer hours.'

Lorna and her husband have accepted, as do so many families, the traditional division of labour because they believe they feel differently about their responsibilities for the child. I heard the same complaint over and over again from working women I talked to, some of whom would have been happy with a greater reversal of roles. Their men simply were not *there* for the kids; they were not emotionally and physically responsible on a day-to-day, hour-to-hour basis. In that situation the working mother appeared to have only two choices: looking after the kids herself or paying another woman to do so. Her husband can pursue his uni-linear career because he simply does not *feel* responsible in the same way.

Again, this situation displays a strong element of *faute de mieux*. Lorna and her husband justify their decisions to each other because they believe that to some extent this is the way of the world, that each of them has different *feelings* and characteristics, that each of them is more suited to their chosen tasks. Although Lorna might not like the consequences of this division of labour, there is a pay-off, and that pay-off is revealed in the other powerful fantasy of the man as stronger and more competent. She, like so many of my interviewees, believed her husband was a much steadier and more secure personality than herself.

In Lorna's case, this assessment is understandable – her own mother died when she was 7 and she feels she missed out badly as a child. Brought up by a difficult and unhappy father, she became timid and withdrawn and felt extremely lonely. But even so, her perception of her husband is as much more straightforward, as stronger and less vulnerable. 'I suppose I'd rather Brendan had a childhood more like Robert's. He had an above averagely happy childhood. Nice parents, nice childhood. I'd like Brendan to have a more settled, more secure upbringing. I want him to grow up more confident and secure, like Robert.'

While Lorna's childhood may not seem typical, it is interesting how many women describe themselves as anxious, neurotic and insecure, while their partners are more balanced, more confident and therefore more competent. It is also interesting that many of the women I spoke to whose relationships had foundered, or failed, described a gradual, though occasionally sudden, realization that this sense of their partner's greater emotional stability was actually quite false. Often, in fact, it was the crumbling of this fantasy that allowed suppressed resentments and anger to surface.

Fiona, who remarried in her mid-30s, described how she fell in love with her second husband John, and in that process idealized him as caring and dependable. 'I had been on my own with my children for ten years. I'd coped very well but I've always had this fantasy of being swept off my feet by some tall strong man and being looked after. I'd known John for a long time but his wife got very ill; she had a severe mental breakdown. In fact she was diagnosed as psychotic. But during that period of her illness, I saw him looking after her so well. He was so wonderful that I began to fall in love with him. He was so full of compassion for her, and love, that I fell in love with him because of the way he treated her.'

When John eventually divorced his first wife, he and Fiona married, but it wasn't long before problems began to surface in the relationship. 'What I didn't realize was that he was that way about her because he felt sorry for her. She was a little child and needed looking after, his child. He doesn't feel sorry for me so he's not nice to me in the same way. He drinks too much. Of course, I knew there were many things wrong with him, obsessive things, but I really thought they were all caused by this dreadful unhappy marriage. Of course they weren't. They were him, and they were the reason he married her, not the other way round. So he still has the problems and I find myself married to someone who is incredibly needful, and we've got two little children and I really shouldn't have children at all. I should be looking after him full-time! He is compassionate with the children. He's able to love them very easily. But he isn't able to love other adults at all. He's very suspicious of everybody.'

Such idealism in love is, of course, extremely common,

especially when one person is seen as a 'solution' to the other's immediate circumstances. Women, in spite of differences in personal history, share a deep conditioning which inclines them to thinking that relationships are likely to solve the problems in their lives. Men, on the contrary, incline towards believing the most important changes and improvements in their lives will come through their careers. This is not to say that men neither idealize nor make terrible mistakes in relationships, but simply that for girls and women there is often more at stake, more hopes pinned on the man who might transform their lives.

Helen, now divorced, gave an account of how she fell in love with someone who seemed to represent the solution to her own difficulties in the family. She says she 'drifted into' a relationship with Stephen rather than having been on the look-out for the right man to marry. But even though she wasn't on the look out for Mr Right, their relationship did feel very good for her at the time. It provides a very clear example of how, when emotional needs mesh, it is easy for the man to be idealized into something he isn't.

Helen describes her adolescence as 'not so much terribly normal as just terrible'. They had a nice modern house in Newcastle, 'all very respectable', but her father used to get drunk regularly. 'He used to come home roaring drunk and abusive. Neither my mother nor my sisters ever stood up to him. But I tried to. I hated him for being like that and I hated my mother for being so meek. Sometimes he hit me, but mainly he insulted me. It destroyed my confidence. In my heart I still believe all the things he said about me. They stuck. But when I met Stephen at college, I found someone who would take my side. Stephen was very rebellious and very clever, and obviously going to be successful. And he sneered at my Dad, and stood up to him, wouldn't let him talk to me like that. It felt great. I just thought he was so funny and clever and strong. I felt safe, and it felt like Stephen had made me safe.'

By the time she had turned 22, Helen had two children and was having to come to terms with the fact that Stephen, who may have stood up to her father, was not able to be a father himself. 'He was still a rebel student. He wanted to sit up all night with his friends, smoking and drinking and playing music. If I said I wanted somewhere decent to live – we were in two rooms – he'd scream at me that I was turning into a petty-minded housewife, like my mother.

When I tried to paint the rooms, he just sat there and laughed or sneered at me. If I took the kids to the park to meet a friend he used to say, "God, you're so boring." He just got nastier and nastier about everything I did.'

They separated when the youngest child was only six months old. Five years later, Helen feels she is only just beginning to understand what happened. 'I have ended up in therapy because I found the process of divorce so painful. Deep down I believed all the things Stephen had said about me, that I was boring, stupid, and a bad mother. They just confirmed what my dad had already made me think, although everyone seems to see me as strong and competent. I still don't understand how it happened. I thought I was escaping my dad and I ended up with someone who undermined me even more. But I really did think Stephen was different, that he was strong and secure when I met him. In fact it's still a problem for me that I do still see him like that – and it's made worse by the fact that he is now a successful musician – even though I *know* he is an even bigger mess than me emotionally and I've had to give up on any hopes that he might be a real father to the children.'

Helen's is a particularly vivid example of how women are often attracted to men who express parts of themselves which have either gone underground or have even been destroyed. In her case, she was attracted to someone who had all the arrogance and confidence to stand up to her father *and* all the obvious competence and talent which she felt she lacked. But finding a person to express these things doesn't necessarily take care of them. For a while Stephen carried these feelings for Helen and it felt like a salvation, but ultimately it created further problems. Her own self-esteem was so damaged that it could only have been a matter of time before Stephen added to her sense of worthlessness rather than bolstering her morale.

This example may be extreme, but the process described is common. Women, who often suffer from low self-esteem, frustrated creativity or an inability to assert themselves, can – subconsciously at least – look for an 'other' who will express confidence, arrogance, purposefulness, ambition and success. A man who will 'carry' all these attributes then feels like a safe haven. And if this is an element in male-female relationships, then it is not really surprising that women have such minimal expectations of male domesticity. They already, without knowing it, feel 'grateful' towards the men for doing another, more serious job.

Finding an 'other' to carry certain buried attributes of the self, and thereby appearing to provide security, must always be a precarious endeavour. Low self-esteem is not necessarily cured by finding someone clever and apparently strong to love you. It may temporarily solve some problems, but they don't go away. Even the more successful and stable relationships founded on this basis are not without their dangers. Caroline, who has been quoted at some length, gives a striking example of the pay-offs and pit falls involved in this characteristically female approach to men.

Caroline, in her early 50s and a mother of three, is now facing up to the need to make changes in her relationship, but she nevertheless feels that the husband she met at university was indeed the best possible choice for someone such as herself. As we have seen, she was still emerging from a desperately insecure and sad childhood and could not face up to her ambition for fear of challenging her mother. 'When I met Ian he seemed very mature – not emotionally, but mentally. I was impressed by his organization and purposefulness. He *knew* what he wanted to do. He wanted to get into the media. Even then he was good at making contacts, using them, spotting opportunities. He was clearly going to be successful. He knew how to cope with life and that is exactly what I needed, so although I wasn't entirely sure I was deeply or passionately in love with him, I did feel here was someone I could rely on to look after me, and I terribly needed that. That may have been a bad reason for getting married, but it was how it was at the time. It made for problems, but at the same time it was a pretty canny move. It was what I needed, and it still is actually. It leads to a certain amount of tension now – which we both know about and are facing – as I am finally, belatedly, beginning to try and emerge as an actual person, rather than someone being looked after or as someone looking after smaller, even more dependent people.'

In Caroline's case the scales seem to tip on the side of happiness rather than grief. The process of finding and feeding the confidence of a successful man is not always bound to fail, and can produce a comfortable relationship. But any process based on fantasy and projection must be risky and what is particularly risky for women in this process is mistaking certain male attributes for others. Women often confuse male ambition and single-mindedness with emotional security, equating that intense, single-minded drive, and men's apparent knowledge of where they are going in career terms, with knowing where they themselves are going and what they want emotionally. It means that women often buy the whole package and cannot either understand or cope when their partners' emotional limitations emerge.

This misrecognition is exaggerated because men's most common pathologies, weaknesses and vulnerabilities are accepted as 'normal' behaviour. Fear of intimacy, especially with the same sex, overdependency on sex as a source of comfort, resorting to forms of physical and emotional bullying – these syndromes are rarely noticed in many work set-ups, let alone become an obstacle to career advancement. But the extreme forms of stereotypical feminine behaviour – emotional displays, sexual wiles or manipulative behaviour – are likely to count very heavily against women. In other words, society endorses male manifestations of emotional weakness and limitations. Even feminism bought into this myth by seeing men as all-powerful, invulnerable. No wonder women in their private relationships often mistake one set of characteristics for another: violence for strength, careerism for inner purposefulness, emotional distance for emotional balance. So the disappointment with men is intense when the problems begin to emerge.

Many women experience enormous disappointment and rage when their lovers or partners either fail to meet the woman's submerged ambition or fail to take care of her low self-esteem. One woman I interviewed was on the point of divorce because of problems which had emerged between her husband and herself after his business failed. It emerged that she had invested enormous amounts of time and energy in helping her husband, and had felt unable to cope when things started to go wrong. 'When I met him, it seemed as if he was on the way up. Then everything changed. He sat around at home moping all day and nothing I said or did made any difference. I felt ashamed of him.' Interestingly, this woman's problems appeared not just at home but at work. She fell out with her boss and spent six months in a total rage about 'men'. Only when her husband got a new job did she calm down. But it was too late for their relationship. 'He doesn't talk to me any more. Neither of

us sees any point in trying to continue. I think he's angry with me for nagging him when he was down.'

Pushing certain attributes on to men, and then idealizing them, is nothing new. Shakespeare captured the process in the character of Lady Macbeth, who thinks of, plans and all but executes the murder which will advance her husband. And he also hints at this curious process of projection when he has Macbeth say, 'Bring forth men children only; For thy undaunted mettle should compose nothing but males.' Is it a supreme irony that should make Macbeth 'praise' Lady Macbeth's ambition and ruthlessness as 'male'? Or is it an extraordinary insight into the 'misrecognition' of all ambition and aggression as male? Either way, the play provides insight into a process which is as true now as it was then. Women still separate off certain qualities which they find unacceptable in their own sex – ambition, ruthlessness, aggression – and project them on to men.

Such processes are not universal, but they are typical, and they do give us a certain amount of insight into how and why some women, often even the most hardened feminists, affirm the same attributes in their male children. A supremely good example of this was the article by Polly Toynbee in the *Guardian* to which I referred in Chapter 4. In it she described how little impact feminism had made on what she was increasingly taking to be the natural differences between boys and girls. The focus of her article was her own children, two girls and a boy, and in particular her little boy's obsession with He-Man and all forms of fighting and warfare.

Ostensibly, her piece was concerned with the difficulty of countering nature with nurture, but what came over much more forcibly was her pleasure in her little boy's unreconstructed masculinity. The otherness of a boy child, his maleness, often the ways in which he exhibits so-called characteristically male behaviour such as aggression, ambition, and single-mindedness – all these are typical, and often praised by the most unexpected sources. I hear women saying, with immense pride, how their sons are 'typical boys', any reservations about what that might entail overruled by the sheer pleasure in having produced a little man where all their own characteristically male attributes can safely be held.

I heard a striking example of this when I interviewed one of the older women who had taken part in the TV series *A Secret World of Sex* (Channel 4, 1991). Ada, now in her 80s, had been raped when she went out one night with a couple of sailors and a girlfriend. She was doubly unlucky. She also became pregnant, and her mother threw her out of the house when she recognized the symptoms (which is more than Ada had done). She had the child, a boy, in the workhouse in 1930, and to her surprise her mother turned up and announced her decision to bring the boy up herself. 'She said, "You get back to service. I'll take the boy. But he's mine and everyone is going to know that."'

So Ada's son has spent sixty years of his life believing that Ada was his sister and his grandmother his mother. While making the programme, the television crew took Ada back to County Durham to speak to her 'son' and tell him the truth before the programme appeared. To her immense disappointment, he seemed neither surprised nor very interested. I asked her whether she felt upset about not having been able to be his mother, even though in her subsequent marriage she was unable to bear children. 'Well, it was hard when he was growing up, although I did try to have him as much as possible. Jack, my husband, and I used to take him places, and I always sent money for his clothes. But no, I don't feel disappointed. Not when I look at him now. He's such a big man, and so handsome, and I think, that man is my son, and I feel proud of him, even though I'm sad not to have a family.'

Pride in unequivocal 'masculinity' in one's offspring is by no means a straightforward matter. Investing the child with all those 'male' attributes denied in oneself is not a recipe for lasting joy. Women can end up feeling envious and destructive towards those who do possess these qualities, hostile to the power they often imply. That hostility often erupts if it is the girl child who exhibits the denied attributes of ambition, competitiveness and single-mindedness. Frances, one of the few women I spoke to who described herself as an out and out career woman, positively winced when we spoke of her relationship with her mother. 'She really finds my competitiveness a problem. When I was little, she used to say to me, "Look, Frances, this is only a game. It's only tennis. Don't be so competitive." But I was always like that. Even if it was only a game of tennis, I was going to win it.'

Looking at how women idealize men, we find further evidence of the deep splitting of emotional attributes which is still very much part of the construction of masculinity and femininity. Women deny certain emotions and attributes in themselves and then try to have them satisfied in other relationships – in their children and in men. When women idealize their male partners they often misrecognize those men as people, but the idealizing confirms a belief that the uncomfortable emotions like competition, ambition and aggression are naturally and inevitably male. In the short term, idealizing men means women do not have to confront uncomfortable attributes in themselves, but the splitting of attributes between men and women has destructive consequences. It is to these destructive consequences that I now want to turn, before trying to understand the root causes of the split between 'masculine' and 'feminine' attributes.

9

Women and Manipulative Behaviour

It might be asked why the splitting of attributes between men and women, and the denial of certain emotions in each sex, is such a bad thing. After all, it makes women appear 'nicer', more caring and more altruistic, the sex that willingly shoulders the burden of caring for the community. However, such denial of emotions involves a considerable unseen cost. Not just in terms of all the extra work which women have to do, but also because any process of denial involves misrecognizing your own needs, misinterpreting the needs of others around you and, quite simply, is likely to result in chaos and confusion when reality can no longer be forced to fit the illusion.

Quite apart from the personal cost of this process, there is also a less pleasant side to women's failure to come to terms with their own emotions: their readiness to resort to emotional manipulation in order vicariously to achieve submerged and less acceptable needs. It is in this realm of emotional manipulation that much confusion around women emerges, for there is still a widespread belief that women are compensated for their compliance with men because of the emotional power they wield.

The idea that women manipulate emotions in order to assume a sort of indirect control is a very old one. In the nineteenth century social theories, derived from biology, asserted that much 'feminine' manipulative behaviour, such as flirtatiousness, passivity, weakness and frailty, was aimed at attracting and keeping a mate, when males by nature were nomadic and polygamous. Theories were constructed about the different forms of marriage in different cultures, where it was assumed that customs such as polygamy were early stages on the path towards monogamy, a state by which women ensured the optimum parenting for their offspring.

While such simple evolutionary interpretations of other societies have now been discredited, there are still many, including contemporary social biologists, who assume that much female behaviour is best interpreted as a strategy to control social conditions for the benefit of their offspring. Even now, it is not unusual to hear the view that women are happy to abdicate economic and political control in return for control of the social and moral environment, an exchange which is supposed to be to the greatest advantage of the children and the social fabric as a whole.

Social theories such as these were used to try to counter the growing influence of feminism in the early 1970s. In 1973, for example, Arianna Stassinopoulos argued in *The Female Woman* that women could not be considered powerless. Not only did some women benefit directly from men's power, but most exercised power within the household in their traditional female roles. At the time, she met with near universal condemnation. It was ludicrous to present women as powerful when they were quite obviously not. Suggestions that women had the emotional upper hand were distortions of reality; women were not only burdened and limited by their traditional role in the home, but were also economically and socially vulnerable should the family disintegrate. To suggest that female wiles could be used to the advantage of women against the real economic and political power of men seemed a complete misrepresentation. Few things could guarantee less security in a culture where a rigid and perfectionist view of the body dominates and where women are under constant threat of losing their appeal with age.

Feminism's insistence on real opportunities and economic independence for women came closer to the prevailing mood than Stassinopoulos' book and *The Female Woman* sank without trace, whereas feminist texts were read by millions. But the belief that women have the upper hand emotionally and extract a hidden payment from men has never entirely gone away. Most people – men and women – accept feminism's insistence on the financial independence of women. But many still believe that if a woman can successfully play the emotional field, she will be well compensated. One woman I interviewed illustrates this belief. At 28, Clare is a co-director of a market research company. She has a high salary but her views on sexual relations are startlingly old-fashioned. 'All my women friends are attracted to rich and powerful men. It all comes back to biology. It's because they are after a successful mate. We're just sophisticated rats, looking for the best provider for our offspring, and that's more important to most women than a good job for themselves.'

In the last ten years, ideas about emotional 'pay-offs' have surfaced in a different form. Now relationships are discussed in terms of an 'emotional dynamic' – of mutual need and dependency – a language which disguises real inequality and stresses instead an autonomy of emotional life in which women can have control or dominance in a relationship as easily as men. The real inequalities of power are neglected once again. Even to talk about these things is seen as passé.

It is easy to understand why a more therapeutic approach to relationships has arisen. One of the reasons for the failure of feminism to dislodge deeply held perceptions of male and female behaviour was its insistence that women were victims, and men powerful patriarchs, which made a travesty of ordinary people's experience of the mutual interdependence of men and women. Something in feminism's language of struggle, oppression and inequalities resonated with women's experience and imaginations. But at the same time the feminist discourse failed to explore the full meaning of 'loving the enemy'. The fact was, and is, that the sexes are locked in a relationship of mutual dependency, undoubtedly often tipping into exploitation, abuse or oppression, but requiring a more subtle approach for its understanding.

These old prejudices about male–female behaviour do in fact still mesh with people's untheorized perception of the complex exchange that goes on between men and women, and also with very deeply held – almost unshakeable – beliefs about the rewards offered by traditional family structures. While I was researching this book I was surprised by the vehemence with which men often secretly believed these things. Many men confided that they still felt manipulated by feminine wiles yet found there was no language to complain since women had monopolized the language of victimization. Some men were angry that they had to stick to the old emotional agendas with women while at the same time being expected to support these women's attempts to achieve in economic and political terms.

The fact is, many women and men privately believe that women are skilled manipulators. And many men feel that women are reaping the benefit of a mild form of positive discrimination while retaining some of their more traditional powers. I do not want to take issue with the feminist assertion that the only real security for *all* women is for women to have the possibility of financial and economic independence. Yet, at the same time, all of us are aware of the uncomfortable truth, that the reality is a lot more complex than some versions of female victimization would have it. Emotional manœuvring is still very much a part of our everyday experience – trying to achieve ends by deflected means, suffering and provoking guilt. Yet this is not power and certainly not a compensation for real social disadvantages.

Emotional manipulation is by no means confined to women, although there are some characteristic ways in which women go about it. Men are just as capable of indulging in forms of emotional blackmail, where people are made to behave in certain ways because of guilt. One friend of mine described how she remained for many years in a relationship with a man who got drunk and threatened to kill himself every time she tried to raise her dissatisfactions with the relationship. Rather than deal with what was happening between them, he tried to make her feel responsible for his happiness, well-being, even his life – a responsibility which terrified her.

Denise is now divorced, and believes her husband is using the children to punish her for initiating this step. 'I don't think he will ever admit our relationship was in bad trouble – that's why I wanted him to leave. He still sees it as me having rejected him and he wants to punish me. He knows I think it's really important for the children to see their father regularly so he constantly threatens to disappear. I don't even try to challenge his version of what happened between us any more because I'm scared he will reject the children for good. I think he keeps me uncertain about how much he cares about them. It's a weapon to him.'

This typical form of blackmail, where the children are dragged in to induce guilt and fear, should make it abundantly clear that emotional manipulation is not gender specific. But the example has also hinted at characteristic differences in how men and women manipulate emotions. Fear and threats are very often at the basis of men's behaviour, but some of the ways in which men manipulate, use emotional blackmail and sometimes even bully are accepted as ordinary behaviour – something which is all too apparent in accepted norms of sexual behaviour. Few people challenge the way in which men criticize and compliment women on their appearance, making this the basis of their decisions whether or not to bother with them. Yet this so-called normal behaviour is a form of manipulation, possibly even of coercion. Women learn that they may be disregarded and overlooked unless they meet certain expectations.

While emotional blackmail is by no means confined to one sex, it is a form of behaviour which is frequently encountered in women because they often do not have a straightforward relation to their needs, desires and ambitions. In fact, such is the difficulty women have with these that many of us fail to recognize them and probably wouldn't act on them even if we could! Women perceive themselves to be less effective in the world, and more dependent on partners to provide emotional and financial security. They learn from an early age that they can make things happen by their behaviour and by responding to or creating an emotional environment, rather than by activity designed to change their situations.

Manipulative behaviour is often a response to feelings of social powerlessness. Historically, since men have controlled household finances and decisions, women have sometimes had to exert their influence in indirect ways. But manipulative behaviour is not only about the vicarious acquisition of status and security, it is also to do with manipulating other people – usually men – to take responsibilities for women's own feelings. As we have seen earlier, certain feelings like competition, ambition and hostility are often repressed, or more often denied, in little girls. Yet they still seek an outlet, and emotional manipulation is often the result.

In moments of honesty, many women will admit to having resorted to illness or some other form of 'weakness' to make certain gains in a situation. Most often women describe trying to provoke 'protective' behaviour, making a man feel guilty so that the woman can get what she wants or deflect a fight. One woman I know said, 'If my partner is horrid and unreasonable with me and I know I can't win an argument I go quiet and depressed. It's not exactly manipulation because I do feel depressed. But I know when I'm like that, he "comes round". He starts looking after me.'

These are fairly obvious forms of manipulation, but there are others about which women are often less ready to talk. Sexual manipulation is something which comes readily to some women and causes resentment among others – far more resentment than there is towards men for falling for it. Brenda Polan wrote in an article about 'women who don't like women' that the competition between women for male sexual approval is still as intense as it is between children for getting everything on offer. 'Today's sandpit is the workplace. The lollipops are promotion, pay, power and male approval – for men are still the bestowers of life's lollipops.' Sexual manipulation is discussed more directly in the following chapter; here the focus is on the less spectacular but more common forms of manipulative behaviour.

One striking fact that came out of these interviews is how much women still manipulate to get men to do things for them. Some women joke about trivial examples of this. Others are more self-critical, aware that they have made it clear that their happiness is dependent on the man's actions; despair and depression will be attendant on his failure to do what is required. One couple I know, now in their late 60s, seem to have spent their entire lives locked in strategies designed to get the other to do or feel something rather than own up what one really wants or needs. To many people the marriage may look ideal. They have recently celebrated their fortieth wedding anniversary and they spend a lot of time together, enjoying the same kinds of outings and entertainment. But in crucial ways their marriage isn't so much a triumph of loyal bonding as a monument to how effective a cement emotional blackmail and mutual guilt can be.

For the last twenty years, ever since their material circumstances began to improve, Mrs Williams has been trying to make her husband take an interest in DIY and home improvements. Mr Williams's lack of enthusiasm has grown in direct proportion to her complaints. Only when the complaints turn first to depression and then to illness does he finally stir himself into action. The jobs are done inadequately – not without a great deal of grumbling and depression on his part too – but they do get done, and the effort is not without compensations. His children and friends tend to take his side, as Mrs Williams is seen as nagging and often vicious, whereas he is seen as mild and gentle. But instead of being a source of satisfaction, the finished rooms seem to be a source of recrimination. Mr Williams feels a failure for not being the husband his wife wanted. She feels bad about the nagging and having been seen to nag by everyone around them.

The solution to this running conflict in their relationship provides a clue as to why it should happen in the first place. Mrs Williams could do the decorating herself, but the fact she doesn't tells us much about why the situation arose. Like many women, she tries to manœuvre a man into doing things she feels strongly about for her. But this desire to manipulate her husband doesn't just come from women having been given a less effective or practical training. In Mrs Williams's case, bringing up her four children and working as a school dinner lady has taught her to reckon with her own strengths and abilities.

What is really at issue here is Mrs Williams's desire for her husband to do something which is an expression of a *mutual* will to 'better themselves'. This is something which she, in fact, feels quite ambivalent about. Her background was poor and her father was an extremely fierce and moralistic socialist who saw material affluence as a sign of greed. She finds it difficult to say openly she wants these things, but she is enormously and often destructively envious when she sees other people's houses. She wants her husband to take responsibility for wanting these things, like a better house, something about which he actually isn't very concerned.

This marriage is an extreme version of what happens in many relationships where individuals fail to take responsibility for, or even to recognize, their own needs and desires. They do this either because they find their own feelings unacceptable or because pushing desires on to someone else and manipulating them into doing things solves certain mutual dilemmas and needs. In this case, both found a perverse satisfaction, since Mr Williams managed to elicit pity from his family and guilt from his wife. It's a mutual enmeshing of needs and dependencies in which men and women are engaged in the same game.

The complicity between these two people suggests that the term 'manipulative behaviour' might well be either an exaggeration or a misrepresentation. But the way Mrs Williams operates is typically 'feminine': she is trying to make men take responsibility for what the women themselves actually want. One of the classic ways in which this emerges is around women's view of their husband's or partner's career, something which I have already touched on. Nowadays, because women are expected *not* to invest their whole well-being and ambition in men, most would deny this. Nevertheless, I came across many women who were engaged in complicated manœuvring around the subject of their husbands' career.

Women often manipulate a situation so that their desires are quietly satisfied while appearing to come from outside, from another person. This can be, and often is, a recipe for disaster, as Carol would be the first to admit. Carol appears to be an extremely strong and forceful woman, but she is angry with herself for having tried to manipulate her husband, something she now realizes is responsible for the current crisis in their relationship. Carol and Ewan met about three years ago. At the time Ewan, who had emerged from a modest background in Wales, looked like a young man on the up. He had his own video distribution company and had made a lot of money. But he had expanded his business at just the wrong moment and the company ran into trouble.

Carol's response to Ewan's difficulties and depression was to give up her job as a PA. Instead, she helped him with trying to sort out his business. 'I spent a lot of time trying to make him "sell himself" more, something he doesn't like doing. I also nagged him about changing career and moving house. I told him what *he* really wanted was a new house and job and that he'd been dragging us down by being so cautious.' When the crunch came with his company and the receivers were called in she took to her bed with terrible headaches. 'At least things improved on the work front. He started making more of an effort because he felt so guilty about me.'

But if Ewan's work improved – he did get a new job – their relationship disintegrated. Carol has become increasingly depressed and has developed a weight problem. Ewan is so resentful he will hardly talk to her. Why, I wondered, had she given up her own job, just at the moment when they needed the stable income? 'I'm ashamed to admit I wanted Ewan to prove he could care for me. My family is really quite wealthy and snobbish. Ewan's isn't. When I met him he seemed just like all my friends' husbands. But once things started going wrong I looked round at my friends' grand houses and I felt terribly envious but guilty for thinking like that. I just wanted him to sort everything out for me.'

Carol has made herself financially dependent and ill in order to try to force Ewan to take care of her, and in the process to become a number of things he isn't. Because she felt ashamed of her envy, she has tried to make Ewan assume responsibility for her own desire for a certain lifestyle. She has been using his guilt about her health to try to force him to make changes she wants, rather than do it herself, a typical blackmailer's strategy.

Carol's story is not unique. Kate, a mother of two, told me her husband had just left her with the shocking revelation that he was having an affair with another woman. 'But the thing that really upset me and that I keep thinking about is not the other woman, but what he said about never being able to relax at home. I always thought I was protecting him – from the kids, from the mess – and letting him get on with his work all the time. Now I'm wondering if it wasn't me that wanted all that, not him. Maybe I was obsessed with him getting to the top and he just wanted to relax at home.' Left on her own with two children, Kate discovered this about her relationship the hard way, but her story is not untypical.

More men than one might imagine find their wives' expectations a pressure and feel they have been given little choice in terms of how they want to live. Sometimes they are even jealous about some of the options facing women. One childless career woman described to me her surprise when she and her partner discussed having children. 'I said to him that in some ways I'd really love to give up work for a bit, just get away from it. I find it so depressing. I think he was surprised at how strongly I felt about it, but he surprised me more. He said, "That's not fair. I'd like to just opt out of my career too. Don't you think I hate some of it? I think it's unfair that women can opt out like that. If I have to go on working, I don't see why you shouldn't. You earn more than me, everyone thinks you're successful, but you want me to keep you." His attitude was, we're in this boat together. It brought me up against the fact that in some way I'd like him to be better off so I could have more options. It would make my life easier if I could say, "He's more successful than me so it makes sense to give up my career."'

Manipulating others, rather than acknowledging or dealing directly with one's own needs and feelings, is not confined to the bedroom or the home. One of the reasons why women sometimes have a difficult time in professional settings is that it is often difficult for them to deal in a straightforward way with their own needs, boundaries and ambitions. Things may be changing now that women are more a part of the professional scenery. But it is certainly the case that in the past women felt powerless and excluded by some of the social pathologies which pass for male professional behaviour.

In my own case, in retrospect, I see that I sometimes used emotional manipulation rather than deal with the situation in hand. One example was when I was being exploited by a department head who was using me more than my contract with the university specified. Did I confront him head on? No. Instead I tried various strategies designed to turn other people against him. I sympathized with other people's grievances, and presented myself as a victim, someone likeable and exploited. I tried to recruit support and I tried to manipulate others to speak up on my behalf, by being clever and therefore desirable to the department, and by making them feel guilty about the privileges they had over me. This was not entirely successful and left me feeling resentful.

I'm being harsh on myself, but there is also truth in the way I'm describing my situation. And the reason for my behaviour was not simply that the department head was a difficult and threatening person. Like many women, playing the emotional field often came more easily to me than taking a more straightforward approach. I know that on occasion I have cried, made myself appealing or even desirable to try to manipulate men and other women into doing what I wanted. In my experience this is due to female conditioning: we fear rejection and displeasure if we directly assert either our rights or our needs. This is made more difficult if we don't even know what we are feeling, especially if it involves anger and envy.

This female conditioning is very hard to throw off, and often begins to change only when age and experience begin to break it down. As Ann Dickson, author of *A Woman in her own Right* (1986), remarks, this kind of emotional behaviour often can change only when you do assert yourself and discover that the world doesn't fall to pieces. Anna, a journalist, gave a very clear example of this. 'I always found it difficult to say no. I used to say this was because I needed the work, "beggars can't be choosers" and so on. But really I just found it difficult to say no. I used to make up excuses, like "My mother is ill" or "I'm ill." Or I'd say "Maybe" and then sometimes, I'm ashamed to say, I'd get someone to tell a lie for me. I went on a self-assertiveness course for women at a local college and – I know it sounds clichéd – it did transform my life. I just had to learn what I could and couldn't do and take the consequences if things didn't turn out as I hoped.'

Why is this inability to be straightforward about needs and feelings part of the emotional baggage of women? Girls learn that achieving things and doing things is in some way (often unclear to themselves) linked with emotional attributes. For girls there's often an implicit message that they can't achieve anything unless they are also nice and accommodating. They learn from a very early age that competitiveness, ambition and anger are very problematic coming from them, and these emotions find other ways of accommodating themselves. But it is also the case that for many women these feelings go underground altogether. Women end up not just feeling bad about them, but begin to consider them as intrinsically bad. This is especially acute for girls because of the potential identification between mother and daughter. If a mother can't accept her own feelings, she's not likely to be able to accept her daughter's. And if these feelings go underground, they then re-emerge in other relationships, with boyfriends, lovers, husbands and partners.

There are many who would and do ask, what's wrong with emotional manipulation? Dependency is part of the human condition, and these factors come into any exchange, even a professional one. What is more, as the drift of this chapter implies, men and women are equally complicit in emotional manœuvring. Emotional manipulation assumes interaction, so it cannot, by definition, be about inequality. After all, blackmail only works if the other partner is blackmailable, so it presupposes some meshing of interests.

Whether or not manipulation is reciprocal is irrelevant. The fact is that it leaves protagonists feeling bad. Women especially end up feeling very bad about 'playing the emotional field', not least because, contrary to popular belief, these strategies are rarely effective, and poor compensation for the real power which men have. These various emotional strategies which women adopt to avoid experiencing their own ambition, competitiveness or envy often misfire. Men walk out and children rebel. The short-term satisfaction of having won a game is no compensation for the possible devastation of losing the match.

10

Slim and Sexy: modern woman's Holy Grail

It is inevitable, when considering the subject of how and why women accept traditional sexual roles, that the subject of sexual behaviour itself should also come up. After all, this is the point where men and women come together and where the foundation for later sexual roles is laid. Traditionalists have it that underneath our complex social structure there is a simple natural instinct, saying we should look no further for an explanation as to why women collude with men in keeping to predictable male and female roles. It ought to be easy to challenge such simplistic biological explanations, but some aspects of recent sexual behaviour make this challenge harder. For in sexual behaviour there seems to be evidence of a backlash against attempts to transform sexual relations – a backlash greater than in any other aspect of male–female relations.

In this allegedly post-feminist era there has been little sign that women no longer care about male sexual approval and the forms of personal adornment that go with that. Instead, over the last ten years or so, women seem to have become more, rather than less, preoccupied with being seen as 'sexy'. The increase in the number of 'successful' women over the last ten years has not been accompanied by a rejection of female sexual wiles and devices, a straight swap of public prestige for sexual prestige. On the contrary, the ultimate accolade for a contemporary woman is that she is not only a successful career woman but sexy to boot.

Is this continuing female preoccupation with 'sexiness' confirmation of the belief that we are all still creatures of biology whose main task is to attract a mate and create a secure environment for our young? Or is it a sign that women are as much as ever tied to male approval, too scared to bring about a situation where our own needs and feelings as *people* come before our need for sexual approval? Of course, there are those who tell us that contemporary women *are* free of concern about male responses. They tell us that contemporary expressions of female sexuality, including sometimes the wearing of all the old trappings of female exploitation, have nothing to do with pleasing men and everything to do with sexual self-definition and self-gratification. In short, they would have us believe that the Utopia envisaged by feminism, where women define their own sexual needs and styles, has already arrived.

The question of women's sexual self-definition was central in the first onrush of the feminist movement. Then it was argued that women had no real sexual rights, let alone sexual freedom. Sexual choice was supposed to reflect women's economic and social dependency on men, a dependency that was played out in sexual and emotional ways. Not only did women want to attract men who could support them, but in order to do so they were prepared to mould themselves to men's desires. Women, it was said, acceded to the male definition of sexiness, and to the policing of their sexuality inside and outside the bedroom. Women displaying sexuality beyond the confines of a monogamous heterosexual unit risked exposure to men's hostility and contempt. Even in the 1960s, when feminism began to gain ground, women were vulnerable to a sexual double standard. They were still liable to be deemed 'slags', 'whores' and 'prostitutes' if they asserted their right to enjoy sex and acted in characteristically 'male' ways.

Feminism asserted that at the heart of all this was a hostility to women's sexual feelings. Men wanted to control or obliterate women's sexuality, or at the very least put it in the service of men. Feminism tapped into a torrent of resentment about this. Women revealed that they felt ignorant of their bodies' functions, controlled by men's interpretation of their sexual history, and belittled or demeaned by prevailing images of sexual desirability. Such discontent fuelled the women's movement, where the call for sexual self-definition was central and where men's control of sexual imagination and imagery was challenged.

For a while these challenges fitted under the broad heading of a

Slim and Sexy: modern woman's Holy Grail 149

call for 'sexual liberation' or, more specifically, women's liberation. But this soon came to be seen as problematic. Women's liberation was something which was all too easily accommodated by an increasingly 'permissive' society. Without a more fundamental challenge to women's economic dependency and prevailing sexual standards, increased sexual expression for women seemed doomed to make them even more vulnerable to men's sexual needs and double standards. Increasingly, women felt that 'liberation' was too limited. Discovering your own sexual needs would be only one part of a wider social and economic independence for women – the real source of security.

Nobody quite knew what a free, self-defined women's sexuality would be like, but many suggestions were made. Some envisaged a sort of unisexual, androgynous sexuality, some the nurturing, natural body of an earth mother. Others suggested that the only free expression of women's sexuality would be with other women. There were other, more nebulous ideas which tried to find ways of making women's preoccupation with sexual attraction less central; women were to concentrate more on their 'sisters', or were to give less time to make-up and trivia. But all these different emphases agreed on one thing: a 'true', free expression of female sexuality would be quite unlike anything that preceded it.

But as the term 'liberation' disappeared, to be replaced by a myriad of different (often competing) descriptions and prescriptions for the problem of sexual redefinition, so too did the groundswell of female opinion cease to call for changes on the sexual front. While many women identified with feminism's economic goals, they were anxious to distance themselves from a *sexual* antagonism to men and from a sexual revolution which they saw as undermining their 'femininity'. The feminist vision of a new sexuality came to be seen as the fevered imaginings of man-haters.

Through the 1980s we heard men and women telling us how it was quite natural for women to enjoy being sexy, quite natural to want to be sexy for men. Only 'uptight lesbian feminists' had a problem with that. As one woman said to me, 'Of course I want men to find me attractive. We all do, don't we? I try to make the best of my appearance and I like it when men respond.' Now, although there may be a much greater variety of female styles, the concern with desirability to men is still uppermost in women's self-presentation. Women backed off from what they saw as a sexual confrontation with men.

In fact, the vision of an egalitarian society, where women would no longer have to use sex to gain power, couldn't be further from what happened in the 1980s. Far from sexuality becoming less central, it seems to have become more so. Far from using the greater equality between the sexes to determine their own sexual image, we have seen women reaffirming the notion that what is most important to a woman is her sexual allure. Madonna is often held up as the young woman's icon of self-defined female sexuality, but she has done nothing to challenge this traditional notion that being sexually desirable is the *ultimate* source of power for women.

So what is the truth behind the contemporary expression of women's sexuality? Is this desire to be desired the fundamental truth of female sexuality or further evidence of a deep collusion, by which women are failing to challenge the traditional exchanges between men and women? The only way these questions can be answered is by a careful consideration of how much has really changed, and how much has been gained, by woman in their sexual self-presentation and their sexual experiences. We can answer this question only by finding out whether women consider themselves happy and free in the expression of a sexuality which still focuses on male approval.

Many important changes have occurred in women's expression of their sexuality. 'Sexual freedom', for all its problems, did make it possible for women to acknowledge their sexual feelings and needs without being instantly categorized as disreputable. Feminism challenged some of the ways in which women were controlled, disregarded and exploited when they showed their sexual needs, one of the most obvious ways being the contempt and disgust to which terms like 'slag', 'cow', 'bitch' and 'cunt' bore witness. Disgust was expressed towards the sexually active woman, as if she was dirty. Women also insisted that their physiological functions were not disgusting and dirty, and insisted on a more open attitude to women's bodies.

Women also gained more practical control over their sexuality. Improvements in contraception meant that, for the first time in history, women could be certain that sex would not end in pregnancy. Abortion on demand was one of the early rallying cries of feminism, and if that battle has not exactly been won, at least most women no longer have to bear unwanted children. Perhaps even more important was the challenge to dismissive attitudes towards women and their sexual and reproductive functions in the health establishment. Women have steadily gained more control over childbirth and now demand the right to information about their bodies. These changes, which younger women can now take for granted, were not easily won.

Even at the level of information about and attitudes towards women's physiological functions, there is still a long way to go, since sexist insults have never completely disappeared and young girls are still anxious about their sexual reputations. There is also evidence that girls are still lacking in basic information about their own bodies and sexual responses. For instance, *She* magazine recently reported that many women still don't give their daughters names for their genitals, preferring to talk about bottom or 'front bottom'. One teacher described to me a class she taught in Birmingham where only two of the children knew what a clitoris was – and they were both boys! She went on to add, 'Some people still complain that children have too much sexual information. I still feel the reverse. Girls are still lacking in knowledge about themselves and their responses. I feel very strongly that we should be educating girls about sexuality and sexual response.'

But in any event, the challenge to sexual coercion was never simply at the level of information and terminology. It was also concerned with sexual self-presentation and sexual image. Women had, in the early stages of feminism, asserted that trying to conform to prevailing stereotypes of sexuality was to conform to male desires or fantasies; it was setting yourself in competition with other women and was also trivializing and degrading. Susan Brownmiller, in her book *Femininity* (1984), gave a clear example of this attitude:

Why do I persist in not wearing skirts? Because I don't like this artificial gender distinction. Because I don't wish to start shaving my legs again ... Because I will not reacquaint myself with the discomfort of feminine shoes. Because the nature of feminine dressing is superficial in essence.

Instead of using sexuality to attract men and gain vicarious power, feminists asserted that women should seek power through personal achievement. The only point of reference in finding their own style should be themselves. This philosophy was at the crux of reactions against feminism, acting as a focus for the hostility that was directed against the movement as a whole. Feminist women were labelled as either 'unsexy' or as 'anti-men' – why else would women reject the usual sexual codes? The tabloids deduced that any woman not concerned with attracting men was a lesbian or a man-hater. Although this was a *reductio ad absurdum* of what feminists believed, the image stuck, and today many young women are still anxious to detach themselves from this caricature.

Many women, even those involved in feminist activities, found the challenge to traditional 'feminine' self-presentation just too uncomfortable. Val is now in her early 40s. She has teenage children and runs her own business – a marketing consultancy. Her style of dress is glamorous and feminine. Fifteen years ago, though, she dabbled in feminist politics and helped produce a small campaign sheet. 'I was never very active because I don't think I'm naturally a very political person. But at the time I was working as a council economist and what was being said by feminists seemed to make a lot of sense in terms of the prejudices I was meeting at work. The women's movement gave me things which I really value, especially confidence at work, and a way of understanding working relationships with men. I consider myself to have been lucky to have had those insights and experience.'

Yet Val claims she always felt at odds with aspects of feminism on a more personal level. 'I had two young children and I'd just broken up with my husband. I was having a few relationships with different men and a lot of men found me attractive, something which I have always enjoyed. I always felt awkward on that front, going to feminist meetings. I don't know if women were really critical of me but I always felt I had to justify myself all the time, as a sexual woman who liked men and who liked dressing up to show it.'

This fear of being seen as anti-men or unfeminine – even among women sympathetic to feminism's general aims – attests to the deep sense of self that attaches to the construction of the feminine sexual being as one who is desirable to men. Rejecting this proved

Slim and Sexy: modern woman's Holy Grail

too uncomfortable for many, and there has since been a retreat, away from confrontational sexual politics and towards a more accepted notion of the feminine. Even among the most ardent of feminists, there has been a resurgence of personal adornment, but always justified as 'doing it for myself, not men'. One woman wrote to *Spare Rib*:

> Recently I have been the target of a lot of criticism from women ... because they do not like the way that I dress and wear my hair (i.e. Mohican, Bondage etc.). They tell me I am ignoring its racist and sexist overtones, that it is not 'feminist' and that I am allowing myself to be exploited by the fashion market ... Is a woman any less emancipated because she chooses to wear make-up and stilettos? Is not the whole point of feminism to help a woman to realize her right to control her own life and make decisions for herself?

Reactions such as these are typical. On the subject of fashion and image, as feminism disappeared as a political force, feminists, like other women, became eclectic. Outside feminist circles there was widespread agreement that feminists had 'got it wrong' about men, and that there was no harm in women's cultivation of their sexual appeal. Accompanying the backlash against feminist puritanism was a belief that fashion and sexual imagery could be seen as a form of play and pastiche. If women adopted particular images, this was no problem, because they could easily be discarded. No woman had to feel trapped and coerced by one prevailing image.

It is a widely held belief that Madonna in many ways expresses this fundamental truth about contemporary womanhood: we are no longer victims. Contemporary women, we are told, are no longer trapped by image and stereotype. And Madonna, embodying this, is in constant metamorphosis, usually one step ahead of a fashion change. She can adopt any image of womanhood – a whore, a porn model, a nun, Marilyn Monroe – but these images never constrict her. They are merely costumes plucked off the rail, open for play and parody, which supposedly makes her the ultimate post-modern woman. When Madonna adopts the attire of bondage and masturbates on stage, it is the audience who is manipulated, not the powerful, wealthy woman on the stage.

Commentators assure us, for example, that Madonna represents a vision of female sexuality that cares little for male sexual approval but is interested in *female* gratification and *female* pleasure. Nancy Friday, documenting what she sees as the profound changes in the sexual fantasies of young women, writes about Madonna:

She stands, hand on her crotch, preaching to her sisters: masturbate. Madonna is no male masturbatory fantasy ... but rather she embodies sexual woman/working woman and yes, I think you can put mother in there too. I can see Madonna with a baby in her arms and the hand still on her crotch. (*Guardian*, September 1991)

Such approval of female pastiche, including sado-masochistic pastiche, extends beyond Madonna herself. Fashion designers have similarly defended their use of the props of sado-masochistic sex as parody and play. These, we are told, no longer represent bondage and humiliation. Instead they represent power, because women are truly free if they can play with slavery without it enslaving their souls.

Drawing on the belief in a new era of post-feminist equality, these ideas seem attractive, but they disguise the reality of women's relationship to their image. Play and parody may have entered the fashion arena, but they have failed to dislodge a fundamental unevenness between men's and women's relationship to sexual display and adornment. Women are still unshakeably concerned with rendering themselves sexually desirable and conforming to prevailing ideals, even if on first glimpse these ideals are many and various. It is still women, not men, who are the aesthetic sex, using their bodies to express prevailing sexual ideals. And overwhelmingly it is women, not men, who try to 'improve' their bodies to make them correspond to prevailing ideals, especially of desirability.

If anything, the concern with appearance, body shape and desirability seems to have grown. Young women flocked to buy Naomi Wolf's *The Beauty Myth* as if hearing for the first time the feminist message that women are coerced by the tyranny of slenderness. It is as if *Fat is a Feminist Issue* had not been written, as if there had been no real systematic challenge to ideals of body shape and the repetitive ideal of the slender, glamorous, sexy woman.

Instead, because women are supposed to be free in their choices, such images can be said to be coming from women themselves. So powerful has this image of thin, glamorous women remained that even magazines which capitalized on it stood back and began to consider its restrictions. In 1988, *Elle* magazine pondered whether or not this image represented a kind of body fascism, by implying that only a certain shape and look could be affirmed and find power in this society.

The female obsession with rendering oneself the aesthetic sex, with making oneself sexually attractive, remains as strong as ever. As Robin Lakoff and Rachel Scherr remark in their book *Face Value, the Politics of Beauty* (1984), concern with beauty obsessed them as adolescents. It was 'what nagged at you privately and as you turned the pages of a glossy magazine, or nudged you in the ribs as you watched the diet drink commercial on TV'. Even younger women remain as much preoccupied with their appearance as did women of the 1950s. A recent Virago book, *How Do I Look?* (ed. Jill Dawson, 1990), is a collection of essays by young women about their body image. The essays certainly demonstrate that for young women growing up in the 1990s these pressures are as tangible and as pressing as they ever were twenty years ago.

The essays of these young women are a useful reminder that current female concerns with body image are a long way away from offering self-satisfaction and personal pleasure. As always, measuring yourself up to a prevailing ideal and finding yourself lacking is a source of discontent and unhappiness, especially as lying behind any contemporary concern with female image and fashion is the obsession with losing weight. Beneath most fashion changes is still the slender female body, exerting a tyranny which has, if anything, become worse. One woman I interviewed gave a shocking account of how much her personal happiness was affected by her preoccupation with her weight and looks. Lucy is, by any standards, an attractive woman. She is in her late 20s, tall and elegant, with thick dark hair and a kind, attractive face. She has done well in a career as an office manager. Again, on the surface, she is a classic contemporary 'have-it-all' woman.

However, it was not long before our conversation turned towards Lucy's anxiety about her appearance. 'I'm really overweight. I've got to do something about it. I'm afraid John [whom she married two years ago] won't want me like this.' After I have dismissed this anxiety once or twice I begin to have a sense that this is really upsetting her. 'Are you really worried about this?' I ask. 'Yes. My day is dominated by thinking about my weight. I don't eat breakfast, and then spend the morning worrying about whether or not I'll give way to temptation when someone in the office goes for a cake at coffee-time. Sometimes I resist, then I get through the day without eating anything, but by five o'clock I'm frantic so I buy chocolate on the way home. I feel desperate after I've eaten it. I hate myself and I often refuse to eat supper. John likes to cook, but recently I've told him he mustn't because I can't bear to have someone else controlling my food like that.'

I found it almost unbelievable that someone like Lucy could dislike her body so intensely. 'Surely you can see that you are very attractive?' I asked. 'I don't think I am. I really hate my body. My bottom is too large. I try and make John stand behind me sometimes because I can't bear anyone seeing my backside. I'm convinced that one day he'll go off with one of these thin women.' Having or not having a career seems completely irrelevant to this issue of self-criticism and anxiety. Most career women I interviewed were convinced that their appearance mattered and that they would not get on so well if they neglected their looks and 'allowed' themselves to get fat. All doors are open to women unless you have to turn sideways to get through them!

Statistics on dieting give a clear indication that as regards positive self-image nothing has changed for women. Two surveys of young girls in the 1980s revealed first that many 10-year-olds, and then that many 8-year-olds were already following some kind of diet. One woman I spoke to described a family argument about her 3-year-old's weight. Her mother and sister had taken it upon themselves to tell her that they were worried that her little girl was too greedy and that she would have weight problems later in life unless her appetite was controlled now. The women pointed out that her daughter was large, like everyone else in the family, and that they had never made similar comments about her boy. She knew she was right to resist their pressure, but she still felt anxious about it.

Recently, American research has indicated that the majority of American women are on continuous diets. Indeed, American doctors have begun to recognize a dieting-related syndrome which they claim affects 80 per cent of all women. They are calling these 'sub-clinical eating disorders', which are eating patterns not extreme enough to fit the clinical definitions of anorexia and bulimia but which nevertheless entail a disordered relationship with eating and a distorted relationship to food. Although it is tempting to dismiss this as just another American syndrome, there can be little doubt that some of the symptoms which they describe are extremely familiar and indeed would fit Lucy's habits. Sub-clinical eating disorders involve becoming obsessed with food, constantly preoccupied with calories and fat grams, always worrying about how much you have eaten the day before and how much you can avoid eating today. Typically women embark on rigid diets, virtually starving themselves for a few days and then giving into cravings, bingeing on 'unhealthy' foods like chocolate or pizzas.

Giving way to these cravings is often followed by extreme guilt, which in turn brings on bouts of masochistic exercising. Sometimes women even make themselves vomit or use laxatives, even though they are not technically bulimics (who have a minimum average of two binge–purge episodes a week). But this pattern of regular undereating and occasional bingeing also has real physical effects, such as irregular or non-existent periods, and a number of symptoms related to a falling metabolic rate – fatigue, cold intolerance, depression, dizziness and constipation.

Almost all the writing on dieting, which seems endless, insists that dieting is healthy. Yet the way this link has passed into popular consciousness is not based on any hard and fast medical facts. There may be a link between *obesity* and premature death, but what is absolutely unproven is a link between women's perception of their ideal weight and good health. The ideals which motivate women to diet are aesthetic, not health-related, and most of the women who diet are by no stretch of the imagination obese or even very much overweight.

I was amazed, in the course of interviewing for this book, by the number of women who said they believed losing five pounds or half a stone would make an enormous difference to the quality of their lives. Women seem to see dieting as a Holy Grail, an endless and painful journey to that magic solution of shedding extra pounds. Most women seem to believe that seven pounds of flesh is all that stands between misery and happiness. Pam, with whom I talked in depth about the problems of looking after two children, doing all the housework and having a job three days a week, commented typically. 'The one thing that would really make me feel better is getting thinner!' She was ostensibly joking, but I had the distinct impression that she really believed it.

Why should it be that women who have had a chance to think about the disadvantages of staking so much on personal appearance should still accede to these ideals? Why is that, when women have so many opportunities to do things for themselves, they remain convinced that if they could lose weight many of their discontents would disappear? The answer lies in a war women still wage with their bodies. Fat is still an insult in our culture, and fat, even plump, people often feel they are seen as weak and inadequate. Such is the horror of flab and fat that women are constantly at battle with their maturing bodies. And even the most successful women seem preoccupied with staying within the prevailing slender ideals.

Rather than rejecting these messages, women have allowed them to influence other areas of their lives. At least in pre-war days, to a large extent, motherhood allowed a woman to drop out of the sexual competition. She could tie an apron around her spreading girth and have a matronly figure without fearing that she would be condemned for having let herself go. But now, thanks to the activities of the likes of Jane Fonda and Paula Yates, mothers are expected to fight against the normal maturation of their bodies. Paula Yates, for instance, asserted in an interview in *Woman* magazine that she was so thin that she had to put on weight before she could become pregnant because the doctors considered it unhealthy. Once she'd had the baby, she immediately set about getting thin again – achieving a weight so low that her body could not function normally. More recently, her views on the 'selfishness' of working mothers have been widely publicized. Her own devotion to her body, which includes hiring a full-time trainer to help her lose weight, somehow does not strike her as selfish, whereas a woman's need to work does. Paula Yates's moral values are clearly muddled, but no one stops to question her because a woman's narcissistic obsessions are taken for granted, whereas a woman's need to work is not.

The comments which women have made to me about dieting suggest that getting thin is as much to do with proof of will-power as it is to do with pursuing a definite notion of personal attractiveness. Women talk about wanting to 'show they can do it' – demonstrating their ability to control their appetite and restrict themselves is very important. Losing weight and staying thin is about demonstrating women's ability to become 'attractive' should they so wish it. This readiness to accept the terms of the sexual game is seen as a statement of sexuality itself, even though the idea doesn't necessarily correspond with what men want when they get into bed. It is not surprising, then, if slimming is about demonstrating personal control, that it can easily become part of more serious emotional illnesses like anorexia and bulimia.

The continuing obsession with dieting is evidence of how important it still is for women to be seen to accede to prevailing aesthetic definitions. In other words, women continue to need to be seen, and wanted, as sexy. And most younger women still feel that their moments of greatest power have been when they feel sexually powerful. Being sexually desired (and acknowledged as such by other women) is more about pure power than about trapping a 'good man'. But many of the old fantasies and dreams of being overwhelmingly desirable still exist. These feed sexual excitement and give the strongest feelings of power, even for women who have been successful in their own right.

Perhaps women's successes in the workplace have made them ever more anxious to please men, for it is certainly the case that being sexually attractive now seems to be *de rigueur* for a successful woman. Expectations have moved very quickly from career women being 'blue-stockings' and therefore unsexy, through the acceptance of women being clever *and* attractive, to the point now where some men seem to think women are not clever *unless* they are attractive. Equally startling is the way in which this desire to attract men, amounting sometimes almost to masochism, has remained central even for successful women wishing to depart from the status quo. Madonna's sado-masochistic displays include both bondage and whips, and a curious identification with the ultimate victim Marilyn Monroe, who was also seen as the ultimately desirable woman.

In Julie Burchill's *Ambition* (1991), the career woman's bonkbuster, the narrative impetus comes not so much from the heroine's quest for career advancement as from the humiliation planned for her by the newspaper magnate who desires her. He says, 'I'm sick of breaking bimbos – it's no fun, no challenge. Strong, hard, career girls – they're the new *filet mignon* of females. They're the new frontier. Girls like you. On, I'm going to have fun breaking you, Susan.' This is a new version of the Mills and Boon romance, where the powerful man sets about subduing the girl. Still the greatest power for women is sexual power, being desired. What is different is the belief that somehow being a successful career woman, being rich and powerful in your own right, means that you can wear the sexual mantle of a masochist without being oppressed by it.

Jessica Benjamin, an American psychoanalyst, shows how much these new images are still an expression of a deep passivity, however actively they are pursued:

> Once sexuality is cut loose from reproduction, a goal the era of sexual liberation has urged upon our imagination, womanhood can no longer be equated with motherhood. But the alternative images of the *femme fatale* does not signify an active subjectivity either; the sexy woman – an image that intimidates women whether or not they strive to conform to it – is sexy, but as object, not as subject. She expresses not so much *her* desire as her pleasure in being desired; what she enjoys is her capacity to evoke desire in the other, to attract. Her power does not reside in her own passion, but in her acute desirability. Neither the power of the mother nor that of the sexy woman can, as in the case of the father, be described as the power of the sexual subject. (*The Bonds of Love*, 1990)

Benjamin believes this to be a fundamental truth that still underlies what she calls women's desire. Not only is women's greatest power still seen as sex, but that sexual power is still essentially passive, courting the approval and response of men. And with the increasing sexualization of culture, a woman is under contradictory pressures: she is still essentially a passive subject, yet she is expected more and more to be defined by her ability to provoke and satisfy a sexual response in men.

This deep feminine identification is a highly precarious route to satisfaction for a woman. In a culture where female sexiness is tied up with a certain responsiveness to men's needs (of which the ability to lose weight is a sign), there is little valuing of older women and the maturing body. Several women I talked to described their acute difficulty in coming to terms with ageing. This wasn't just concerned with the difficulty of getting old, because that brought certain satisfactions. There was a constant fear of no longer being valuable, a fear of male contempt, and a self-disgust that their own bodies were undesirable.

Diana is a television researcher for the BBC. She is in her late 30s and she described to me how the whole ethos of her institution is hostile to the ageing woman. 'I've noticed how women producers and researchers mysteriously disappear in their 40s. That's partly to do with the fact that many drop out to have children and then fall behind in their careers. But it's also to do with the fact that the BBC – I suppose like many establishment institutions – tends to be very prejudiced against older women. Just look at what happens on the screens. Very few older women are kept on as presenters – there are hardly ever older women on chat shows and intellectual discussions. The shows are forever changing last year's model for this year's. Well, it's the same behind the scenes. It makes me feel very insecure. I never thought I'd be someone affected by growing older because I'm a strong person and I value myself. But in the last couple of years I've been assailed by doubts. I think these up-and-coming young men are going to want to surround themselves with attractive young women. I'm horrified to hear myself say that. I didn't think my confidence at work depended on my being young and attractive, but I can see it does.'

No one understands better those fears and anxieties, and how to capitalize on them, than the extreme conservative. Conservative views of a woman's traditional role feed off women's fears and their anxieties about sexual desirability as the basis of self-definition. Older women I talked to were all of one mind about the precarious exchange that had taken place around women and sexuality. One older woman said to me, 'I feel sorry for you lot. You'll never keep your men if you don't marry them or if the men don't believe in the old morality. Why should they stay when you are getting older and there are all these young girls around?'

Victoria Gillick sums up this approach. She insists that women have been fools to trade in a moral and religious basis to marriage for a sexual one. In an article on the subject of marriage she describes how a male journalist came to visit her and her husband Gordon to talk about their views on marriage:

We asked him why he was interested in the subject, was he married himself perhaps? No, he was cohabiting, he said rather sheepishly ... Was his girlfriend at work? Yes. What kind of place did they live in? They had two homes – one in London and a country cottage. Joint mortgage? Naturally. Separate bank accounts? Of course. Any kids? No, they didn't want any ... Who did the housework? She did. Did he intend to stay with her for the next thirty years? He couldn't answer that one. 'Well', said Gordon. 'You're on to a winner, aren't you? You've got two homes, two incomes, the minimum of responsibilities, an open-ended sexual relationship and a free cook and housekeeper – what more could a man want?'

Like many extreme conservatives, Gillick believes that the shift from a moral to a sexual marriage is following men's desires, not women's. If women go along with it, it is only because they have no alternative. 'If the men in their lives had been adamant that their love was so passionate, so total and so unconditional that they were prepared to pledge themselves publicly to cherish the woman and any children they might be blessed with, for the rest of their lives, then precious few women in love would turn down such a time-honoured proposal.' The hostility which many conservative women feel towards the sexual revolution is based on a fear that the traditional 'deal' between men and women has been eroded. Men, no longer held by traditional morality and Christian duty, will have no reason to stay with women. Sex will become uppermost, men will shirk their responsibilities, and women will be left alone. This vision is only marginally less alarming to them than the possibility that women actually want to survive alone!

Ironically, these traditional notions of male sexuality are much closer to contemporary views than traditionalists such as Gillick might assume. There may be some who think that men can change and will respond to their wives as equals because they understand the changes that surround having a family and growing older. This type of man will have the same commitment to the family unit as the woman herself. But for all those women, I could easily find ten others scurrying around fighting their wrinkles, having face-lifts and torturing themselves in aerobics classes with the nagging fear that, without sexual allure, men just will not stick around.

What is startling is how little headway women have made on the sexual front. Not only have they accepted the increasing sexualization of their world – of motherhood, of working life, of old age – but they appear to have accepted it as an inevitable part of female desire. Women have only themselves to blame if they continue to accept willingly that sexual value is women's greatest value. It is true that women are in a situation where the goal posts are constantly being moved – first we have to be sexually free, then sexual *and* careerist, then sexual *and* careerist *and* a mother – but few women are challenging this. Naomi Wolf's *The Beauty Myth* is the only real sign that there is any resistance to the coercive belief that sexual desirability is overwhelmingly important. Yet she recycles the old feminist analysis that women are the dupes of men's needs. The real problem lies in women's readiness to buy into the myths of sexual desirability as the ultimate source of female potency, as if for women the only power they can wield is sexual power.

11

Women as Victims

In the previous chapter it became clear that women's sexual power is still focused on a contemporary version of female passivity, which manifests itself in the continuing anxiety to please and attract men. This passivity is rarely admitted, let alone analysed. Instead, there is a myth – disputed in the previous chapter – that contemporary female sexuality is powerful and free. But in contemporary discussions of sexuality, there is one note that is particularly troubling. Alongside all the celebration of sexual power and the insistence that men and women are sexual equals playing a sexual game, there is another message coming through loud and clear: women still perceive themselves as sexual victims. Even in this period, when everyone appears to accept that sexual discrimination is a thing of the past, women do not *feel* free; they fear sexual crimes and believe these are on the increase. Even for those most wedded to the myth of post-feminist equality, these are troubling reminders that all is not entirely well in male–female relationships.

Several incidents forcefully brought home to the confident womanhood of the 1980s the message that perhaps, after all, contemporary women did not have quite all the freedom and power they imagined. One was the attack on a young woman in daylight in Central Park, New York. She was a successful career woman, going about her normal daily routine, which included jogging in the park. She was attacked by a group of young boys (most no older than 13), gang-raped and very nearly killed. Few people could wholly comfort themselves with an explanation for this attack based on the disintegration of New York. Above all, it was a reminder that even the most powerful contemporary women could easily become sexual victims. In England, the disappearance of Suzy Lamplugh – abducted in the course of her work as an estate agent – conveyed the same message.

These attacks were many women's fears writ large. Post-feminism might be the name of the game in the world of work, but few women were deluded into believing that they were no longer potential victims of sexual harassment, violence and rape. In the 1980s while interest in those areas designated 'women's issues' declined, anxiety about sexual crime did the opposite – it shifted and grew. Rape continued to hit the headlines in the form of concern about campus rape or well-publicized cases of particular rapists. Sexual harassment continued to simmer beneath the surface, finally erupting in the very public case of Judge Clarence Thomas in the USA. A number of serial murderers were at large, and the ghoulish interest which film-makers took in these fed a persistent anxiety among women that they were in real danger. Admittedly, none of these issues was at the basis of sustained political campaigning as they had been in the days of active feminism, but they nevertheless niggled away, occasionally erupting as anxiety and outrage.

However, rape, sexual murder and harassment were not the only issues around which women's concern about victimization by men continued to be heard. By the end of the 1980s the sexual abuse of children had become a major social issue. The social work budgets of most local councils were ploughed into providing resources to detect and prosecute those involved, and to counsel both victims and perpetrators. The public discourse surrounding this area tended to represent the issue as one of 'parental' abuse of children; nevertheless, within it there lurked an unspoken fear of men, and an unspoken anxiety about how far men were to be trusted as sexual beings. Several 'babysitting circles' acted upon this underlying assumption by no longer accepting fathers as babysitters. If the fathers were unknown to the children, they were automatically considered untrustworthy and, by implication, potential abusers.

This was a clear indication that at the centre of many of the sex-abuse scandals was an anxiety about men's sexuality and men's untrustworthiness in relation to the powerless. Even in England's most notorious case, in Cleveland, such anxiety never became explicit. But several articles appeared providing a context for the widespread abuse which had allegedly taken place. Many mentioned high male unemployment and the increased time men were spending in the home. In America the anxiety about men was more at the forefront. The most notorious case, and the first involving 'satanic abuse', was directed against the McMartin Day Nursery, in particular against a male nursery worker who was alleged to have dug tunnels under the nursery where he proceeded ritually to abuse those in his care.

Leaving aside the question of whether or not these incidents actually happened, public concern about them indicated two things. First, that women continued to be anxious about male sexuality; but second, that many would rather not admit it, feeling happier to describe the situation as 'parental abuse' or abuse by 'satanists'.

In the newspapers, the reported statistics appear to show that rape has been on the increase throughout the 1980s, and was not attributable just to an increase in the number of women reporting attacks. In addition, there was a growing sense that social changes had made women more rather than less vulnerable. These changes, leading to declining public transport services and greater social isolation in neighbourhoods, affect the 'quality of life'. Far from feminism having ushered in a new era of male decency, women continue to feel restricted – even victimized – by aspects of male sexual behaviour. But most rejected feminism as an explanatory model and most refused to think about the problem explicitly in terms of a problem of *male* sexuality.

We have only to look at the experiences of many young girls to find that they too feel extremely vulnerable to unwanted sexual attention, and that this often has an undermining effect on their social behaviour. One woman with a 6-year-old daughter described what happened after her daughter's photo appeared in a local newspaper, regrettably captioned with her name. 'For several weeks, a man kept ringing up and asking for my daughter by her name. The other children always fetched her. Then, when she was on the phone, he'd start making obscene suggestions. He'd traced us by our unusual surname.' As unwanted attentions to young girls go, this one is pretty mild. But many women I know have had to fend off early, and unwelcome, sexual attention. One young woman I spoke to felt her current sexual timidity could be traced back to a horrific experience at 14 when she and her friend agreed to meet up with a couple of young men who took them back to their flat, forced them to drink alcohol and then molested them.

Teachers I have spoken to confirm the impression that unwelcome sexual attention is common for young girls. One London teacher, who has now left her job and is a full-time mother, said that on average about seven out of ten girls she taught had been 'frightened and upset' by sexual incidents. 'I was glad to give up my job when it came to it because I was spending so much of my time counselling the girls about difficult sexual experiences. And I just wasn't qualified to handle some of the problems that came my way.'

Carrie Herbert, who has written a book about the sexual harassment of schoolgirls called *Talking of Silence* (1991), feels it is a hard task trying to get anyone to take this routine imposition on young girls seriously. 'Most people still insist that what happens between boys and young girls is just horse-play or "normal" adolescent behaviour.' Herbert argues that this myth of 'normal' behaviour stops the girls from realizing what is happening to them. It also sometimes stops them from reporting incidents. 'If everyone agrees that pushing girls around, looking up their skirts, taking a quick grope and talking in innuendos is just boys being boys, then no one will take a stand. That means even schools aren't safe and girls are not being protected from routine but systematic harassment.'

Herbert asserts that sexual harassment is a serious educational problem:

If girls are frightened and ashamed, they can't learn properly. If they have to be continuously on their guard about what they say or do, or how they dress, they can't concentrate properly. I tell head teachers to look at what happens to girls after 12 or 13. They lose confidence, they don't use the playground or the extracurricular activities like the boys, they leave earlier. Any business would be very worried if that happened to half its workers.

It is a well-documented fact that many girls lose confidence around the time of puberty. When I interviewed two groups of 10-year-olds in South London primary schools I was struck by their enthusiasm and idealism. Most, even those from poor and troubled homes, had great ambitions for themselves and great drive, which I recorded in a newspaper article. But I was reminded by letters in response to this article that girls often change dramatically between the ages of 10 and the onset of puberty, when they become more conscious of, and more awkward about, the sexual agenda between boys and girls.

It has to be said that even these 10-year-old girls, who at one level showed such ambition and enthusiasm, also already felt weighed down by some of the sexual attentions paid to them by boys. Almost all described their exasperation at being followed in the street and having sexual comments passed about them 'all the time'. Several had disturbing accounts of sexual attacks. One girl had been attacked in a lift and had then been blamed by her family for leading the boys on. Rhea and Charlotte, both from West Indian families, talked about how 'the boys put us down all the time' and 'don't respect us'. They described the girls as 'having to put up with a lot' from the boys. Emma, whose parents are divorced and who is being brought up by her father, claimed that girls had to make themselves stronger so they could stand up to the continuous harassment from boys. 'We have to be stronger,' she said, 'because we have to cope with the boys being so disgusting.'

Lavinia, a 10-year-old from a mixed-race family and already verging on puberty, summed up some of the problems awaiting the pubescent girl. She felt resentful at constantly being reminded of her sex, since her real passion was for horses and riding. She wanted to be a jump-jockey and spent all her spare time at a local riding stables. 'It's embarrassing being a girl. Boys are just too fast. When we walk down the street we get whistles and everything. I really don't like all that.' Yet the picture involves more than the simple imposition of an excessive male sexuality on innocent and passive girls. Most of the young girls I have spoken to are, as I said earlier, extremely concerned about their appearance and seem to fear more than anything the possibility that they might be called ugly or be seen to be out of line in the way they look. Several of the young girls I interviewed said that the thing they would most like to change about themselves was their appearance. This included Emma, an extraordinarily pretty girl who said she 'liked everything about being a girl, except that she wished she was a bit prettier'. Several of the girls were already quite preoccupied by their appearance and many wanted a future career based on the cult of female beautification, such as hairdressing or fashion design.

Understanding all this is a delicate and difficult task. There is an old school of feminism which interprets both the harassment itself and the girls' internalizing of prevailing sexual values as a form of social control of women's sexuality. Girls and women have to 'buy' into the sexual terms of boys and men for fear of harassment and even violence. If they follow their own course of development and their own interests they run the risk of shaming and coercion. This school of thought also tends to interpret increased concern about the victimization of women as a sign that the situation is getting worse, because men feel more threatened by women's independence and therefore have stepped up their use of violence as a form of social control. However, this kind of understanding is as limited as the opposite approach, which believes that boys will be boys and that a form of harassment is part of 'natural' sexual behaviour. Again, what it fails to address is the much deeper agenda by which both feminine identity and typically 'female' responses to emergent sexuality are being shaped.

While almost all teachers who have dealt with young girls recognize the problem, many are hesitant to use the term 'sexual harassment'. Pat, who is head of an all-girls' comprehensive school, explained her dislike of the term. First, she feels it detracts from the broader issue of sexism, which affects girls at all levels, such as in expectations about appropriate female behaviour, in how they are taught as well as in the specifically sexual form of unwanted attention. But she also dislikes the term because she feels sexual harassment defines the problem in terms of an excess of male sexuality which has to be controlled, rather than looking at the ways in which boys and girls interact. 'There is a lot of "silliness" around sex but this relates to too little information for both sexes. Of course the boys can be thorough nuisances, but that only becomes a problem in the context of an overall sexism where girls are unassertive and don't feel in control of their sexual responses.'

Pat's comments about the ways in which female passivity and lack of control feed into the problem of unwelcome sexual attention returns us to the central concern of this book. Her remarks remind us that at the heart of the two recent manifestations of female sexuality – as powerful siren, and as victim of unwanted male attention – are the same problems: female passivity, female sexuality as a lure, and the lack of a sense of a woman being a *subject*. From the girls' point of view, there is a confusion between 'ordinary' experimentation and unwelcome sexual attention. Adolescent girls are rarely encouraged to assume responsibility for their sexual feelings, so that even pleasurable experiences can seem as if they are imposed from 'outside'. And boys are still conditioned to take the initiative in sex. Hence the situation where girls can feel guilty about genuinely unwanted attentions and boys feel aggrieved about misleading signals.

My contention is that there remains a terrible muddle around passivity. Although girls are sometimes now encouraged to recognize their sexual feelings, they still do not learn to take responsibility for them – at least not until they are much older, with much painful experience behind them. Sexual initiative and sexual responsibility (other than the possibility of saying and meaning no) are still largely the prerogative of boys. This situation creates a very thin line between normal sexual experimentation or development, and harassment or attack. Many women still prefer to fantasize about a sexuality which comes to them from outside, one which they respond to rather than initiate. This, after all, is the impetus behind both romantic fiction and the fantasies of men being unable to control their desire for us. Although such fantasies are sexy and assume female sexual pleasure, they still assign active sexuality to the man. Female sexual excitement and pleasure remain essentially passive responses.

So, in spite of apparently sweeping changes – in spite of the 'sexual revolution' – the psychological structures are still intact, and sexuality is externalized as male need, male impulse and male initiative. This means that, from a very early stage, girls and women, although they may well be conscious of sexual desire and sexual need, don't go through the same processes as boys in terms of either acknowledging their sexuality or competing with others for their chosen object (except in the passive ways of trying to be the most attractive); they don't risk rejection; and they rarely find themselves in a situation of being able to assess whether they can find a person to meet their sexual needs. It is this division of sexual roles and responsibilities which then confirms the appalling mismatch of male and female sexual feelings. But leaving that aside for the time being, what is relevant here is how, for many young girls and young women, sexuality remains a source of confusion. It is something which many can relax about only when they find a partner who wants them and whose needs take care of their own greater ambivalence and uncertainty.

I am not trying to create a picture of male adolescents at ease with their emerging sexual needs and happily taking responsibility for them. On the contrary, adolescence is clearly an unsettled time for both sexes. But 'experimentation' is extremely harzardous for girls. This is a crucial point of divergence between the sexes. Girls develop a moral sense at the cost of sexual feeling; boys cultivate a sexual imperative at the cost of moral sentiment. Few women are able to confront their own role in the dynamics of female passivity, which are potentially so hurtful and destructive. This sexual division again seems part of the process in which certain uncomfortable feelings – in this case, strong sexual feelings – are projected by women on to men. I am well aware of what might appear to be a dangerous logic in this. Am I suggesting that extreme manifestations of male sexual violence, such as rape or child sex abuse, are part of a confused and malfunctioning division of sexual responsibilities, in which women are in some way answerable? No, not quite. These are crimes, and the victims are never responsible for crimes inflicted upon them. But there clearly is some kind of continuum which needs to be looked at.

In 1990 the book *Understanding Rape* was published. Based on interviews with convicted rapists, and providing acres of methodological justification, it contained a kernel of uncomfortable fact regarding male attitudes towards rape. The great majority of the men believed that their victims had actually enjoyed the experience. Rape is a violent crime against the person, and as such involves a denial of the victim's needs and humanity. But there are disturbing ways in which the attitudes of these rapists corresponded with other views about sexuality expressed in different contexts. Carrie Herbert's book, for example, cites a disturbing case of sexual harassment in a school where the harasser simply would not believe that the girl had not in some way invited the attacks.

Rape is an extreme manifestation of a state of affairs in which men are associated with initiative, activity and potency, and women still do not feel fully in control of their sexuality. At the same time, our culture inflicts on young girls what amounts to a belief that being sexually alluring is one of the deepest female achievements. This is a fatal combination, mainly because men, having been forced to believe themselves the most significant bearer of sexual responsibility, often cannot see girls and women as real people, but only as repositories for their sexual needs. In cases of disturbed individuals who commit the crime of rape, the victim can often be psychologically obliterated altogether. Thus the work of those dealing with rapists has to centre on the apparently obvious fact that their victims do have feelings, and have been hurt by them.

One interviewee provided me with an example of just how thin the line between 'normal' sexual exchange and rape can be. She moved from having unpleasurable sex with her husband to being raped before she fully realized what was happening. Her history and her own confusion around her responsibility for this seemed to go to the heart of some of the questions about the link between a deep female passivity and actual vicimization. Valerie, now separated from her husband Owen, feels intense rage towards him. But more surprising is the fact that she also feels guilty.

Valerie is now 36, with three daughters all under 7. She met her husband when she was 28 and, as she describes it herself, 'on the rebound from a very intense relationship'. 'I had been living with another man for three years. I think I was very "in love" with him but he didn't want children and I did. We kept quarelling about marriage and commitment and children. In the end I stopped taking the pill and I got pregnant. I miscarried at about ten weeks and Peter just seemed relieved. I felt incredibly hurt and convinced myself the relationship was going nowhere. I moved out and met Owen almost immediately. He really pursued me and that made me feel good again. He seemed the opposite of Peter. He was talking about marriage after we'd been going out together for about three months and was saying he'd found the person he wanted to spend the rest of his life with and have children with.'

Valerie got pregnant within a year of meeting Owen and they married as soon as they found out. Was she in love with him, I wondered. 'I don't really know. I can't remember. The main thing I felt was how much I wanted a child. After the miscarriage, it became an obsession really.' After the birth of their first child, Valerie, like so many other women, felt less interested in sex. 'I didn't feel like having sex and I was also in pain after the birth. My stitches had been done badly and sex really hurt me. At first he didn't insist too much but he made me feel bad because he'd suggest sex every night and I kept refusing. Sometimes I'd force myself to go through with it, but it hurt and I didn't enjoy it, and often I tried to stop him when we were actually making love.'

Valerie was pregnant again when the first baby was only four months old. She hoped her pregnancy would put a stop to Owen's demands but it didn't. 'I think that was the point at which I began to hate him. I just wanted him to go away. I longed for the times when he had to go abroad to work. Sometimes I'd force myself to agree to sex. Sometimes I couldn't stand it. By the time the second child was a year old I was so tired I couldn't care less. I used to say to him, "Get out! Go and find someone who does want sex with you. No one is keeping you here." He didn't go, said he couldn't afford to find somewhere else to live, and that's when he started raping me. In the end, he just said, "You're my wife, I want sex." We had terrible, terrible scenes. He even dragged me out of bed and downstairs. I got a carpet burn on my arms.

'When my two eldest children were only 3 and 2, he raped me and I got pregnant again. During that pregnancy I just decided, this child is nothing to do with him. That was when I knew I had to do something. This baby was going to be mine and I wasn't going to let him near her. In the end I was quite literally rescued by a friend. She lent me money to pay off my mortgage, but only on condition Owen moved out. He's moved in with a girlfriend now and he comes to play with the kids once a week. He's like another child, a big brother; it's as if nothing ever happened between us.'

I wondered how they both understood this period now, whether she was worried he might rape again or whether she saw what happened as something specific to their relationship. 'We don't talk about it. I still hate him. When it was happening I hated him so much, I'd have killed him if I'd had a knife. I mean that. I don't think he'd rape again because basically he's not violent. Well, I don't know. He's obviously got the capacity for violence because he did it to me. But I think it was specific to our relationship. I think it was because it went wrong sexually and I didn't want sex with him. All the time it was happening I thought, this is my fault because I won't have sex with him. I still do think that deep down. It makes me feel a bit better that the law now recognizes rape in marriage as a crime, but I still feel somehow it was my fault.'

Valerie still feels responsible for the rape, even though she knows she was the victim of an actual crime. Most therapists dealing with victims of criminal assault, rape or abuse are all too familiar with the feeling of guilt which follows the experience. Even women who have been assaulted or raped by complete strangers often feel not only invaded, degraded and made dirty, but also intensely self-doubting, questioning how far their own behaviour could have contributed to what happened. It is a feeling which has been compounded by the convention of defence lawyers trying to pin the blame on women and accusing them of ambiguous sexual messages.

But why should a woman like Valerie feel guilty about something which is recognized not just as a crime, but as a crime often associated with highly disturbed and damaged men? The answer almost certainly lies in the muddle which surrounds women's feelings about their own sexuality. Valerie would probably be the first to admit an ambiguity in her own sexual life. 'I don't think of myself as a very sexual person. I've had satisfactory relationships but, even before children, I often got turned off sex. I've had a long history of being involved with men who want sex more than I do.' If a woman habituates herself to a reluctant acceptance of sex, from which arousal sometimes follows, it is not surprising that when an extreme and criminal version of this dynamic comes her way she should question her own complicity.

When I use the word complicity, I am not referring to ambiguous sexual messages or women inviting rape. I do, however, remain convinced that there is often a confusion in women themselves about what they want sexually and how to get it, and how much they 'owe' men in return for other things. It is this confusion with 'normal' sex which creates inappropriate guilt in a criminal situation. In Valerie's case, there is obviously a great deal of guilt about whether or not she 'used' Owen to get her longed-for baby, and then about whether or not she owed him sexual services because she had wanted the baby (and loved it) more than him. Another, younger, woman talked to me of a similar but less extreme version of what happened to Valerie. Her partner forced her to agree to sex by threatening to leave her for 'someone who would give him what he wanted'. She gave way, with increasing reluctance, because she was frightened he would leave her alone with their baby. She too felt that he was owed something because she was gaining so much satisfaction from the baby. Again she talked of her guilt about how intensely she loved her baby.

Leaving aside the question of why so many men should seek to satisfy all their emotional needs through sex, what I am emphasizing here is how women are still growing up extremely unclear about what they really want from sex and what they expect to 'give' in return. And this stems from their habitual expectations of not taking an active part in defining their sexual needs. I believe that women still leave the definition of the sexual dynamic in their relationships to the man. So long as their needs are compatible, the relationship will appear to be just fine; as soon as their needs change, especially after the birth of children, any sense of mutual agreement breaks down, often with dire results.

Thus women are caught between two powerful forces: on the one hand the compulsion to 'be sexy', and on the other a persistent denial of their sexual needs. The two add up to an identity that still centres on the need to be desirable, to be the object of men's desire. With the increasing sexualization of culture, a woman is expected more and more to be defined by her ability to provoke and satisfy a sexual response in men and this is still essentially a passive aim. Women's by no means unfounded fears of becoming a victim of male sexual aggression show that this passivity does not breed contentment. In the final chapter, I will look at why this deep passivity still prevails in the female psyche.

12

Are Women Passive by Nature?

Throughout this book I have asserted that, although there have been great changes for women over the last twenty years, many aspects of what is considered traditionally feminine behaviour still pertain. The previous chapter showed how female passivity, the desire to be desired, and the tendency to hand over control to men exist from a very young age and are part of women's most profound expectations about sexual behaviour and sexual roles. This leads to the uncomfortable question of whether or not women are, by nature, passive, an assertion which, if true, would explain certain emotional structures which this book has explored.

The idea that women are, by nature, more passive has a long history in Western culture. Indeed, prior to Freud, middle-class morality also tended to deny the very existence of such a thing as female sexuality. Women's role in sex was seen as entirely passive, their only interest in sex being to procreate. Freud challenged these assumptions by insisting not only that sexuality was evident in children from infancy, but also that initially this sexuality was the same in both sexes. Male and female children, he claimed, started out with both active and passive sexual drives and aims; they settled into their characteristically 'masculine' (active) and 'feminine' (passive) forms as a result of social repression. It was in the unconscious that Freud found evidence that the route to a mature sexual identity was a precarious and difficult one.

Freud's ideas were revolutionary. He rejected biological explanations of maleness and femaleness and instead tried to trace the complex development that produces 'masculinity' and 'femininity'. Female masochism was seen by Freud as an extreme result of this process of acquiring 'feminine' passive aims. The girl child was forced to abandon her active sensual drives and transfer her desire into passivity. The 'typical' route by which this process of sexual differentiation travelled was, according to Freud, through castration anxiety in the boy and the castration complex in the girl. Put very briefly, this leads the boy, fearing castration by the father, to identify with him instead and put his desire for the mother into abeyance. The girl, disappointed with her mother for her 'castration', transfers her desire to the father, and then to a man of her own who will eventually offer a substitute for the desired penis in the form of a baby.

In America in the 1950s Freud's ideas began to appear as a justification for male domination and female passivity. Freud may have described femininity and masculinity as *constructions*, but what interested the therapists of the time was the *outcome* – a true or proper femininity with passive aims, the desire to be loved and, in its extreme form, pleasure in pain. The expansion of individual psychoanalysis in America in this period coincided with an extremely passive and domesticated stereotype of femininity.

When certain clichés of passive femininity came under attack from feminists in America in the late 1950s and early 1960s, the theory and practice of psychoanalysis were prime targets. Psychoanalysis was regarded as part of a conspiracy to brand any woman who stepped outside the limited stereotypes as a neurotic. The discontented housewife – and there were plenty of those in the 1950s – was the woman with the unresolved castration complex. The career woman was the woman who identified with the phallic father, and so on. Yet the masochistic woman who was prepared virtually to obliterate herself in a passive collaboration with men's desires was seen as an extreme form of normal femininity.

One by one the leading feminist writers of the early period turned their attention to what they saw as the Freudian myth. Shulamith Firestone in *The Dialectic of Sex*, Kate Millett in *Sexual Politics*, Eva Figes in *Patriarchal Attitudes* and Germaine Greer in *The Female Eunuch* all attacked Freud for his patriachal view of women and, in particular, his notion of female masochism. They set to work proving that women's subordinate position in society had nothing to do with inferior organs. Instead, it had everything to do with men's power and control over the events and social structures which most affected women's lives: the family and childbirth.

Each of these writers detailed the ways in which men had excluded, manipulated and bullied women over the centuries. Greer's *Female Eunuch* traced the oppression of women far back into the emergence of the patriarchal capitalist family, where inheritance and property accumulation required the control of women's reproductive capacities. Now, she argued, women should throw off all shackles of sexual repression and find their true sexual selves. Kate Millett railed against the images of women which *men* like Freud had created to delude women about the reality of their sex. Statistics were wheeled out to prove that female submission was actually female oppression.

These feminists all asked a similar question: how could Freud talk of the passivity of women's desires when women had had no chance to discover themselves? Women had been coerced and controlled by men's rules, men's laws, men's desires, and defined, not in God's image, but in men's. So many sexual fantasies, it was clear, were dominated by male imaginings and male wishes about what female sexuality should be, rather than what women really wanted. So-called masochism often turned out to be men's fantasies of what women wanted, like Norman Mailer's insistent presentation of his heroines as begging for violation and sometimes even pain. How could people know the truth about feminine imaginings or needs or desires when so little had come from the pens and tongues of women? No wonder Julia Kristeva, the French feminist theorist, should have claimed it was impossible to talk of women because they didn't yet exist (*Desire in Language*, 1984).

Yet even in these early heady days of feminism, dissonant voices were heard. The most significant of these was probably Juliet Mitchell, who in *Psychoanalysis and Feminism* (1974) acknowledged centuries of prejudice against women but at the same time recognized that some aspects of the female condition were tenacious, not easily overthrown by political good will. Unlike many of her contemporaries, Juliet Mitchell did not try to shirk some of the more uncomfortable aspects of female behaviour, and she insisted that Freud still offered the most plausible starting point for examining these. Only his perspective could explain the deep hold which female passivity in its broadest sense had on the imaginations of both men and women. It was a brave assertion in the face of the growing idealization of women and femininity within feminism.

This feminist idealization was not only concerned with the bonds between women, although 'sisterhood' and mother–daughter love were constantly held up as examples of the naturally supportive and egalitarian love within the female personality. It was also asserted that women were by nature more caring, more nurturing, less competitive than men. The triumph of female values would mean a better, more caring, more egalitarian society. In addition, women's natural sexuality, when finally liberated, would also be wholesome and egalitarian. Freed from the shackles of patriachal repression and violence, love would no longer involve domination and submission, certainly not sadism and masochism.

As it turned out, Juliet Mitchell's insight that 'femininity' might be deeper rooted than many feminists imagined was borne out by events. By the 1980s, it was obvious that some feminist Utopias were in fact delusions. Disillusion grew, not just from the bitter political disagreements which were emerging from within feminism, but also from honest discussions in which some feminists began to 'own up' to the waywardness of their desire in relation to political correctness. Not only had it become clear that not all Western women were prepared, on hearing the call of feminism, to forsake traditional roles, but it was now becoming evident that even the most committed feminists often found themselves deeply embroiled in what was called 'loving your enemy'. This ranged from supporting the traditional family and loving men, to asserting that dominance and submission were part of many sexual relationships, including even lesbian relationships.

In the 1980s some feminists began to analyse 'the problem' of desire, which did not follow political prescriptions. In particular, they asked how women could understand enjoyment of deep passivity and of losing oneself in another, which sometimes amounted to masochism. These discussions were the source of much bitterness and division. For some women (both heterosexual and lesbian), wedded to the idea of a nurturing, egalitarian female sexuality, these questions were offensive enough. The enactment of these scenarios by some lesbians was the final straw, especially for those already jaded by the endless divisions and bickering within the feminist movement. Combined with apathy on the wider political front, the divisions spelled the end of many women's active involvement in feminism.

Throughout the 1980s, defenders of the idea of the nurturing, egalitarian female sex found a new home in New Age related politics – in the alternative health movement, humanistic psychology and the mystical side of green politics. There the idea of the peace-loving female principle acquired a new centrality, although everywhere else the unsettling aspects of female sexuality began to have prominence. Masochism and domination appeared constantly in women's sexual fiction and Hollywood films, and at the same time sado-masochistic scenarios of chains, thongs and leather bondage were evoked by female fashions. By the end of the 1980s, one of the most consistent representations of women's sexuality – whether in films, novels or fashions – was as female masochism. Its most common embodiment was the successful 'modern' woman embroiled in a steamy, masochist sexual relationship.

In part, these fashions, like any fashions, were simply 'cultural borrowings'. They aped sexual subcultures where sado-masochism was no longer merely a theoretical possibility but a flourishing practice. And the fashion industry as always reached out for what might shock, provoke and appear 'new'. These fashions also had another appeal for a generation where sex, death and danger had once more become linked through Aids. But none of these factors fully explains why fantasies of female masochism became acceptable at the very point when we were told that we were entering the era of the successful woman. Here, after years of women demanding that they should define their own sexual needs and asserting that these needs would not involve power and submission, were films and novels which focused on sex as if it were only about dominance and submission.

These images and fashions might simply be taken as proof that men still dominate the leisure and entertainment industries. But there has been little protest about such images. Indeed, women themselves have taken the lead in saying that in a post-feminist era such protests are redundant. But does this lack of resistance mean that 'ordinary' women live out their real sexual relationships in a passive and masochistic way? The answer is almost certainly not, or not in any direct sexual way. The interviews throughout this book have given evidence that men and women are highly conscious of the problems of female subservience, even if they are not very creative in their solutions to it. The glamorous career woman in her obligatory suspenders gasping with masochistic pleasure in films like *Tie Me Up, Tie Me Down* or *9½ Weeks* are a far cry from these real women's lives.

Obviously we do have to be very careful about making deductions about the reality of people's lives, or indeed about what they 'really' want on the basis of these fantasies. Fantasies are just that; they cannot be assumed to express a straightforward wish. Indeed, according to Freud, the unconscious is made up of wishes and fantasies which are unacceptable to our conscious selves. In psychoanalysis, the psychotic is precisely someone for whom dreams come true. But if these images do not correspond to women's real lives, there is still a question about why this fantasy should have taken hold at this particular time. Why should a 'grotesque' of femininity – the successful woman who can survive sexual submission – be appealing at this time?

Some of the more astute theorists have noted that fantasies concerning domination and submission offer the viewer/reader the possibility of occupying *both* positions: the dominator and the dominated, or the passive and active sexual subject. One lesbian theorist, for example, defended the use of some sado-masochistic clichés in a collection of 'erotic' fiction because she believed that these scenarios allow women to experience the flow between aggression and passivity, domination and submission. She argued that these feelings were integral to sex but are normally confined to one sex or another according to gender conventions. She went on to assert that when women allow themselves to enjoy these fantasies, they can enjoy aggression, dominance and control, things which are normally submerged in women. Such an assertion might explain why women sometimes seem loath to challenge the conventions of pornography and erotic films. It could be argued that women's relation to these fantasies is more complex than a passive confirmation of submissive roles.

But while fantasies may in theory allow men and women to occupy the positions both of dominator and of dominated, in practice the situation is neither so fluid nor so comfortable. After all, it is invariably women who are represented in the masochistic position, usually in the most clichéd ways, and that remains a problem when women are still subject to real sexual assault and real sexual victimization. In addition, when masochistic fantasies are explored in a more profound and analytical way – as has been done by several contemporary women novelists – they find that the reality behind feminine masochism is pain, despair and self-annihilation. The post-feminist myth that it is now possible for women to explore sexual extremes without harmful consequences would appear to be just that – a myth.

Margaret is one woman who has thought a lot about these issues. After two relationships with men significantly older than herself, she eventually married a man twenty years her senior. Many problems emerged when in her mid-30s she discovered that he did not want her to have children; he already had three children by a previous marriage. Margaret went to see a counsellor about her marriage. She describes herself as starting the counselling in 'a complete rage with my husband, Mike', and ending up 'trying to find out why I was always attracted to a certain type of man'. 'When I started the counselling I just thought I was attracted to these men because they were more interesting; they had seen more of the world. It never occurred to me it was a pattern. But I began to realize I wanted someone to approve of me and look after me as if I was a girl. It was the only way I could feel safe.'

Margaret describes her childhood as 'unhappy'. Her mother had been very depressed, and often ill, throughout Margaret's childhood and adolescence. 'I think my mother was always terribly unhappy with my father and with us. She couldn't ever really cope with the five children, although she did try. My grandmother – my father's mother – lived with us, and she made sure we were all basically all right. But my mother was terribly unpredictable. She would start a game and then something would go wrong and she would scream at us. Then she would cry. I think we must all have felt in chaos. It was a sort of relief when Dad got home from work, even though he was often very unkind. My grandmother used to get us all organized for when he came in. Then things started happening – "Get this, do that!" "Have you done your homework?" "Who was top of the class?" '

As soon as Margaret left home, she got into a relationship with an older man – one of the lecturers at college – and that set a pattern. Margaret describes how all her fantasy and desire centred on older, more powerful men. 'It was a case of finding all my contemporaries callow. I never thought about older men ageing and having different needs from myself. I just found them sexually very attractive; their power turned me on. I never stopped to think about it because I had a certain prestige, living with one of the lecturers. But now I think I just didn't know who I was. I hadn't found myself at all in the family, I'd just survived. With Tony [the lecturer] I felt real. It was as if he was the only safe point in the chaos.'

But she found sex itself more problematic. 'Again, all my relationships have followed a pattern. At first they are very charged sexually but I felt very panicky about sex. Then abruptly the sexual side came to an end. Now I see that my relationships have all been dominated by fantasy and have quickly died when reality gets in the way. The whole question of having a child has made me realize this. The desire for a child came on me very gradually and there I was married to a man who was nearly 60. I suddenly thought, I'm never going to grow up.' Margaret's childhood is by no means typical but her desires and fantasies are only extreme versions of what passes for normal in our society – the fantasy of the powerful man who allows a woman to lose and find herself simultaneously.

So why is it that, in spite of great social changes and new opportunities for women, there is still a sexual pull in women towards passivity – by which I mean a general tendency to pass control and responsibility to men, rather than a specifically passive position in sex itself? Jessica Benjamin describes this as 'the problem of domination'. According to her, sadism and masochism in both the boy and the girl child derive from the infant's erotic relationship with its mother. She argues that this sensual relationship with the mother is a mixture of two things, one a vital, intimate and necessary relationship of dependency, the other a struggle for separation which stirs up issues of mastery and control.

Benjamin suggests that two fantasies predominate in the very young child. One is the fantasy of the all-powerful mother who will do everything for the passive child, control it totally and never let it go. Should this 'really' happen the child would in fact never become a fully autonomous individual and would therefore, in effect, be destroyed. The other, equally strong, fantasy is of omnipotence. The child imagines that it can demand everything of its mother, that these demands will always be met and that there will be no separation between the child and the mother, since in this fantasy the child can totally control the mother. Again, should this 'really' happen it would be disastrous, since the mother would metaphorically disappear and the child would then feel abandoned.

The 'healthy' child is supposed to emerge from somewhere between the two fantasies. Enough of the omnipotent feelings have to be met to allow the child to feel safely dependent, but the mother must be sufficiently powerful not to allow the child to annihilate her. To find this balance the child needs a parent who is strong enough to be used, if that doesn't sound too much of a paradox. It requires a parent, usually the mother, who can sympathetically understand the child's needs and respond to them, but is neither so weak she will become a slave nor so strong she will crush the child. In other words, the mother must have, in the language of contemporary psychotherapists, strong 'boundaries'. In Margaret's case, the chaotic and ill mother would have been fertile ground for fears and fantasies to grow, and not a good situation for her to find her own boundaries.

Benjamin believes that these fantasies of domination and submission remain in the unconscious and play a vital part in adult sexuality, which is precisely about abolishing and maintaining separation and boundaries between individuals. Adult sexuality is, she says, infused with this tension between the desire for the other to take total control (masochism) and the desire for the destruction of the other (sadism) so that you can experience your own separation and mastery. 'Healthy' sex is a play and equilibrium between the two poles, and both males and females have the capacity for these feelings in equal proportions, although in 'normal' sexual relations women incline more in one direction and men more in the other.

Benjamin also has an explanation for why men and women on the whole tip one way rather than another. She claims that the reason behind the traditional division of sexual responsibilities is the 'escape' that conventional gender positions offer the child from what it perceives as the all-powerful mother. In opposition to Freud, who suggested that children see the mother as castrated or weak, Benjamin says that because the mother is largely responsible for the day to day care of infants she appears all-powerful. But with this proviso, Benjamin thinks Freud's original ideas about castration anxiety and the castration complex leading to the adoption of normal 'masculine' and 'feminine' positions still hold true. It is the gradual apprehension of the father's difference to, and prior claim on, the mother which allows the child to relocate itself and develop its identity separate from the mother. In particular the child relocates itself around the polarities of sexual difference.

The boy child recognizes paternal difference and the power of the outside world which the father represents, and sees the chance to identify with the father as a means of escape and separation from the mother (albeit temporary, given that the heterosexual male can always hold on to the fantasy of 'returning' to women). For the girl child, too, the external, different power of the father, symbolized by his penis, also offers the possibility of escape. She too recognizes the significance of the penis, but has to deal with the disappointment of not having one. Her 'solution' is to defer 'having' a penis – making the famous connection of a baby representing a penis originally asserted by Freud – until she can have a baby herself. The result is that desire is split up according to the masculine and feminine polarities of activity and passivity, dominance and submission.

In an ideal world – of true quality between the sexes – this division between masculine and feminine roles would not be rigid or obsessive. The typical solution of 'masculinity' and 'femininity' (activity and passivity) would remain the cultural 'solution' to the struggle for autonomy from the mother, but the child would have developed a secure enough sense of its own boundaries and its mother's boundaries for it to be possible to move between activity and passivity, control and submission. Yet much of the evidence is that, in spite of contemporary changes in the family, girls and boys are not free to break with deep feminine and masculine identifications.

As sexual identity is currently formed, taking up positions around the father's desire is not a neutral acceptance of difference. It is still importantly about boys identifying with power and about girls handing over power to another. I have described time and time again in this book how the female psyche still turns around the desire to hand over power and responsibility, to merge what is perceived as a 'weaker' personality with a 'stronger' one. This is the basis of the splitting of emotions and of the idealizing of the potent father (or man). In sexual terms it becomes the desire to be desired. Margaret's case may be extreme because her mother was literally in chaos, but it is also typical because many mothers are not secure enough in themselves to 'hold' the child. Then the father will become the obvious solution. In Margaret's case it became the quest for the literal and authoritarian father. In less extreme cases, it is finding oneself in being desired, and finding the potent father in other men who can then carry various uncomfortable feelings for the woman.

Contemporary changes in the family have done little to challenge this deep structure. In fact, if what is crucial in determining the child's conventional gender identifications is the quest to escape from the mother who is simultaneously all-powerful and insecure, then there are some changes which may have made things worse rather than better. Many social changes have made women more central in the family rather than less – the increase in single mothers, the absence of any imposed childcare routines, the fact that for the most part children are still looked after mainly by their mothers, and the rejection of patriarchal and external authorities. The paradox is that, unless the woman is exceptionally strong – both financially and emotionally – the power that women appear to have gained is illusory. These changes simply place women in the eye of the storm, leaving them alone to field and structure the child's evolving identity.

A potent mother does not imply a socially powerful mother, but simply the mother who is in charge of childcare and largely has to 'hold' the child's development on her own. Because the father is no longer evoked as a distant authority, or is absent, the mother appears to the child as psychologically even more powerful. The more potent the mother, the more ferocious the need of the child to distance itself, not literally but symbolically, in forming its own sense of self. This process would be all well and good if the mothers, at the centre of these changes, were strong, well supported and had a secure sense of their own boundaries. But as I have found in the course of interviewing for this book, contemporary mothers are in their own ways just as self-doubting, self-critical and anxious as those of any previous generation. Indeed, it may well be that some of the conventions around mothering in previous generations gave women some protection. In the 1950s, at least, there were set routines around children, and pretty minimal expectations about what a mother should do for a child. There were also 'external' authorities to be called on for support and discipline – the church, the school, the father. Now, as they increasingly bear the burdens of educating, disciplining, stimulating and comforting the child, women are suffering further erosion of their personal boundaries; their success or failure as mothers is more critical, yet they still receive little validation from outside.

While I would never advocate a return to the practices of forty years ago – practices which often neglected the children's emotional development and relied on harsh discipline – at least women at that time could fall back on the old routines and customs around children. For example, children were expected to sleep and eat at set times. These routines ensured the mother had some separation from her children, and they were validated by family and neighbours, even if women did not receive the external validation of a working identity. Now many women no longer accept such routines, nor will they accept external sources of authority. Their reasons are often excellent, but it has left them without any external props while the child is forming its own boundaries. The fact is, contemporary mothers pretty well have to reinvent the wheel when their children are born in terms of routine, authority and boundaries. Their journey is thus far more intense and perilous than when these things were more clear-cut.

Catherine, who described her troubled relationship with her young daughter in the chapter about guilty women, is relevant here also. She found that she had no real boundaries between herself and her daughter – only the external boundaries of going to work and meetings. She found her daughter's whingeing and incessant demands maddening and frequently lost her temper. She halted a slide into violence only by taking classes in 'parenting'. The most important thing she learnt there was 'not any tricks about how to manage my child, which is what I had initially hoped for. Instead I found I had to understand my own needs and limits. Most important for me was learning not to feel guilty because I've got needs as well as the kids. Before that, I'd been using work as the only way I had of setting limits. When I was at home I felt my daughter should be able to have me completely, but I couldn't cope with that.'

The breakdown in traditional ways of caring for children means that the dynamic between mother and child is potentially far more intense, especially in the context of a growing ideology about maternal stimulation. This, paradoxically, means that the child can now experience the full force of its mother's insecurities and anxieties. Women's identities may have been strengthened by work, but sometimes this is not an inner strengthening – work can simply be a boundary imposed from outside, while within the family mothering remains without real boundaries. In our culture, with its inadequate provisions and scant rewards for working mothers, maintaining your identity by working is often just another pressure.

No wonder traditional gender identities have held firm over the years. Taking up traditional male and female roles around paternal authority is one solution to a muddled and ambiguous relationship with a mother from whom it is difficult to separate. Even in families where the mother is on her own, the father is still relevant because this is a symbolic, not a literal, issue. The father does not have to be literally present for the child to recognize that the gender polarities implied by the father's role offer a way to separate identity. But the tenacity of extreme gender division is not evidence that things will never change. It is evidence that at the heart of our culture it is women who – unsupported, undervalued and insecure – are still being asked to shoulder the lion's share of caring for the future generation. In such a context it is often difficult for women to feel secure enough about themselves to allow their daughters to separate without adopting a traditional role.

There are, obviously, important ways in which changes in women's employment patterns have helped open up the way for new 'female' possibilities in the future. There is, for example, some evidence that girls with working mothers are more ambitious and less traditional than those whose mothers have stayed at home. But other changes are more ambiguous. Ironically, the 'power' which women have been given and have taken up in the family – the power that comes with defining all the rules yourself – can create a backlash. For girls, the struggle to become autonomous from the mother is especially perilous because the boundaries are unclear and the mother's identity can be precarious. Identifying with paternal authority and accepting passive feminity is one way out of this. Perhaps women have accepted the wrong power in the family. By accepting emotional power, they have let themselves in for the burden of emotional responsibility. This may mean that it will continue to be difficult for women to break the legacy of passive femininity.

Conclusion
The Complicity of Women

Social commentators will continue to tell us that the bad old days of female subordination are over. They will try to convince us that women are now free to choose their lifestyles, and that if these women choose the traditional ways it is because this lifestyle makes them happy. When they say these things, it may be useful to remember the anxieties and dilemmas of the women interviewed for this book – their difficulty in straddling the different ethos of work and home, their insecurities in the face of impossible ideals, their guilt at the inability to get things right, their discomfort when suppressed emotions and feelings erupt, and their financial and social hardship when the traditional family fails. Since many men still see their responsibility for the family in financial terms, they are not so liable to experience these anxieties. The female condition in the 1990s is far from being as happy as the media would have us believe.

Many of the 'bad old things' about women are still in play – female passivity tending towards victimization, female anxiety for male approval, female readiness to bury their own needs in others (usually unsuccessfully) and female vulnerability when men's support and approval is absent. But there are also new stresses. There are the difficulties of combining work and mothering on both a practical and a psychological level. And there are stresses created by the new middle-class ideals, where mothering can turn into a form of slavery to the children and where competition and anxiety can run amok.

The ideals which women set for themselves can create extremely unpleasant feelings. It is, for example, not easy for women to cope with guilt, envy and jealousy. Nor is it easy for women to convince themselves they are 'nice' people when they envy the achievements of their friends' children, when they become a demented monster at a school open evening, or when they scream at their children because – this time – things have gone just that little bit too far. It's not *nice*, feeling all those emotions, especially when a person has spent a lifetime trying to deny she has them. Nor is it pleasant for women to pass their lives in a haze of anxiety about the future, wondering: Will my children be deprived if I work? Will I go mad if I don't? Is the local school good enough for *my* child? What will happen to the kids when they leave home? More important, what will happen to me?

It is hard work, these days, trying *not* to come to terms with what one's real needs and feelings are, but one of the ways in which women successfully avoid confronting them is by endlessly thinking about the future. Imagining a future where all current decisions and difficulties are validated is something women do habitually. The myth of the future that has always held women in sway is the vision of their perfectly adjusted, perfectly brilliant grown-up children, the end product of years of getting it right. Germaine Greer has added her version of this myth. Now, she tells us, women can dream of life after 'The Change'. Then, when the children have left home and hormones no longer drive women into the arms of men, clutching their pension books and tottering on their walking frames – then, at last women can be themselves.

In the meantime, although women's anxieties and dilemmas may be as great as ever, they lack a language of social complaint. Complaining is seen as an embarrassing feminist habit now that the 'real' women of the 1980s and 1990s are reconciled to their feminine destinies. Women now seem to believe that everything that happens to them results from how they *individually* choose to settle their dilemmas. If women love men and want children, then they have to accept the ways of the world, with the bulk of domestic and moral responsibility falling to them. If they want to work and have children, it is up to them as individuals to resolve any contradictory feelings and find private solutions to the practicalities. If they want good things for their children, it is up to them as individuals to get them, and hang the consequences of becoming ever more burdened with hopes and fantasies for somebody else's future. It is up to them as individuals to make things work in their families.

Yet if women of the 1990s don't want to complain, they certainly know how to worry. Worrying is what self-fulfilled 'real' women of the 1990s do best. They worry about themselves and their looks when their husbands leave home; about their children's behaviour and the quality of their maternal attention. They worry about themselves if they lose their tempers. They worry about their children's schools. All the while they tell themselves and each other that they are at least doing better than their mothers' generation because *they* have a degree and a part-time job, and they have chosen their lot. Try telling that to the children when they grow up. As they are shuttled to and fro to their violin lessons, their home tuition and their French clubs, they'll be storing up the same reaction to parental over-investment as the last generation did.

In spite of all this worry, most women seem to have swung round to believing their lot is inevitable. Although feminism challenged the old inevitabilities, they have returned with a vengeance. Now people believe that if women fled from the feminist visions, it must have been because women themselves wanted the old ways. And women are also saying that the satisfactions outweigh the disadvantages. Given the choice, they would rather be women than men. Most women still seem to feel that their careers are unimportant compared with the overwhelmingly significant task of caring for and educating the future generation. Even the most successful career women seem to think that, come the crunch, they could shed their working identities much more easily than men. And many seemed more prepared to shoulder extra domestic burdens than to share them with men.

This is partly because women still want to see themselves as altruistic and selfless: caring for children is where these qualities can most readily be expressed. Taking care of the needs of others – especially those who are dependent – can be a way of dealing with your own needs. Some of the demands of a career – long hours, devotion to a 'selfish' institution, sometimes ruthlessness – contradict this self-image. And when the two different requirements clash, many women opt out or reduce their career expectations rather than attempt to find a way to combine them. Those who remain within the career structures find other women – nannies, childminders or nursery teachers – to offer the quality of attention which they can give only sporadically. Very few insist on renegotiating home life with their men.

I have argued throughout this book that, if only it could be recognized, many aspects of women's ambivalence towards work and career could be put to radical use. It could lead to a more general challenge to the work ethic, which is, with its inflexible requirements and antisocial hours, responsible for many women's hardships and dilemmas. It could (and sometimes does) produce awareness of 'quality of life' issues – environmental campaigns, good provision for children in terms not just of childcare but of more general social improvements which would benefit women from all walks of life. It could lead to confronting men about the way they sometimes split off morality, humanity and emotion in the workplace. But more often than not this radicalism is absent. Instead, women justify their adherence to traditional male–female roles and their ambivalence about work in terms of either the specialness of the maternal bond or the greater decency of women, attuned as they are to the more important, more significant, more enduring things of life.

Both these notions – the specialness of the maternal bond and the greater decency of women – obscure the criticism of real social relations, pitching the debate in terms of how much mothers and children need each other or how much humanity needs womanly values. Maternal bonding and womanly values may give women short-term power, but they are part of a much less desirable package where the process of child-rearing is idealized in order to justify the status quo, and the male structures of work are left unchallenged. The power women acquire is the wrong power, placing them again at the centre of the family, but leaving them unprotected against all the new pressures which have been gathering force there.

I understand both the way in which a uni-linear career can lose its appeal after children come on the scene, and the attractions of the traditional family. I gave up my own university career to go freelance because it gave me more flexibility to look after the children. I was lucky, because I had that option and because I had a partner whose earnings made it possible. The satisfactions were greater than I could ever have imagined in pre-children days – satisfactions of being able to structure my own work, to set my own priorities, and above all to feel I was there when the children needed me. But I have also experienced the perils of this route – the fear of becoming dependent, the fear of future economic insecurity, the sense of hovering between 'doing fine' and ending up with no money, no career, no identity. I have also experienced first-hand the sapping of political will: energies previously directed towards the greater good can easily be channelled into unproductive anxiety about children's achievements.

Money does to some extent cushion women against some of the perils of the family, but it can never wholly obliterate them. Any woman dependent on a man for financial security is potentially vulnerable. And all women are vulnerable to the emotional disappointments of the contemporary family. Today's women are, no less than the women of previous generations, involved in a massive effort to banish uncomfortable feelings outside the family, either by projecting them on to men or by denying them altogether. But this rarely works in the long term. Buried emotions eventually erupt, and envy, jealousy, anger and competitiveness are often worse within and between families than in any workplace. Some women leave the workplace dreaming of harmony only to sink into depression at the chaos and conflict in their families. Children have their own agendas, and rarely oblige by returning altruistic educational devotion with endless displays of creativity, brilliance and gratitude. The result, for women in families which simply do not correspond to their ideals, is guilt.

Living an illusion is uncomfortable, and often women hover on the point of exposing the illusions of their lives. But most back off, prefering the illusions to the difficulty of personal change. And this is ultimately what I mean by complicity. Complicity is about not telling the truth – to other women or to ourselves – and not confronting men about the areas of our lives that don't fit the illusions. This complicity means that women don't pass on information and knowledge about their condition, and disparage those who try to do so. Complicity is about continuing to delude yourself about yourself, and not being able to sort out what comes from outside and what from within. It means that instead of recognizing who they really are, women continue to project on to men and children what they haven't dealt with properly in themselves. It means they continue with miserable obsessions about what men can do to make them happier, and what children can achieve to make them feel better about themselves. Those without money cannot cushion themselves by buying time away from children and making their working lives easier. Without choice, there is less reason to mystify. But the less affluent do not have power in the public domain. The voices heard there are the voices of women who are fed lies and try to believe them.

Two interviews I conducted with women living close to each other within the same area of London seemed to sum up this whole area of complicity, and indicated why some women stay with the illusions while others are forced to reassess and change their domestic situations. The first interview was with Elizabeth, who is a mother in her mid-30s with two girls, aged 9 and 7. Although not an active feminist, at university she had been one of a circle of friends who considered themselves socialists and feminists. She'd married one of that circle, Ian, whose politics were left-liberal. During the 1980s Ian became very successful because his career as a journalist took off. Elizabeth, who had been working as a medical researcher, gave up her job when she became pregnant for the first time and had not worked since then until six months ago, when she started a part-time research job two days a week.

Elizabeth employs an au pair and two years ago moved her children from the local primary school to a small private school. I asked her how this related to her former sympathies. 'I employ an au pair because the children's school is quite a distance away and I could spend my life in the car if I didn't get someone to help. I do feel guilty about the school but Sophie wasn't doing well at the local school. I went to see this private school, which was right for her, so we moved her.' Had Sophie been unhappy at her other school, I asked. 'No, but her reading wasn't all that good and she's a very intelligent child.' What did she feel about perpetuating a class division were some women pay and the rest are left to make do? 'Everyone should have the right to a good education, and I hope we get it, but it might be too late for my child.' Was she trying to shield her child from the racial and class mix of the area? 'Look,' she said, finally, 'when we took the decision to move Sophie, I was at the end of my tether, I was drinking a lot, every evening. My husband was having an affair, I was awake every night worrying. I knew I had to get a job. But if Sophie had stayed where she was, I wouldn't have been able to get a job. I'd have felt guilty. I'd have felt I had to do more for her by way of helping her with reading and writing and getting involved in the school. I had to get some time for *me*.'

Here, in a nutshell, is the complicity of the 1990s. The family has internal and impossible tensions – in this case a successful husband who doesn't help in the house and is having an affair. The woman sees herself sinking in it. She uses work as a 'solution' to her own personal disintegration and a private school as a 'solution' to the anxiety and guilt she suffers as a working mother. She feels better. But she has failed to confront her husband: his success means more to her than negotiating a change *within* the house. And secondly, she has passed the problem along, buying into a system where she tries to quarantine herself from the aspects of her worries. She thinks that sending her children to private school will buy her some respite from one of her worries – which it probably won't – but in doing this she inevitably spoils the chances of an improvement in social provision for all women.

Less than a mile away from Elizabeth is Linda, quoted at length in the chapter about guilt. The contrast could not be more sharp. Linda is the woman who abandoned being a full-time mother when she felt tormented about how badly she was coping with it. She went back to work as a school secretary and rose from there to her current position as a computer trainer. But her attitude to the relationships in her home, her child's education and to dealing with guilt are utterly different from Elizabeth's. Instead of 'buying' solutions, Linda made changes at home. She says she stopped feeling guilty once she went back to work – her guilt had come from feeling she wasn't enjoying mothering and she was able to admit this to herself, which included deciding not to have more children. 'But I didn't behave irresponsibly. Claudio was always well cared for and I didn't go back to work full-time until he was at school. Also, my husband has helped a lot. At first I kept on going for things because he said I'd never be able to manage it. But he's very proud of me actually and he's made a lot of compromises with his work. He could have travelled a lot more but I think he felt it would leave Claudio too vulnerable. So maybe he hasn't done as well as he might have done. But I think we all feel it's the right decision.'

Conclusion

Linda has already been quoted as saying her 14-year-old son boasts about his mother, 'the computer buff'. She is equally proud of him. 'He went to local schools and has a lot of friends round here – from every background. I can trust him to travel about London on his own – he always tells me where he is going. He never lets me worry and actually I don't much because he's so sensible. He's also got a lovely relationship with his dad. They really love each other and I think it's because my husband looked after him a lot when he was little.' Rather than adapting to the existing parameters, Linda has found herself changing some of the male expectations and values. She recognized her true feelings in the situation and acted on them. In short, she has done what one of my interviewees said was 'the most important thing', which is to look after her own needs without shirking her responsibilities. We could add to that: without letting men get away with it.

It goes without saying that men, if women do let them get away with it, will do so – providing too little childcare, working ridiculous hours, taking too little responsibility for their homes. They may not like having to be the repository of all the ambitions, competitiveness and anger of a family, but they do recognize that it brings less stress and burdens than the female side of the equation, with all its guilt, morality and anxiety. The impression formed from women's accounts is that the picture is gloomy as regards men making real changes in their behaviour. Women really have let them get away with it. One television executive summed it up when asked by a woman why his company was no longer committed to showing films by and about women. 'Because,' he answered, 'you lot haven't kept up the pressure.'

Women have let men get away with it. When it came to the crunch, most made it quite clear they didn't want conflict with men. Rather than have conflict, which they saw as a symptom of disturbed and angry people, they would prefer to keep the traditional structures of masculinity and femininity intact, even if it meant not coming to terms with themselves, even if it meant burying aspects of themselves in men and in children, even if it meant harder work and more pressures for women. In exchange, they have ostensibly been given more power in the family by accepting a new mythology concerning childbirth, mothering and nurturing. But that 'gift' is ambiguous. As their significance as mothers has increased, so have the pressures to live up to the ideals of being educator, therapist and friend to their children, while at the same time bearing all the weight of decisions and responsibilities for them in the absence of any secure external authority.

Contemporary women are in something of a mess. Already burdened with an inheritance of obligations, guilt and splitting off uncomfortable emotions, they have taken on even more. When the possibility of real social change was opened up, they failed to tackle on the one hand their real feelings and needs and on the other the real contradictions and difficulties of their situation. Instead, women were going to combine perfect mothering with a faultless career or they were going to give everything up and put themselves in touch with feminine values. More likely they were guiltily going to try for both, and feel inadequate about both. Everyone I spoke to seemed to think the answer lay in themselves, rather than recognizing dilemmas and anxieties that reflect real social problems, requiring social and political solutions.

I am not saying that women ran away from feminism, and that feminism could have provided these solutions. Feminism disintegrated as anger, divisions, accusations and guilt erupted from within, and for many – especially those who were wedded to the 'idealizing' of the feminine in feminism – these emotions were intolerable. What is more, feminism as a movement subverted itself. In what could almost be seen as a parody of stereotyped feminine behaviour, feminists experienced themselves as powerful and promptly turned on each other. The 'Utopian' and 'egalitarian' movement disintegrated and left in its wake a travesty of feminism – the media association of feminism with careerism.

I am not talking about restoring old-style feminism. But I do think that some of the simpler things that feminism said were important – about the pressures on mothers because of their lack of support and validation, about the need for women to recognize who they are rather than be coerced by imposed ideals, and about the way in which any real improvement in the lot of women will entail changes in social, economic and political priorities. Perhaps that unavoidably 'socialist' message scared many women as much as a threatened confrontation with men. Whatever the reason, women retreated from the stridencies of feminism and turned instead to a new myth – one that declared the problems confronting women to be individual, not social. Like every other myth women have bought into this will continue to oppress them.

It remains important for women to find out who they are and to take responsibilities for their feelings without abandoning their obligations to those around them. This applies to women who work and to women who give up paid work. And it is crucial for women to refuse to be coerced by a society like ours, which needs women to assume 'feminine' positions so that it can maintain some moral fabric. Clearly there are pleasures in women's responsibilities which have been underrated by feminism, but these do not amount to a feminine destiny in which most women drown. Instead, women need the freedom to understand themselves, their individual strengths and needs, and what they can best contribute to others. If this involves, for instance, deciding not to have children at all, or being a full-time stay at home mother, so be it. Such choices might well mean that these women are being more honest about themselves and have more to contribute to society generally than if they force themselves to perform the social and psychological gymnastics required by the prevailing ideals of womanhood.

Women are rather too skilled at performing such gymnastics for their own good. Not only do they contort themselves to accommodate all the contradictory expectations of the prevailing ideal, but they try to fend off social problems with individual solutions. Viewed from one side, such gyrations are heroic. But viewed from another, they show a failure of will, an acceptance of the status quo, and a collusion with men's expectations of women. When I told one woman that the subject of this book was women's collusion with men, she said, 'Oh God! It's going to be about me, isn't it? You're going to say how dreadful I am.'

I shall end with my reply to this woman. I told her that this book is not prescriptive, and is about myself as much as it is about any other woman. In it, I am trying to describe the feminine condition in order to understand which of our prevailing beliefs are choices from within and which are prescriptions from without. The last thing women need are any more prescriptions about how to live their lives. I hope if this book contributes anything, it will help release women from the burdens of other people's prescriptions. But, above all, I hope it will encourage social, not individual, solutions. Because if women try to lighten the burdens imposed by society only as individuals, it is other women who will pay the price.

Index

abortion, 50, 151
abuse: of children, 165–6, 171; and cycle of dependency, 11; and guilt, 174; women's complicity in, 10
activity/passivity, 176, 185
adolescence, 167, 170, 171
ageing, 161–3
aggression, children's, 62–8
Aids, 180
alternative health movement, 180
altruism: and the family, 44; and motherhood, 43, 74, 81, 85, 110; and older generation, 101, women appearing more altruistic than men, 135; and women's self-image, 192
ambition, 102, 114, 146; in a boy, 132; for daughters, 95; and the family, 61, 73, 81, 197; and girls, 133, 139, 145, 168; and identification between mother and child, 62; male, 120, 123, 124, 125, 129, 132, 134; own mother's frustrated, 98; at work, 17, 20, 27, 31, 33, 35, 37, 38, 41, 43, 44, 124, 125
Ambition (Burchill), 160
ambivalence, 106, 111, 114, 116, 171, 193
anorexia, 157, 159
au pairs, 33, 53, 195

babies, 7, 55, 56, 58, 60, 185, 97
babysitters, 165
Backlash (Faludi), 11–12
BBC, 161
Beauty Myth, The (Wolf), 154, 163
Benjamin, Jessica, 160, 183–5
blackmail, emotional, 138, 143, 145
body image, 155
Bonds of Love, The (Benjamin), 160
boys: and aggression, 63, 66, 67, 68; identification with power, 185, 186; and mothers, 44, 185; sadism and masochism in, 183, sexual harassment by, 167–8; and sexual imperative at the cost of moral sentiment, 171
breast-feeding, 70
Brown, Helen Gurley, 16
Brownmiller, Susan, 151
bulimia, 157, 159
Burchill, Julie, 160

Campbell, Bea, 49–50
career women, 25, 31; and appearance, 156, 159; giving up work for motherhood, 16–29, 30, 123; and their mothers, 93–6, 133; opting out or reducing career expectations, 192; and sexiness, 147; and sexual mantle of a masochist, 160; as supermums, 2
careerism, 23, 28, 31, 124, 125, 131, 198
castration complex, 115, 116, 177, 185
Central Park, New York, 164
childbirth, 7, 49, 151, 197
childcare, 46, 193; absence of routines, 186, 187, 188; altruistic, 86; and companies, 4; demands for improved, 5; funding of, 8; in the future, 16; haphazard organization of, 106; inadequacies of provision, 122; by man, 8, 26, 96, 121, 122, 123; manuals, 76, 82; new philosophies of, 74; by other women, 40; and Thatcher, 7; working mothers pressurized by worries of, 85
childminding, 58, 59, 84, 95, 96, 105, 106, 108, 192
children: and aggression, 62–7; autonomy and parents' needs, 72; 'being creative' with, 77–9, 112, 117; and competition, 63, 67, 71–2, 74, 88; criticism of routine by grandmother, 98; dependency of/

dependent on, 58; 'early learning', 81–3, 87–8; fantasies of young, 183–4; father's custody of, 8; female friendships broken over, 63–4, 65; having own agendas, 194; identification between mother and child, 62–74; and identification with own mother, 96–7; mother's encouragement of intellectual development, 5, 77, 192, 198; music lessons, 79, 192; nurturing, 7, 78; sent to private schools, 87, 195, 196; and road deaths, 5, second child and professional women, 21; sexual abuse of, 165–6, 171; social life, 79–80; as a traditional need, 1; women as slaves of, 86, 102, 190; and women's individual choice, 191
civil rights movement, 94
cleaning ladies, 4
clerical work, 5
Cleveland child abuse cases, 166
communism, 8
competition/competitiveness, 90; between women for male sexual approval, 140; over children, 63, 67, 71–2, 74, 88; escape from, 61, 97; and the family, 44, 45, 61, 73, 194, 197; and feminism, 62; and girls, 133, 139, 145; and identification between mother and child, 62; mother-daughter, 72–3; seen as inevitably male, 134; sexual, 158, 170; women's avoidance, 146; at work, 30–33, 38–44, 66, 124, 125, 194
complicity, 9–10, 194–6
Conservatives: and the family, 6, 15, 45; and funding of educational, health and childcare resources, 8
contraception, 50, 150–51
Cosmo, 16
crèches, 7, 19, 111
cycle of dependency, 11

Daddy, We Hardly Knew You (Greer), 92
Daily Mail, 18
day-care, 84
Dialectic of Sex, The (Firestone), 177
Dickson, Ann, 145
dieting, 156–7
discrimination, and legislation, 3
division of labour, 10, 113, 122, 126
divorce, 3, 6, 11
domestic planning, 7
domestic service jobs, 4
domestic tasks, 6, 7
domination/submission, 179, 180, 181, 184, 185
Down Among the Women (Weldon), 19

dress, 7, 151, 152

early learning, 81–3
education, 8, 17, 150
elderly, women's responsibility for, 5
Elle magazine, 155
'empty nest' syndrome, 57
environment, 2, 5, 193
envy, 91, 191; and the family, 61, 194; and identification between mother and child, 62; mother-daughter, 72–3; of other mothers, 76, 77, 80; own mother's, 98, 101; at work, 30, 33–4, 38, 43–4, 194
equal rights, 94
equality: economic, 2, 11; myth of post-feminist, 154, 164; professional, 2, 28; social, 2; and Thatcher's leadership, 1–2; and traditional relationship between the sexes, 1
erotic films, 181
Evening Standard, 81

Face Value, the Politics of Beauty (Lakoff and Scherr), 155
Faludi, Susan, 11–12, 86
family: and altruism, 44; and competitive work, 30, 31; disintegration of, 136; egalitarian, 91; and 'empty nest' syndrome, 57; and envy at work, 30; extended, 6, 9; flaunted by public women, 7; greater fluidity of structure, 3; and guilt, 109; 119, 194; ideal, 77–8; income, 41–21; male commitment to, 162; and male partner's work, 123, 124; and media, 2, 12; morality, 45; myth of, 2–3; patriarchal, 91; and pollution/environmental hazards, 5; roles within, 6–9; 'second', 58; swings back into fashion, 5–6; traditional, 1, 6, 9–10, 102, 119, 179, 193; women as emotional centre of, 57–60; and women's economic inequality, 11; as women's prime responsibility, 5, 16
fantasies: assigning active sexuality to the man, 170; of baby, 114–15; of child, 183–4; of female masochism, 180, 182; and Freud, 181; of men about women, 120; of 'returning' to women, 185; sexual, 178; of women about men, 120, 121–2, 126–7
fashion, 5, 153, 154, 155, 169, 180
Fat is a Feminist Issue (Orbach), 154
fathers: as babysitters, 165; custody of children, 8; daughter sharing mother with, 115; and gender polarities, 188; and power, 185; and psychological

responsibility for children, 106, 113–14; women's idealization of amount of domestic input, 120–22; work of, 121–3, 126
Female Eunuch, The (Greer), 92, 177, 178
Female Woman, The (Stassinopoulos), 136
femininity: deep rooted, 179; flaunting, 7; and Freud, 177; and masculinity, 133–4, 176, 185; and media, 2, 12; myth of, 14; old forms of, 9, 197; passive, 189; and sexual revolution, 149
Femininity (Brownmiller), 151
feminism: and abortion, 151; apparent redundancy in 1980s, 2, 3; backlash against, 11–12, 153; and boy-girl differences, 132; challenge of the old inevitabilities, 192; and complaining, 191; as daughter's revolt, 91–2; disintegration of, 5, 7–8, 12, 180, 198; and 'exempted man' syndrome, 120; fear of loss of identity, 94; and fight for professional women, 2; and financial independence, 11, 136; 'lesbian' feminists, 149, 152; and 'loving the enemy', 137, 179; and male sexual behaviour, 166; and the media, 12–13; sees men as all-powerful, 131; and motherhood, 18–19, 47, 68; of 1970s, 1; novels of, 19; and peace-loving, non-aggressive child, 67; and pleasures in women's responsibilities, 199; and publicly successful women, 7; and Second World War, 101–2; and selfishness, 100; and sexual self-definition, 148; and sisterhood, 42; and social theories, 136; and solidarity, 42, 62; sees women as victims, men as powerful patriarchs, 137; and women's attraction to 'successful' men, 123; and women's showing their sexual needs, 150
Figes, Eva, 177
films, erotic, 181
Firestone, Shulamith, 177
First World War, 91
flexitime, 40
Fonda, Jane, 158
food scares, 5
Forster, Margaret, 19
French, Marilyn, 19, 92
Freud, Sigmund, 82, 115, 176–7, 178, 181, 185
Friday, Nancy, 154
Friedan, Betty, 4

Gillick, Gordon, 162
Gillick, Victoria, 100, 161–2

girls: and aggression, 64, 67–8; and ambition, 133, 139, 145, 168; and appearance, 168–9; and competition, 133, 139, 145; development of a moral sense at the cost of sexual feeling, 171; and father's power, 185, handing over power to another, 186; lack of information about their bodies and sexual responses, 151; loss of confidence at puberty, 167–8; and mothers, 44, 145, 185, 189; sadism and masochism in, 183; sexual harassment of, 166–70, 171
Godley, Georgina, 81
green politics, 180
Greer, Germaine, 6, 92, 177, 178, 191
Guardian, 15, 67, 132
guilt, 191, 197, 198; and ambivalence, 106; and children, 3, 76, 78–9, 81, 87, 88, 105, 106, 107–118, 196; and emotional blackmail, 138, 143; and the family, 109, 119, 194; and feminism, 12; and food, 157; and husbands, 105; and 'protective.' behaviour, 139; and rape, 172, 174; and women's mothers, 94, 105; and work, 3, 31–2, 106–9, 111–12, 113, 118
Gyngell, Kathy, 18

Halsey, Nigel, 37–8
Haran, Maeve, 17, 18, 19, 41, 108
Having It All (Haran), 17, 108
health care, 5, 8
Herbert, Carrie, 167, 171
Herman, Nina, 115–16
homelessness, 2
housekeeping money, 24
How Do I Look? (ed. Jill Dawson), 155
humanistic psychology, 180

identity, 117, 118; absorbing husband's, 123–4; gender, 188; loss of, 94, 95, 96, 113; and work, 188, 192
independence, 45, 96; children becoming independent, 97; economic/financial, 11, 24, 50, 94, 136, 138; and violence as a social control, 169
Ita, 17

jealousy, 91, 191; at work, 30, 34, 35, 39, 40, 41, 194
Jenkins, Simon, 12
job-shares, 28, 40
journalism, women's-issue, 12
Junior, 16

Kenny, Mary, 22

Klein, Melanie, 84, 106, 111, 114–15, 116
Kristeva, Julia, 178

labour, division of, 10, 113, 122, 126
labour market, 3, 15, 122
Lakoff, Robin, 155
Lamplugh, Suzy, 165
Leach, Penelope, 71
legislation, and discrimination, 3
lesbians, 149, 152, 179, 181
Lessing, Doris, 19, 82
'Love, Guilt and Reparation' (Klein), 114–15

McKee, Victoria, 16
McMartin Day Nursery, 166
Madonna, 150, 153–4, 159
Mailer, Norman, 178
Major, Norma, 22
manipulation behaviour, 135–46
market economy, 4
marriage: connotations of possession, obedience and subordination, 3; in different cultures, 135–6; disintegration, 9, 54; Gillick on, 161–2; old attitudes to, 102; statistics, 6
masculinity, 119, 133, 134, 176, 185, 197
masochism, 176–81, 183, 184
 see also sado-masochism
masturbation, 153, 154
maternal bonding, 51; altruism of, 43; and career women, 18, 28–9; and identification with one's children, 65; and motherhood, 47; and short-term power, 193; social ideologies surrounding, 57
maternal instinct, 18, 29, 47, 51, 57
maternal love, 18, 20, 21
maternalism see motherhood
media: and career women, 2, 16, 20; and feminine women, 12; and feminism, 12, 198; and idyll of family, 12; and popular retreat into traditional values, 13
men: and abuse of women, 10; and amorality, 44–5; and childcare, 8, 26, 96, 121, 122, 123, 197; dependence on, 10; domination by, 177, 179, 180; and equality, 1, 2; and feminism 7, 91; and guilt, 115–16; importance of career to, 128; and narcissistic identification, 37; and networking, 36–7; power of, 11, 123, 136, 137, 146, 177, 183; and role within family, 6; women scared of fundamental confrontation with, 8; women servicing career, 37; women's desire for approval of, 10; women's

idealization of, 10, 119–20; and women's 'manipulative behaviour', 135–46; women's need to be sexually attractive to, 1, 7
Millett, Kate, 177, 178
Mitchell, Juliet, 178, 179
monogamy, 136
Monroe, Marilyn, 153, 159
mother–daughter relationship, 67–8, 72–3, 90–104
motherhood: altruism, 43, 74, 81, 85, 110; and career women, 16–29, 30; dangers of trying to meet all needs in, 55–60; and dependants 51–2; desire for babies, 55; and feminism, 18–19; ideal, 75–89, 110, 111, 113, and maternal bonding, 47; obsession with being a 'carer', 52–5; 'power' of, 46–7, 197; self-assertion v fears of annihilation, 45; and sense of belonging, 50; and sexual competition, 158; sexualization of, 163
mothers: all-powerful, 183–6; competitiveness, 71–2; contemporary mothering, 71, 72; 'escape' from, 185; fights between, 61–2; identification between mother and child, 62–74; infant's erotic relationship with, 183; and strong 'boundaries', 184, 187; traditional mothering, 71; women's, 70, 71, 90–104, 105, 107, 116;
see also working mothers.
mothers' helps, 4
Mother's Tale, A (Gillick), 100
myths: of family, 2–3; of femininity, 14; of individual problems, 198–9; of nature of feminism, 18–19; of womanhood, 14; of sexuality, 182–3

nannies, 4, 15, 21, 53–4, 93, 99, 107, 114, 192
National Childbirth Trust, 49, 85
networking, 36–7, 76
Networking and Mentoring (Segerman Peck), 36–7
New Age, 42, 68, 180
9½ Weeks (film), 181
nurseries, 16, 166, 192

Observer, 18
One Mother's Daughter (Herman), 115
one o'clock clubs, 75
one-parent families see single parents
Options, 42

parenting: classes, 112, 188; fashions of, 98; good, 83; and husband's career, 126;

Index

and monogamy, 136; 'parental abuse', 166; and prescriptiveness, 74; shared, 19;
  see also single parents
part-time jobs, 5, 25, 26
passivity, 176–89; child, 184; dynamics of, 171; 'muddle' around, 170; and unwelcome sexual attention, 169; and victimization, 170, 172, 175, 190; and women's sexual power, 160, 164
Patriarchal Attitudes (Figes), 177
patriarchy: arrogance or bossiness, 8; defence of, 46; family, 91, 178; rejection of patriarchal authorities, 186; repression by, 179
pay, 4, 5, 7, 36, 60
Phoenix, Ann, 50
physical abuse, 11
  see also violence
Polan, Brenda, 140
pollution, 5
polygamy, 135, 136
pornography, 181
post-feminism, 165
power: boys' identification with, 185, 186; emotional, 135, 189; and father, 185; female, 13, 135, 136, 150, 152, 153, 154, 160, 163, 164, 189, 193, 197; male, 11, 123, 136, 137, 146, 160, 177, 183; of mother–child bond, 18; relationships, 102; sexual, 150, 152, 160, 163, 164; short-term, 193
pre-school care provision, 5
pregnancy, 48, 49, 50; colleagues' attitude to, 23; discomforts of, 47–8; feeling clever, 48, 49; feeling powerful, 48, 49; teenage girls, 49–50
professions: exclusion of women, 1, 2; and ideals of mothering, 6; top jobs for women, 2, 3
  see also career women
psychoanalysis, 181
Psychoanalysis and Feminism (Mitchell), 178
psychology, humanistic, 180
puberty, loss of confidence at, 167–8

race, 2
rape, 164, 165, 171–4
Reality Attuned Parenting (REAP), 83–4
remarriage, 6, 11
returnism, 16
role reversal, 8, 26–7, 126

sadism, 179, 183, 184

sado-masochism, 154, 159, 180, 181
'satanic abuse', 166
Scherr, Rachel, 155
Second World War, 91, 101–2
Secret World of Sex, A (Channel 4 TV series), 132–3
Segerman Peck, Lily, 36–7, 38, 40, 41
sexiness, 160–61; female preoccupation with, 147, 149–50; male definition of, 148
sexism, 3, 169
sexual abuse: of children, 165–6, 171; and cycle of dependency, 11; and guilt, 174; women's complicity in, 10
sexual discrimination, 164
sexual experimentation, 170, 171
sexual exploitation, 10
sexual freedom/liberation, 102, 149, 150
sexual harassment, 165–70, 171
sexual manipulation, 140
sexual murder, 165
Sexual Politics (Millett), 177
sexual roles: division of, 170–71; and guilt, 105; and male sexual approval, 12, 140, 149–50; being sexually attractive to men, 1; stereotypical feminine behaviour, 131; women's acceptance of traditional, 147
sexual self-gratification, 148
sexuality, male, 162, 165, 166, 168, 169, 170
sexuality, women's: and double standard, 148, 149; education on, 151; liberation of, 179; male imaginings and wishes about, 178; and men, 148; myth of, 164; nurturing, egalitarian, 179; practical control over, 150–51; and rape, 172; self-definition, 148, 149, 150; and social changes, 91; 'social control' of, 169, stereotypes, 151; unsettling aspects of, 180
Shakespeare, William, 132
She magazine, 151
single parents: moving into other families, 6; rise in numbers, 3–6; and social security, 9, 22, 41; women as, 3, 4, 186
single-mindedness, 123, 131, 132, 133
sisterhood, 42, 92, 179
slimming, 156–7
social security, and single parents, 9, 22, 41
socialism, 8
Spare Rib, 153
special needs, public spending on, 5
Stassinopoulos, Arianna, 136
sub-clinical eating disorders, 157
Summer Before the Fall, The (Lessing), 19
supermums, 2, 97

Talking of Silence (Herbert), 167
taxation concessions, 16
teachers , 5, 167, 192
teenage girls, and pregnancy, 49
Thatcher, Margaret, 1–2, 8, 22, 43, 100
Thomas, Judge Clarence, 165
Tie Me Up, Tie Me Down (film), 181
Times, The, 12
Toynbee, Polly, 9, 67, 132
traffic congestion, and child deaths, 5

Understanding Rape (Herbert), 171
United Nations, on abuse of women, 11

victims, women as: and emotional manipulation, 144; and feminism, 137; Madonna as ultimate victim, 159; and passivity, 170, 172, 175; women's perception of themselves, 153, 165, 166
violence, 10, 165, 169, 171

wages *see* pay
weight loss, 155–9
Weldon, Fay, 19, 82
Wicks, Malcolm, 4
Wigan Pier Revisited (Campbell), 49–50
Winnicott, D. W., 82
Wolf, Naomi, 154, 163
Woman magazine, 158
Woman in her own Right, A (Dickson), 145
womanhood: confident, 164; ideals of, 91, 199; images of, 153; myth of, 14; and tradition, 22
Women's Room, The (French), 19, 92

work: ambition, 17, 20, 27, 31, 33, 35, 37, 38, 41, 43, 44; ambivalence to, 29, 30, 32; competition, 30–35, 38–44; conditions, 36; drive to make money, 30, 37, 40, 41, 56; envy, 30, 33–4, 38, 39, 43–4; freelance, 193–4; full-time, 8, 11, 25, 26, 33, 78, 102, 103; giving up for motherhood, 16–29, 30; and guilt, 3, 31–2, 106–9, 111–12, 113, 118; hours, 33, 34, 36, 192, 193, 197; and ideal of motherhood, 76–7, 78, 80, 82, 84–9; jealousy, 30, 34, 35, 39, 40, 41; low-paid, 4, 5; low-status, 5; man's idealized, 121–6; networking, 36–7, 38; part-time, 5, 25, 26, 40, 46, 77, 86; in professions, 1, 2, 3, 6; and role reversal, 8; self-advancement, 34, 35, 40, 45, 56, 112; and traditional relationship between the sexes, 1; values of, 28, 30, 38; and women's internal sense of their boundaries and needs, 117–18
working mothers: and competition, 40; and domestic tasks, 6; end of stigma attached to, 3; expectations, 15; guilt, 3, 106, 107–8, 111–12, 113, 118, 196; and ideals of mothering, 6; inadequate provisions and scant rewards for, 188; increase in, 6; and individual choice, 191; mother–daughter relationships, 90–104; and Paula Yates' views, 158–9; statistics, 5; supermums, 2; support from other women, 40

Yates, Paula, 47, 158
Young Mothers (Phoenix), 50